TEXAS Toys and GAMES

TEXAS

and GAMES

Publication of the Texas Folklore Society XLVIII

Edited by Francis Edward Abernethy

University of North Texas Press
Denton, Texas

Second Edition 1997

5 4 3 2 1

Requests for permission to reproduce material from
this work should be sent to

Permissions
University of North Texas Press
Post Office Box 13856
Denton, Texas 76203

The paper in this book meets the minimum requirements of the American
National Standard for Permanence of paper for
Printed Library Materials, Z39.48-1984.

Library of Congress Cataloging-in-Publication Data

Texas toys and games / edited by Francis Edward Abernethy. — 2nd ed.
    p.   cm. — (Publications of the Texas Folklore Society ; no. 48)
        Originally published: 1st ed. Dallas, Tex. :
        Southern Methodist University Press, 1989.
        Includes bibliographical references and index.
        ISBN 1-57441-037-7 (pbk. : alk. paper)
1. Toys—Texas—History. 2. Games—Texas—History. 3. Folklore—Texas—
History. 4. Toy making—History.   I. Abernethy, Francis Edward.
    II. Series: Publications of the Texas Folklore Society; no. 48.
                    [GR1.T4 no. 48]
                    [GV1218.5]
                    390 s—dc21
    [745.592]   97-10584
                                                  CIP

Unless otherwise credited, photographs are by
Francis Edward Abernethy.
Chapter opener art by Barbara Clark.
Cover and title page art by Barbara Whitehead.

Contents

Preface

It is interesting, this chain of often unrelated events that culminates in a happening of some consequence, with that consequence becoming a cause in another line of causes leading to another consequence and on *ad infinitum*. That is the basis for the study of history, of course, and because the Society is always in the midst of history and is presently compiling its own, it seems fitting to discuss the history of *Texas Toys and Games*.

In which the editor discusses recent Texas Folklore Society history

Lee Haile is responsible for its conception. In 1982—on Saturday, April 10, at 11:00 A.M., to be exact—at the Sunday House in Fredericksburg, Lee, then a student of Texas A&M, presented a paper with the most unacademic of titles, "Seven Toys We Made for Free." He spun, whirled, bounced and talked about his toys for his allotted twenty minutes and instructed and delighted all present. He expanded his talk and discussed home-made toys again in the spring of 1984 for the Texas State Historical Association. Then in 1985 when I started filling in folk topics for the *Handbook of Texas*, getting Lee to do the entry on "Folk Toys" was a natural conclusion.

At the same time that I was filling the Texas folk toys entry for the *Handbook*, I was looking for someone to do the companion entry on "Folk Games." Martha Hartzog of the Alta Vista Productions in Austin volunteered for that topic, and I had the beginning of *Texas Toys and Games*. I didn't consider the two for a PTFS though, even after Suzanne Comer, then with the University of Texas Press, said that she was interested in seeing a book on Texas toys and games.

Then in the July 1986 newsletter I asked for suggestions for special PTFS topics, and Janette Swadley wrote that she and Don and Ben Capps, during a deliberation over libations, had decided that we should have a volume on toys and games. She very generously volunteered Ben's services, and this present book was under way.

That was two years ago, and how I ever thought I could assemble, organize, and illustrate a book of this magnitude in one year illustrates a problem I share with King Lear: the acquisition of age without the acquisition of wisdom. Thus, it is a year late, but closer to expectations than it was last year.

The contributors—so many of them for this book!— deserve all our applause. We have included a special index of contributors as well as one for the toys and games. I have gleaned this manuscript, and truly hope that I have not left out a contributor's name.

I hope that I have not left anyone's toy or game out of that index also, although I know that I have left many of them out of the book. Collecting for this book could have gone on forever. Each chapter could have been expanded with more toys and games, and the book could have included more chapters on other kinds of toys and games, a chapter on tricks and puzzles, for instance.

I want to thank the Stephen F. Austin State University Board of Regents for giving me a development leave this fall of '88. They really gave me the time off to work on the TFS history, but I had to get *Toys and Games* out of the way before I could start the history, and they are a good sort and will understand.

On behalf of the Texas Folklore Society, I thank William R. Johnson, President of Stephen F. Austin, and Kirby L. Duncan, Chairman of the Department of English and Philosophy, for continuing financial and moral support. And I sincerely thank two of the Society's secretaries, Carrol Daniels and Carolyn Satterwhite, one for getting the manuscripts started and the other for finishing them.

Carolyn Satterwhite is also the assistant editor—*sine qua non!*—of *Texas Toys and Games*, which means that she did the hard work in getting this manuscript ready for the press. She has my appreciation and respect.

Francis Edward Abernethy
Stephen F. Austin State University
Nacogdoches, Texas
October 18, 1988

Part One

Folk Toys

Folk toys are those that are made with natural or available materials by amateurs in the tradition of the area's culture and ancestors and for personal rather than mercantile reasons.

Folk toys are made with natural materials, such as forked sticks for slingshot stocks, or cornhusks and cobs for dolls. Or they might simply be made from available material—old inner tubes for rubber-gun ammunition or cowboy chaps, or an old tire for a swing, or a buggy wheel bolted to a tree stump for a merry-go-round. One might search through a scrap pile to find a suitable 2×4 for a skate scooter, but he wouldn't go buy one. Folk toys are made from whatever is handy or can be scrounged.

Folk toys are made by amateurs of varying degrees. This includes a wide range of building skills, from those of a ten-year-old boy hammering on a stilt step to grown men whittling out paired giraffes for a Noah's Ark or a seamstress grandmother making doll clothes. These craftsmen are true amateurs, building for the love of the creation and the craft and/or for the love of some child or grandchild. They don't build toys to sell. The ten-year-old usually builds from necessity, knowing that the only way he is going to get a tree house is to build it himself. But for most there is the challenge and joy of creative building, and the resultant toy is an object of personal pride.

Folk toys are built in the style and tradition of the neighborhood or the area's culture or the elders and ancestors. The younger children watch the older and covet their toys and their expertise and try to build their own go-carts or flying jennies. The toys they build might be a bit different from their models, but the toys are recognizable as being in a tradition, a pattern passed from generation to generation in a fairly fixed form.

The term *toys* covers a multitude of things to play with. Some toys are to be manipulated—tossed, flipped, bounced, hit—to test and develop agility. Some are used to gamble with, some to activate mentalities. Some toys are played with to satisfy a desire to create and control small people and the miniature worlds they live in.

But if they are folk toys they don't come from Toys R Us and aren't moulded plastic. And even though some promoter might have gotten the idea for a toy from some traditional top or yo-yo, the mass-produced-in-Korea, all-alike, for-sale items on the toy counter at Woolworth's are not folk and are not the province of this part of this book.

I

Wheels

The wheel has been around five thousand years, more or less, so archaeologists tell us. Someone of our forefathers early on noticed that a round log was easier to roll than to carry. The next step was to figure out that heavy objects could be moved by rolling them on three logs, keeping two logs under the load and shifting the log that rolled out the back up to the front. In order to lighten the weight of the logs to be shifted, some inventive soul cut two cross sections out of a log and put a pole through the middle of both, making a wheel and axle. The next step was to fit a platform on the axle in such a way that the axle stayed in one place and the wheels turned round and round. This ancient inventor had thus invented the wagon that five thousand years later became an Olds 88. The wheel business began, speculatively, in Mesopotamia and from there spread to the rest of the Old World—Europe, Africa, and Asia.

Strangely, the wheel did not become a part of New World culture until the Spanish brought it in 1519. As sophisticated as the Mayas and Incas and Aztecs were, and as many round calendars and columns as they built, they had no wheeled vehicles. Perhaps this was because they had no large draft animals to pull a load that might require wheels. Mesoamericans understood the principle of the wheel, however, because they made toys with wheels. Archaeologists have uncovered models of small animals that rolled on wheels attached to their feet (Leonard, 83, 119). These could have been made for religious purposes, but by the looks of them they are toys. And they do not look much different from a Texan's own animal toys, some of which had axles or were on platforms with wheels.

Children from Texas and elsewhere early took to the wheel. The simplest use was the paddle and hoop.

The Paddle and Hoop

Mrs. George Van Burrows of Nacogdoches tells about her association with this toy: "My father made and repaired wagons and as a result there were always iron hoops off the wagon wheel hubs available. The hoops were about eight inches in diameter and an inch-and-a-half wide. My brother and his friends rolled their hoops with paddles which consisted of a handle with a crosspiece on one end. They rolled these hoops for miles and sometimes the hoops would be rolled so much they would shine."

Wheel-hub hoops were the best to roll and were the most popular hoops, but coming in a close second were barrel hoops, which were made out of lighter metal. Center hoops on small casks were favored. The outer hoops on a barrel had the disadvantage of being slanted and thus harder to control. Some hoops were made out of green branches, stripped and circled and tied. A piece of garden hose circled and doweled together with a stick also served the purpose, as did old plates, abandoned doll buggy or Radio Flyer wheels, or anything that was round and would roll. Someone identified only as TMP wrote: "I don't know what it was or where it came from, but I had a metal hoop, about as big around as a car tire, but it was thin—about a half-inch wide. I rolled that thing for miles with a stick with a shorter stick nailed across it at the bottom. Some kids used barrel hoops, but mine was not a barrel hoop. I remember I was most careful every night to put it up in the garage."

The previously described paddle was one means of rolling the hoop. Some used any stick or limb handy. A wire with three-quarters of a loop in the rolling end was common. In countries unblessed with the presence of Toys R Us and where grandparents have not the wherewithal to drown a child in every item out of a Sears toy catalog, the considerable skill of hoop rolling is still a popular pastime with children.

Chris Wick of Nacogdoches played a game with a larger hoop: "My grandfather, Fred Winters of Boerne, Texas, taught us a game with a hoop. All you needed was an old iron wagon wheel rim and somebody to compete with. We would get the rim rolling as fast as we could and then try to run through the hoop as it rolled. The one who could make the most complete passes through the rim before it was knocked down or fell over won the game. It was also a good game for one child to entertain himself with."

Car tires were sometimes rolled as a hoop and were many times suspended from a limb and swung in. And I was once of a size that I could ball up in a tire and roll down a hill into a hogwire fence. My dog Jack enjoyed the trip as much as I did and barked and snapped at the tire as we bounced down the hill. I think he thought the tire was running away with me, and he always greeted me with much relief and happiness when I emerged from the tire and the sagging fence.

The spool tractor is a more complicated toy but was equally popular. Spool tractors and descriptions were sent in by Elton Miles, Lee Haile, Ben Capps, Robert Metcalfe, Joseph Jones,

Gayla McLain Sanders, and Willie Hudson. All spool users be-
moaned the passing of the wooden spool.

A spool tractor is a self-propelled toy made from a sewing-thread
spool, a rubber band, matchsticks, and a bit of soap. For traction
the flanged edges of the spool ends are notched all around. For
lubrication a disk of soap about the size of a nickel is carved, and
a hole is drilled through the center. For power a rubber band is
passed through the spool and secured on one end with a short
piece of matchstick. At the other end, the rubber band is passed
through the soap and secured by one end of a full-length matchstick. For resistance—or breeching—this stick must extend well
beyond the rim of the spool.

    To operate the tractor, the rubber band is wound tightly by
means of the match stick. Released, the long stick drags the
floor, the rubber band begins to untwist, and the tractor begins
its short, erratic journey. When it stops, wind it up and watch it
again, taking pride in the fact that what you made, works.

    In the 1920s in Gatesville, Texas, we six- to ten-year-olds
made and ran spool tractors when we could think of nothing
better to do.

**The Spool
Tractor
by
Elton Miles**

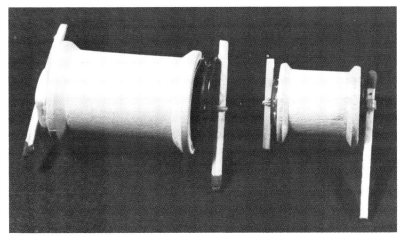

Spool tractors by
Willie Hudson.

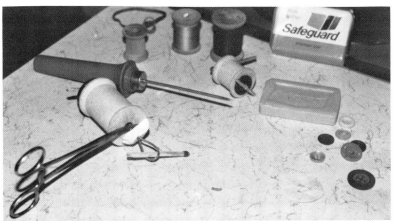

Ingredients for spool
tractor (Willie and
Linda Hudson).

Cranking a spool
tractor (Karen Haile).

◆ The rubber-band car is built on the same principle as the spool tractor but is one spool more complicated:

The Rubber-Band Car
by
Lee Haile

For the rubber-band car you need two spools, a rubber band, and a wire clothes hanger. Cut the hook off the hanger with a pair of pliers, and cut a piece of wire about two feet long. Bend the wire into a U shape with the bottom of the U about three inches across. The angles need to be sharp corners. Now, put the thin rubber band through the hole on one of the spools. There should be a little loop sticking out of each end of the spool. Stick a pin or drive a small nail into the hole at an angle so that the rubber band passes on each side of the pin. Slide the loops at each end of the spool onto the ends of the wire; then slide the spool to about one inch from the bottom. Turn in the ends of the wire to where they just match and form a box. Next spread it apart enough to put each end of the wire into each hole on the second spool.

To wind up the car, just roll it backwards until the rubber band is twisted tight. Then let the car go. It will go pretty fast. If it spins out, then the floor is too slick. It works better on a surface that is a little rough, such as a sidewalk. We would stack stuff across the wires so that the cars could "haul it." This extra weight would also keep it from spinning.

◆ Dorris Tull sent in a twin-spool car that was simply pulled by a string rather than powered by a rubber band. Toy vehicles were made from all sorts of materials. Patricia Hurley sent in small wheeled carts made of medicine, match, and oatmeal boxes. Ruben Villareal described a Mexican toy cart with the tongue, bed, and sides made out of dried corn stalks and with wheels made out of dried cow patties. I truly admire that sort of imagination and ingenuity. To pull the corn-stalk cart, Mexican children made their oxen to scale out of clay and fire-hardened them.

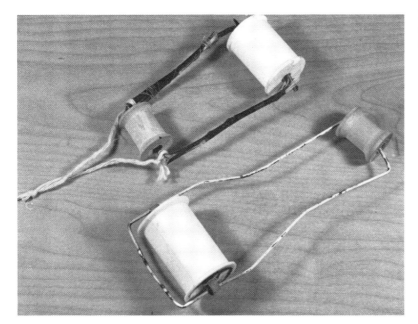

Dorris Tull's spool car and Lee Haile's rubber-band car.

In the 1920s in Gatesville, Texas, children (six to ten) made toy cars from pieces of scrap lumber, using shoe polish cans for wheels. We got the empty cans from the shoeshine man at the local barber shop.

    Making each car was a creative job, depending on the sizes and shapes of the many scraps we scrounged. The most common model was a squared roadster, or racer, with a bit of 2×4 for the hood and a shim-wedge of 2×4 for the "turtle." Leaving space for a driver, we nailed these onto a chassis of 1×4, then mounted the wheels by driving nails through the shoe polish cans. We nailed another can on the turtle for a spare. Whenever possible, the five wheels were matched. We made the steering

Shoe-Polish-Can Cars
by
Elton Miles

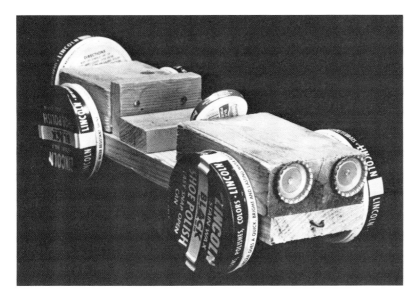

Elton Miles's shoe-polish-can car (Mark Weatherly).

wheel out of a jar lid or a flattened bottle cap with a nail driven through it.

After driving a staple or bent nail into the front, we attached a towing string and drove barefooted all over the block at breakneck speed.

Prince Albert Cars
by
Billie B. Kemper

My brother and I played many hours with homemade trucks on elaborate road systems which we built. The trucks had a cigarbox bed and a hood made from a Prince Albert tobacco can. The rest of the truck was made from wood from apple and orange crates. We used keyhole saws to cut the wheels and put a bolt through the front axle so that it would swivel. My brother worked to improve his trucks with such extras as a steering wheel, running boards and fenders, and license plates, all made from Prince Albert cans, and hubcaps from Dr Pepper bottle caps. The performance of the vehicle depended on the imagination and skill of the driver, and they were excellent for transporting imaginary people, cattle, and cotton over our country roads.

We graded up a roadbed wide enough for one truck, which was the way country roads were made. When our trucks passed, the right wheels were on the shoulder, unless some road hog forced the other truck into the ditch, where it often stuck. Then the driver of the other truck pulled his unfortunate neighbor out of the ditch with a rope (a kite string). Our roads had at least two bridges, some grades, and a number of sharp curves.

Racing toy cars (Marvin Gorley).

We had no towns because we lived in the country. Neither did we have a railroad because cars and trucks were our only means of transportation. Although we could hear the Cotton Belt trains blowing for Pinnacle Switch five miles across the woods, and we saw big locomotives pulling boxcars when we went to Big Sandy, we only imagined where these places were and how they looked. We lived under the air lane between Shreveport and Dallas, but we only saw the airplanes overhead and did not associate our lives with them. At night we could see the beacon lights in the east and west that kept the airplanes on course. Therefore we knew that they did not have the freedom of trucks that could be driven on any road or in fields without artificial help. Maybe we were the first generation of Texans to replace the horse with the truck.

◆ Larger wheeled vehicles were constructed in the same way, with whatever materials were at hand. Reverend Arthur Smith, in an interview for Gary High School's *Loblolly* (Spring 1979), tells about building a wagon two generations ago:

A Wagon from Scratch
by
Arthur Smith

We made a homemade wagon from scratch. We'd just go out in the woods and find a good straight-bodied sweet gum that was just as round as we could find it and about ten inches or a foot thick. We'd take the old crosscut saw and saw it down, and then we would saw off rings. These were the wheels for the wagon. Dad would usually help me with this. And we would bore an inch hole in the center of that wheel. If you didn't have it centered well that thing was a real Leaping Lena when you would pull it.

Then we would take some good hard oak or hickory, a piece about two or three inches around and about two feet long. We would whittle out a spindle on each end of it. Then we would take a handsaw and saw around them and make a shoulder and then whittle it out. We made that spindle round and smooth, where it would fit in that hole as a loose fit. We would drill a small hole in the end of the axle, out past the wheel, and make a real nice hardwood peg to fit the hole to hold the wheel on. Then we would grease that thing with axle grease, and boy that thing would really roll. That's the way poor folks could get a wagon without having to go to town and buy one.

◆ Ben Myers of Fort Worth also tells about a homemade wagon built with more ingenuity than money:

Wheels for the Poor
by
Ben Myers

Even in the old days there were such things as red wagons and bicycles, but they were expensive. It was every boy's dream to own a bicycle, but until that day he just *had* to have wheels.

There were not many things that were thrown away. But now and then a very old cultivator or planter would become unrepairable. Sometimes a trashed reel-type mower could be

Rebecca Yarbrough's
apple-box truck.

found. The parts from these things could provide wheels, of sorts, for a poor boy's toy.

The old planter wheels, which were about three feet in diameter, were the best. You mounted those wheels on a three-and-a-half-foot-long axle. An eight-foot-long 2×4 split into two pieces made the left and right sides of the frame for this vehicle. This was about all you needed for a cart in which to haul things. However, for a wagon to ride down hills in, you needed two more wheels.

If you had two old reel-type lawn mower wheels, these could hold up the front end. The wagon slanted from back to front, but it was long enough that the slope wasn't too steep. The lawn mower wheels were mounted on a 2×4 in the front with a center pivot pin. This allowed the steerage of the wagon. There were two ways to do that. One was to put one foot near each front wheel and push on the side opposite to the direction of the turn. The other was to tie a rope onto the 2×4 near each front wheel and pull on the rope in the direction of the turn.

About the only means of locomotion was to have someone push you. Or you could get up on a hill and let gravity do the work. Of course, you had to push the cart up on top of the hill in the first place.

One such hill was Bloomer's Hill, on the back of Mr. Bloomer's pasture, by Post Oak Creek, east of the old Highway 75 south of Sherman. The area was covered with trees, but a trail had been cut up the long axis of the hill. It was used on the weekend by motorcyclists, to test their climbing ability. The trail led up from the creek bank, where the motorcycles started their climb. We would drag our cart to the top of the hill during the week to see if we could come all the way down without hitting a tree. To let the cart go as fast as gravity would propel it was the most fun—the biggest thrill of all.

The trail was about the same grade all the way up, except that about halfway up it leveled off for about twenty feet. This was good for the motorcycles, giving them a little relief halfway up. But when we would come off the top of the hill in our home-made cart, that level spot was disastrous. If we didn't drag our feet to impede speed, the flat spot would throw the front wheels off the ground. This minute or so without steerage usually would head the cart right toward the tree.

One time George let the cart go full tilt, and it hit a tree. The cart turned over and the iron planter wheel hit his head. He was bleeding and unconscious. We took him down to the creek and were washing off the blood when he finally became conscious. His first words were, "Don't get my shirt dirty, my mom will kill me."

◆ As children got older their requirements in toys changed. A big boy wanted a big toy, and he usually had to build it for himself. Two standard toys a couple of generations ago were the skate scooter and the soapbox racer, or go-cart.

The Skate Scooter

I apologize for the looks of the skate scooter made as an illustration for this chapter. Not because it looks so bad, you understand, but because it looks so good. Your usual skate scooter was battered and skewed, wood-split and nail-bent, and it looked like it had been built by a twelve-year-old, which it usually was. My only excuse, in this case, is that after I decided I would build a scooter for an illustration, I decided that I would build it for my grandson. That is when things started going wrong. I squared boards, measured, centered—drilled! I even used new and matching nails, screws, and bolts. The best that I can say for myself is that I used materials that I had on hand, just as I did when I built my last one fifty years ago. I just have better materials on hand now, if that happens to be one advantage of getting fifty years older. Outside of using what was lying around under the house, however, this scooter was not built in the traditional way.

On the other hand, I haven't seen many properly built skate scooters in several decades. I guess they have evolved into the omnipresent, commercially manufactured skateboard. There was a time when a natural part of a boy's learning to build started with his constructing—no, knocking together—a skate scooter.

Coming up with a skate wasn't much trouble during a time when just about every kid had skates and when you could skate the bearings out of half a pair at a time. Then, when you got tired of doodling around on one skate, you built a skate scooter. Finding a good piece of 2×4 could get to be a problem when the only thing left over after a Depression carpenter built a house was a small pile of sawdust. Nails were scrounged, pulled from some existing structure if necessary.

The building was elemental. The skate was separated at the joint, and the heel piece was hammered and worried flat. Then the two parts were attached to the 2×4 by as many nails as one could drive into the board and clench over to hold the skate. The weight of that many nails surely must have provided some

Skate scooter.

lower stability. The upright piece was a 1×4 that was bound to split when it was nailed to the 2×4. Braces helped but it was a rare scooter that didn't wiggle at the handle. The best of handles was a part of a broomstick or hoe handle that was nailed at the top of the 1×4.

Ornamentation was minimal. Nehi bottle caps artistically nailed onto the heel served as taillights. Reflectors fastened as headlights always looked good. I remember one scooter that had Prince Albert cans wrapped around the upright. That was a very classy set of wheels!

Skate scooters made a great racket clickety-clacking down a concrete sidewalk. Skillful scooter riders maneuvered their wheels over cracks and curbs and around corners with considerable dexterity, never envying—as far as I remember—those kids who had regularly wheeled, store-bought scooters. Three or four scooters rattling down a hill, shooting in and out of walks and driveways, and sailing off curbs were an exciting sight. I have no doubt that our modern skateboard was invented when the 1x4 finally fell off one of these scooters and the maker was too aggravated to nail it back.

The Soapbox Racer

The only thing that made more noise than a herd of skate scooters rattling down a concrete sidewalk was a single iron-lawn-mower-wheeled soapbox racer. They were later called go-carts, probably after P&G quit shipping soap in good, solid wooden boxes. Soapboxes made good hoods and seats and struts for go-carts, so I've been told. Personally, I never knew anybody who used a soapbox to make a go-cart. Apple and orange boxes—those crates of many uses, components of every shop and garage and many apartments well through the 1950s—were used whole or in parts in the making of go-carts in my time and neighborhood. But we frequently referred to our go-carts as soapbox racers and

Soap Box Derby contestant in San Antonio, 1941 (Bert Rees).

fantasized regularly on building a proper entrant for the Soapbox
Derby in Akron and whizzing across the finish line in record
time, faster than any other twelve-year-old in these whole
United States! To be a kid-sized, heroic Barney Oldfield was a
widespread dream in the Twenties and Thirties.

The best that Jack Deerman and I did in Palestine was to
push each other—alternately—to John hill (a one-block, low-
traffic hill on John Street) and then go rattling down that incline
until a wheel came off or the seat collapsed or the front steering
axle whipped a wheel around and under the body. Soapbox racing was really a lot more trouble than it was worth, come to
think of it. We spent more than half of our time pulling the
ungreased dead weight of it back up the hill and half of the other
half putting it back together. And if the older kids came and
wanted to play skate hockey, we had to quit. But to cross that
finish line in Akron just once. . . ! (—*He had built it himself and
it was sleek like an arrow, with rubber-tired wheels that spun so
smoothly that you could barely hear them roll. He looked to his left:
five soapbox racers almost as streamlined as his own, poised at the
starting line. To his right four more race drivers tensely prepared
themselves for the long roll down the hill to the Soapbox Derby
finish line—and fame! He snapped the flaps of his aviator cap
that he had gotten for Christmas and then pulled down his goggles.
He could see the starting flagman walking up to the line, and he
looked in the grandstand down the hill and could see Betty Walker
and his parents and his girl cousin from Tyler, who was prissy and
one year older than he. Betty's eyes looked into his own and then
she threw him a kiss . . . and winked. The starter raised his flag,
dipped it, and they were off!—And he was about halfway down
John hill when the back wheel went skeeting off to bang into a*

curb. The dragging axle threw him off balance, and he jerked on the right wheel which went under the frame, and the whole thing came to a grinding halt. He heard, "Get that junk out of the street!" and a car honking. He wondered if he might be broken or bleeding, hurt enough to make the man feel bad about hollering at him. And the man would rush him to the hospital, with sirens, and he would lie there wrapped in bandages and Betty Walker would write him notes and come to see him, and his mother would bring him a chocolate meringue pie. "You're gonna get yourself killed, rolling that thing down the middle of the street," the man said as he drove around him and went on down the street. —)

But as I was saying . . .

I apologize once again for the looks and the construction of my wheeled vehicle. I tend to get carried away with the crafting of an object and forget the utility of it. I have a chuck box, fully outfitted and sitting in our entrance hall, that I wouldn't think of taking to the river or on a camping trip because it looks so good. It's the same with this go-cart; I don't want any frazzling kid whipping it around on a public street. But that's not the way it's supposed to be. A go-cart was built primarily for utility, for wheeling along; and the basic go-cart was a frame, axle, and wheels—sometimes without even a seat on it—steered with a rope. Older, more practiced builders—fathers, even—added the soapbox to the front for a hood and made a steering wheel that really worked. Elemental niceties, such as reflectors, tin-can headlights, radiator caps (usually stolen), and coats of paint were added when handy or fortuitously acquired.

Elemental go-cart.

The basic go-cart was a 2×6 frame with a 2×4 fixed back axle and a 2×4 rotatable front axle. The wheels were off a push mower and were iron because that was the only junk wheel to be found. No kid that I knew had the money to buy a set of rubber wheels. I remember one cart with a set of old Radio Flyer wheels, but it was a rarity—and the object of envy.

The main problem in the building of a go-cart was getting it wheeled, that is getting the wheel on some kind of spindle on the 2×4 axle. Lag bolts screwed in the 2×4 were sometimes used but were hard to come by and soon got wobbly. The absolute worst—the "poor white" of axle spindles—was a glob of big-penny nails, enough to fill the wheel hole, pounded through the wheel hole and into the defenseless 2×4. I confess to being a party to this kind of butchery once, and I am sure that I am still compensating: the axle shaft in the illustration was purchased at a hardware store. Bolts, iron rods, telephone-pole steps—anything that was near the diameter of the hole in the wheel—would be attached to the 2×4 with the usual bent-over and pounded-down nails. The use of fence staples was considered a refinement. A go-cart builder understands early in life how it happened that the Mayas had round wheels but were never able to come up with the principle of the axle and the resulting go-cart.

The reader must note that the traditional lawn mower wheel is being used on this demonstration model. Granted that it is modern and much superior to the old iron wheel off a push mower, it is still from a lawn mower and is the most common junk wheel found lying around houses and junk piles. I have trashed out many a cheap lawn mower in my time and have as yet to throw away a useable wheel. Thus it was an easy matter to resurrect the great wheels you see on this cart. If I had had these wheels when I was a serious go-cart builder, I would have been the envy of all—and perhaps would have become a famous Soapbox Derby racer and married Betty Walker.

II

Kites and Other Flying Things

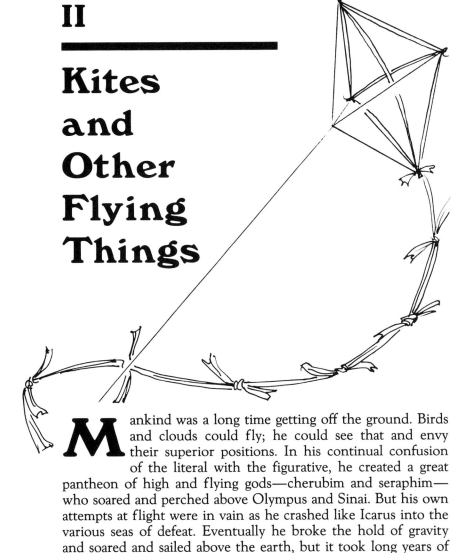

Mankind was a long time getting off the ground. Birds and clouds could fly; he could see that and envy their superior positions. In his continual confusion of the literal with the figurative, he created a great pantheon of high and flying gods—cherubim and seraphim—who soared and perched above Olympus and Sinai. But his own attempts at flight were in vain as he crashed like Icarus into the various seas of defeat. Eventually he broke the hold of gravity and soared and sailed above the earth, but it took long years of cumulative science to do it. Left behind on the trail to Phantom Jets and Concords were all sorts of flying things—gliders of many shapes and sizes, propellers that twisted into the atmospheric pressure, and kites hung high in a balance between their slim hold to earth and the winds that wanted to take them off to a far country.

The relics of aeronautical science became the stuff of toys, the fliers that youths soared with in their imaginations.

A lard- or syrup-can lid is a flier, and if properly thrown against a wind can get up in the air and stay there, for a while anyway. The Reverend Arthur Smith of Gary reported on this childhood practice in a Spring 1979 *Loblolly* interview: "Lard

A paper glider attack (Mark Weatherly).

came in buckets of different sizes. The eight-pound bucket had a lid on it which was about seven inches in diameter. It was turned down on the edges. You could take one of these bucket lids and sail it for a long way. I found that you could throw it against a pretty good wind, and it would go way up there and come back nearly to the same place you were standing. We would play with them just like a frisbee."

Balloons, inflated and turned loose to jet around a theater's interior during a Saturday matinee, are fliers. This was done before the Tom Mix movie began or between the Three Stooges and chapter five of the Buck Rogers serial; fliers never violated the holiness of film time. Variations on a simple balloon launch included the balloon with a split-bamboo squealer or a tin whizzer in its orifice, or one partially tied in such a manner to make it sound like runaway flatulence. The joy of these toy jets was increased manifold by the fact that as soon as one lost its propulsion and dropped back into the squirm, a child's breath could send it soaring again, perhaps all the way up into the balcony where adolescents of opposite sexes sat close to each other—and touched!

The paper plane or glider, however, is youth's first real hands-on experience with aerodynamics. I can vouch for my generation's expertise in making paper planes of all sizes and shapes, and my mother says that they were sailed during her school days in Wolfe City, so we are talking about schoolroom aeronautics soon after Wilbur and Orville flew their kite with an engine above the sands at Kitty Hawk. Who knows how long before that? I collected the paper planes for this chapter from one class of college students and English department faculty members. Most, if not all, of the boys in the class could make a flyable plane; a few of the girls could. The planes were variations on four basic designs. The long triangular model won the grace and distance contests. The half-sheet-size darter with folded-up wing tips was the acrobatic winner. I am sure that if I were to

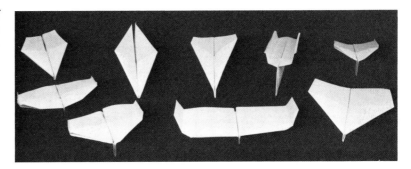

walk into any public school classroom, from junior high to senior, I could get an equal number of paper gliders, if not more.
Given a little lead time one could assemble a fleet of these creative and enduring toys.

Billie Kemper sent in a description of an elemental flying
toy, a single propeller that screws its way through the atmosphere, which her uncles had built for her and her brother.
Leonardo would have loved it. "The staff of the whirligig was
made of old telephone wire (not cable) which was soft and pli-
able. My uncles held the wire in a vise while twisting it with
wire pliers. The twist had to be uniform so that the propeller
would slip easily and smoothly off the staff. The propeller was
made of a thin metal such as a Prince Albert tobacco can. The
Siamese twin holes in the center of the propeller were so designed that the propeller would slip easily on and off the staff
without being too loose. While holding the staffs in our left
hands, we used the thumbs and forefingers of our right hands to
push the propellers off the staffs with as much speed as possible.
If a propeller caught the wind just right, it would sail some
distance."

Lee Haile, who has more skill and takes more pains with
the construction of toys than do most of us, describes the quali-
ties and construction of more elaborate flying toys:

**The Flying
Propeller,
Whimmy
Diddle, and
Boomerang
by
Lee Haile**

The hand propeller is an easy toy to make and use. It consists of
nothing more than a propeller and a round stick, and it is operated by hand. It was known as a helicopter when it was patented
on February 6, 1906, by L. B. Mathison under the name Flying
Toy (Provenzo, 163), even though there were many references to
this toy in paintings and illustrations dating from the Renaissance in Europe (Provenzo, 166; Fraser, 62, 89; Schnacke, 203).
A company in California now mass-produces them and sells
them as Puddle Jumpers.

The first thing you do is carve a propeller. Next, drill a hole
in the center of the propeller small enough that a round stick
will fit very tightly in it. The round stick should be about the
size of a pencil or smaller. Sometimes it is easier to make the
hole oblong and then carve the end of the stick so that it fits
the oblong hole. This keeps the stick from slipping around in

Flying propeller
(Karen Haile).

the hole. Stick the stick in the hole and maybe add a little glue to help hold it. It now looks like a capital T.

To fly it, you just rotate the round stick between the palms of your hands, like you roll up playdough. How high it flies depends on how fast you slide your hands when you spin the prop and the amount of twist in your prop.

The flying Whimmy Diddle is like the helicopter toy but only the propeller flies. It consists of a handle, a wooden spool, a piece of string, and a propeller (Henderson and Wilkerson, 61).

The handle can be a stick big enough to grip comfortably in your hand. The end is carved down small enough to fit in the hole of the spool so that the spool can turn easily on it. Or a nail is driven into the stick so that the spool can rest on it. Neither the nail nor the end of the stick should stick past the spool when it is set on the handle. Two smaller nails are driven into the spool at one end on opposite sides of the hole. The heads of the nails are then cut off. The propeller can be carved of wood, cut out of a flattened tin can and given a twist, or as the man who first showed me did it, made from the top of an old Prince Albert tobacco can lid with a twist in it. Two holes are drilled in the prop to match the small nails in the spool. They should be big enough so that the prop will come off easily. The small nails are bent in opposite directions so that the prop will stay on when you pull the string. The twist in the propeller should match the way the nails are bent. Make sure the up-twisted side of the propeller is in the same direction as the bend in the small nails.

Now wind the string around the spool in the right direction (the direction that the small nails are pointing). Hold it above your head pointing up and pull the string as hard as you can and watch the propeller fly.

Flying propeller with "launch pad" and pull cord.

The boomerang is thousands of years old and is still one of the most fascinating of toys. Although it is most commonly associated with the Australian bushmen, it was found on every continent in the world (Provenzo, 55). It was known to the ancient Egyptians and was found in India and Polynesia. In North America, the Hopi Indians had a hunting stick that resembled the Australian-type boomerang (Mason, 8; Ruhe and Darnell, 12).

The word *boomerang* comes from a single tribe of natives in New South Wales and is the accepted name for this type of throwing stick (Mason, 55). There are two types of boomerangs, the return and the non-return type. The non-return type was used strictly for hunting and has little value as a toy or for recreation. The return type was used for fun even by the Australian bushmen. The English explorer James Cook introduced the sport to modern Europe in the first half of the eighteenth century (Provenzo, 55).

There are also two types of the return boomerangs. There is the curved-stick kind and there is the cross-stick kind of boomerang. The cross-stick is really just two curved-stick boomerangs back to back. The principle to making either one is exactly the same. First, you carve down the top side of each wing until the edges are rounded. Leave the bottom side of each wing flat. They should look like a half moon when viewed from the end. Then you put a slight upward bend to each wing to give a slight dihedral. These two steps are all there is to any type of return boomerang.

The cross-stick boomerang is much safer as a toy and is a lot easier to throw, so this is usually the kind I recommend to make. The easiest way is to use a wooden yardstick. The nice thing about yardsticks is that the centers are already marked for you. Cut it in half at the 18″ mark. Now leave the center (the 9″ mark) of each piece like it is and carve down each of the four wings starting 1″ on each side of the center. Give each wing its bend. Wood bends when it is wet and warm. You can hold it under a warm water faucet, or if the wood is clean, just lick it on the 7″ and 11″ marks. Now bend it upwards and count to twenty. It should hold its bend. Now connect the two sticks together in the center to where they look like a cross or an X. You can glue it, staple it, or use baling wire and wire it together. Once it is connected, you can go fly it.

The big reason most boomerangs do not come back is because they are not thrown correctly. To make a correct throw, remember that the 'rang will turn in the direction of the side that was carved. Also, remember that the 'rang makes its turn perpendicular to its own plane. When you throw it, it should leave your hand perpendicular to the horizon. Make sure you put lots of spin in it so that it can stay in the air long enough to come back. The spin gives it lift. You should throw it into the wind if there is any. It works best when there is no wind at all. Any wind will cause it to land downwind from you. You adjust your throw a little one way or the other from the perpendicular to make it land in front of you or behind you.

Cross-stick boomerang (Karen Haile).

There used to be this guy that lived on South Padre Island that made his money selling boomerangs. He went by the name of "Billy Boomerang." He would show up on the beach with a bunch of boomerangs and stick them in the sand. Then he would start throwing them out over the ocean to attract a crowd and then sell his wares to the tourists. His personal record at consecutive catches was 338! Charles Kuralt did a documentary on him in his "On the Road" TV series. He was well enough known that when he died, his obituary was carried by the UPI (Ruhe, 34).

◆ And then there are those angels aloft, the princes of all fliers, the kites, of which Jack C. Phipps writes: "Because I was born in March, the beginning of the windy part of spring, I frequently received kites and kite string on my birthday. This period of vernal equinox was an annual season for kite flying, and merchants, cognizant of the market potential, always had a supply on hand when it began. My enthusiasm was due to the facts that building a kite required some creativity, flying it could be done alone, and it was probably the most animated inanimate object ever devised by man. The performance of a kite is primarily a function of the force and gustiness of the wind, the angle at which the wind strikes its surface, and the length of the tail, which is the stabilizer of the aerodynamics involved. The various combinations enumerated can cause the kite to dive, dance, be almost motionless, and even appear berserk when the string breaks. Sending paper 'messages' along the string to the kite and releasing handkerchief parachutes as they went to the top of the string added to the enjoyment of this pastime."

The Kites of March

It was all over school that Friday: Frank Hastings and his older brother and some other of the big boys were going to fly a kite that was six or eight or ten feet tall, depending on the time of the day the story was told. And they were going to send up a cat in a basket—or a German police dog—or a boy! By the sixth period (on that springtime Friday in Palestine, Texas, of the late Thirties), twelve-year-old mere-mortals were in such a frenzy of expectation that they were chewing on pencils, eating paste, and knocking over ink bottles. A pronoun or stated problem or Hannibal on an elephant on an Alp was a thing of no interest, was beside the only point that ever mattered: Frank Hastings was going to lash himself to a twelve-foot kite, and his big brother was going to fly him high enough to see all of Palestine and some of Elkhart. Like Christ on a flying cross! Now that was something that would get parents' attention when the tale was told at suppertime.

Springtime kite flying was nothing new. On those first promising March days—when the wind was still resentful of being dragged back to the frozen north to make room for the warmth of spring—we made and flew kites on Andrew Carnegie's library lawn. I was very happy with the simple two-stick kite that I made from anything handy and that was covered with newspaper. It was heavy, usually unbalanced, and required optimum wind conditions to make a decent showing. Three-stick kites of varying sizes, sometimes bought though usually made, were popular and flew with more stability on less tail than two-stickers. Periodically someone would show up with a box kite that his father had helped him build, and we all would admire its complexity and give it our full attention and let it have the sky to itself. Sometimes, when we got bored watching the kites just hang there in the sky, we would rein them in short and have kite fights, banging them into each other, which inevitably resulted in tangled lines and crashing kites. The kites of March were a tradition preparing the way for the marbles of April, and we flew them for an afternoon or maybe a few or until they went into a tree or power line. We recovered what string we could and went on to something else.

A twelve-footer soaring aloft with a human being was another matter.

The site of the ascension that Saturday morning was a hill pasture surrounded by a post-oak woods. A road ran through the center of the pasture on a gentle incline to the top of the hill. Jack Beard and I arrived before the kite crew but not before some of our peers. A half a dozen of us hung around—and chased and frogged and Indian-rope-burned and wrestled—for an hour before Frank and the kite came in a car with his brother George driving and the kite covering the top of the car like a huge cap. It was an impressive entrance.

The kite was a huge three-sticker covered with brown wrapping paper. It could have been twelve feet tall, for all I knew. It was almost as long as the car that carried it, and the light breeze that was picking up whipped it off the top of the car as soon as they untied it. They finally got it pinned, and they held it down with no little effort as they tied on the bridle and the tail of tow sacking. Jack and I looked around for a basket in which to loft a cat or a German police dog, but we didn't see one. A half a dozen small boys were handy, but none of them was fool enough to let himself be tied to a kite. And in the end it took just about everybody there, Frank Hastings included, to get the kite off the ground. Disappointingly, nobody was left to go up with the kite. We were soon so immersed in the problems of the kite that we forgot that we had expected a passenger.

Frank laid out about a hundred feet of towline from the kite bridle and looped it around the back bumper of the car. George sat on the spare tire with line to play out when the kite became wind-borne. We dwarfs got to help hold the kite up as a Big Boy in the car eased out the slack. There was a lot of yelling back and forth and finally George yelled, "Go!"

The kite went! The car accelerated and the kite went up about twenty feet and then nose-dived and slammed into the earth, with everybody cussing and screaming for Big Boy to stop. He did, after he had dragged the kite another twenty feet. Miraculously the kite survived intact. The paper was not even torn.

We carried it back up the hill and propped it up again, this time with the tail laid out behind instead of in front and with twice as much towline as we had had out before. Big Boy started out a little slower and smoother and the kite really went up this time! And everybody ran along cheering and yelling and awed by this thing that the Big Boys had wrought, this wonderful thing flying free of earth, looking down through kite's eyes and seeing us as birds and gods saw us. The great kite waltzed around a little at first, but after it got up a hundred feet or more it settled down to a steady slow rock, like a woman walking.

Big Boy stopped the car and George started carefully playing out line. This giant of a kite, which could have lifted a very small boy had one been available, slowly rose, maybe a hundred feet more, but then would go no higher. The wind had lifted all the kite and line that it had the strength for. We sat on the ground and marveled, and soared our hearts, tied like Christ's on the crosspiece. At this stage of life, this was as close as one could get to real flight.

A heavier wind came along a little later and raised the kite a few more feet, but a gust eventually broke the line where it was wrapped around the bumper. The kite sailed up the hill, bobbing and dropping as it went and as we raced to rescue it. It flopped down, out of breath, then cartwheeled and somersaulted as the wind blew and continued to punish it for its presumption.

We finally caught up to the dragging towline and stopped its runaway. Big Boy drove the car up the hill, and the fliers pinned the kite down and woefully began to examine its injuries, the main one being a broken strut. After much deliberation and

study of the situation, they decided that the kite had made its last flight for the day. They wrestled it on top of the car again and lashed it down, all the while trying to figure out how they could make the kite lighter and how to get stronger and lighter towline. They let the kids ride the running boards until they got back down to the main road.

I have never had a kite experience to equal that one. I made and flew kites at the instigation of my growing children, but once I got a kite hanging high on two balls of twine, I lost interest. I got kite fever when I saw the beautifully artistic kites of Singapore and Malaysia, but I was more interested in hanging a wall-full of the treasures than in flying them. I ached to get hold of a kite string in Tian An Men Square in Beijing when a young Chinese was flying a dragon kite that must have been thirty or forty feet long. It flew with ultimate grace and swayed in delight and rippled in the wind that held it. I watched as he reeled in this awesome flying thing that had seen from on high the Forbidden City with its Gate of Heavenly Peace and the Great Square where Chairman Mao had christened the People's Republic of China, and then this god-like creature slid to earth and became an artistically intricate series of bamboo hoops wrapped in colorful tissue paper.

The History of Kites

Legend has kites first appearing in China around the fifth century B.C. This is the general time of the Greek Periclean Age, of Buddha, Confucius, and Lao-tze, a great time of beginnings, when ideas were sent aloft that are still flying. And so are kites! (For the history of kites see Streeter, 153–164, and Hart, 23–32.) Historically, around 200 B.C. Chinese General Han Hsin flew a kite between his army and a palace in order to ascertain the distance a tunnel had to be dug to come up inside the palace walls. From China the tradition of kite flying went to Korea and Japan, the Malay Archipelago and Oceania, through Burma and India to Arabia and North Africa, and then to Europe from the Middle East and by the ocean trade routes (see map in Hart, 32).

My favorite Asiatic kite legend is about a famous Japanese outlaw who had himself flown in a great man-lifter kite over the palace of Nagoya so that he could steal the gold scales off two fish that adorned the steeple of that royal abode. The above-mentioned General Han Hsin is also legendarily associated with a man-lifter. In a campaign against an enemy, it is told that he had himself flown over the enemy camp at night, and he spook-ily called down to the soldiers to return to their homes or be destroyed, which they did, leaving the field to Han Hsin. A Ko-rean legend has a general launching his men in kites from a ship offshore to within the walls of the enemy's castle.

In Japan, kites were early flown for ritualistic purposes, ris-ing to invoke blessings from the gods in the form of sons and rich harvests and asking protection from all the evils that flocked under the bowl of the sky. As a custom the people of Nagoya celebrate the emperor's birthday by flying and fighting kites; in China the customary day is the ninth day of the ninth month. The giant ceremonial *wanwan* kite of Naruto, Japan, was round and sixty-three feet in diameter. Ready to fly in the nineteenth century, it weighed 8,800 pounds and required 150 to 200 men to control it. It crashed in 1914.

Beginning in the eighteenth century, kites were used for the exploration of the upper atmosphere. The most famous of the early meteorological scientists was Benjamin Franklin, who violated every rule of safe kite flying when he flew a kite up to a thunderhead to confirm the electrical nature of the atmosphere. The electricity flowed down the wet kite string to a suspended key. When the grounded Franklin held his finger near the key, a spark jumped. Fortunately, the charge was light enough to satisfy Franklin's curiosity about the nature of electricity without killing him. In 1910 a train of ten kites reached an American record height of 23,385 feet, and in 1919 in Lindenberg, Germany, a train of eight kites set a world record of 31,955 feet. Airplanes—and the Wrights began their invention by flying kites—and balloons have now taken the place of kites in atmospheric exploration (see *World Book Encyclopedia*, "kites").

Making and Flying Kites

I observed kites this spring. I toured parks and fields and saw that there was really a lot more kite flying than I had imagined. I did not see any tissue-paper kites—or newspaper kites, for that matter. They were all plastic-covered. And most had been bought. I saw Asiatic-looking bird and butterfly kites in their Oriental splendor. But they looked out of place in Nacogdoches. One young man had a train of four two-stickers flying very authoritatively. Three-stickers were popular among college kite fliers who hadn't quite left their childhood behind.

One spring Sunday afternoon a young Catholic Franciscan group helped kids make and fly kites at one of the city's parks. The most popular, and the best flyer that afternoon, was the sled kite, which was new to me but was very simple and once aloft held the wind nicely. The kite makers also favored the Conyne winged kite, which was more complicated than I was used to. Some of the kids made box kites, but the wind wasn't strong enough to keep them aloft for any length of time.

All the kites were made of plastic, mostly black and green plastic garbage bags. And the plastic was fastened to the sticks with Scotch tape. Kites were more efficiently made than I remember. Certainly no flour paste appeared among the kite makers.

For those who are seriously interested in making and flying kites, I recommend David Pelham's *The Penguin Book of Kites* and H. W. Fowler's *Kites: A Practical Guide to Kite Making and Flying.*

Building box kites.

The Flat Kite   Flat two- and three-stick kites can be made with purchased
dowels—1/8″, 3/16″, or 1/4″, depending on the size of the kite—
and plastic garbage bags. Struts and spines are also made from
split bamboo, window-shade sticks, and any other light stick that
is handy. After the struts have been cut and tied into the desired
frame, a string is run through precut grooves at the tip of each
strut, outlining the area of the kite and providing the frame for
the sail, or skin. The frame with string is then laid on a sheet of
the plastic, which is cut to the outline of the kite with a one-
inch outside margin. This margin is then folded over the string
and fastened with Scotch filament tape.

The traditional two-sticker (figure 1) has a twenty-four-
inch strut on a thirty-inch spine. A four-inch bow in the strut
will increase stability and negate the need for a tail, if the kite
is well balanced otherwise. Square kites (figures 2 and 3) fly well
with twenty-four-inch struts and spines. The three-sticker
(figure 4) can be made as a perfect hexagon, with thirty-inch
struts, although it is usually constructed with the cross-strut
unbalanced toward the top. The conventional three-sticker (figure 5) has thirty-inch diagonal struts and a twenty-four-inch
horizontal strut, unbalanced toward the top.

Flat kites usually require tails for stability. A tail can be
made of leftover plastic strips or cloth. The length of the tail

1.

2.

3.

depends on the size and balance of the kite and the force of the wind.

Most of the two-stickers can be flown with the string run through a hole in the skin and tied directly to the cross of the struts. For the traditional two-sticker in figure 1, a bridle can be attached through a hole to the spine three inches from the top and seven inches from the bottom. The kite is held in the wind by this bridle to find the point of the best flying angle, and the flying string is tied to this point. This same test is used when flying on a three-point bridle tied from the tips of the two struts and top of the spine.

4.

If the ordinary flying of an elemental kite is not interesting enough, there are several ways to add a dimension. Flat kites can be made in many different forms and still be aeronautically sound. They can be painted and tasseled and streamered, belled and whistled. The maker can leave about an inch of stick exposed on a three-sticker, cover and seal a long strip of plastic on the exposed string, and he has a hummer. Handkerchief parachutes can be sent up the line till they hit a trigger, which separates them from the line and allows them to float down.

Kites can also be fought. I doubt that anybody in the States gets involved in kite duels as much as do the Japanese of Nagoya, but it is something most adolescent kite flyers get into if they fly long enough. Ralph Miller of Ingram flew kites long enough and learned some devilish ways to cut a string and eviscerate an opponent's kite. One weapon was a tongue depressor with razor blades fitted on it and through it at ninety-degree angles and tied to the end of a kite's tail. Even deadlier was a foot-long piece of bamboo lethally armed up and down its length with halves of double-edged Gillette razor blades, edges up. Mothers frown on this sort of thing, as well they should.

5.

The sled kite (figure 6) is the simplest kite to make and fly. The plastic skin is cut to the proper dimensions, and the two struts are taped to the skin. The bridle points should be reinforced with tape. This kite, when properly made, needs no tail. The sled kite has twenty-eight-inch spines, parallel and sixteen inches apart. The overall width of the sled kite is thirty-four inches between the bridle points, which are on a perpendicular ten inches from the top of the spine. The bridle consists of two twenty-four-inch lines extending from the bridle points to a tow point, where the kite string is attached.

The Sled Kite

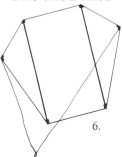

6.

Sled kite.

The Conyne Winged Kite

The Conyne kite is popular with present-day kite fliers. Optimum dimension of the struts are forty-two by forty-two inches. The leading strut is the point of a fourteen-inch free triangle. The frame for the Conyne kite is made the same way as a flat kite, although two temporary crosspieces braced between the spines help hold the form in shape while the cover is being applied. The Conyne kite was invented in 1902 and was early used as a man-lifter. It was also known as a French Military box kite, or Pilot kite.

The Box Kite

The box kite is basically four struts—forty-two inches is a recommended length—cross-braced to make a twenty-one-inch-square box with a twelve-inch skin cell at each end. A single flying string adjusted below the top cell or a bridle tied on the leading edge at the center of the two cells can be used. The box kite, which was invented in the 1890s, has a strong lift, and the Wright brothers' early versions of airplanes were variations on the box kite.

Conyne winged kite.

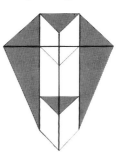

Box kite.

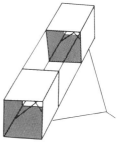

III

Floaters

Lift any adult male's shirt and you will find a faint longitudinal scar running down the side and length of his rib cage. This is the result of a universal insanity that occurs among young males during adolescence. Twelve-year-old boys are convinced that they can dive through an inner tube an unlimited number of times without ever getting raked down the ribs by a valve stem. Like the pitcher that took too many trips to the well, the boy will try one too many dives—just one more from a higher bank, or one more and this time he will hang the tube by his knees or toes as he passes cleanly through—and that is the time that he will miss the exact center of the tube target and scrape a streak from his armpit to his ankle. He will recover and try again because he is "enjoying" the basic floating toy of the last hundred years, the inner tube.

Inner tubes are popular because they work and they used to be readily available, several old patched ones sitting in a box in the back of every garage. Parents still never take children swimming in a noncommercial creek, tank, or lake without taking also a bunch of inner tubes to float in for pleasure and protection. Inner tube rafting has even gone commercial in some of the fast-moving streams and rivers of Central Texas. And one of the finer fishing devices is a commercially constructed inner tube cover and seat for fishermen who like to be down in the water amongst the creatures. These tubes come equipped with pockets for baits and candy bars and with holders for the rod.

Inner tubes work. They certainly work better than a washtub, which I once tried so diligently to make into a floater. Lawrence Farr, a young neighbor in Beaumont, did much better

with a modern bathtub. It did float, and with him in it, and if my memory serves me right, he even rigged a mast and a sail. I cannot imagine that he covered much water in his bathtub, but then he accomplished something by just staying afloat. George Ewing, who was blessed in having a very creative older brother, tells about his adventures afloat in Mercedes in the Thirties:

Canal Canoeing

by George Ewing

It's an ill wind that blows no man good." My daddy's statement, even with his grin, was hard to believe. We had just pushed the old thousand-pound Metropolitan player piano over against the north wall of the front room, along with the heavier furniture, and the whole family was huddled next to it, trying to keep the little box-and-string house in Mercedes, Texas, on its foundation. It was about midnight, and the 100 + MPH winds of the 1933 hurricane had begun to raise the floor an inch or two and drop it back onto the cedar posts obliviously designed to hold the house *up* rather than *down*. But the piano, with probably the hand of the Lord on the keyboard, did keep the house in place, and though we had to move everything to the south side after the passing of the storm's eye along toward morning, we made it through the twenty-four-hour ordeal with the loss only of the sleeping-porch roof, the barn, and the pigpen.

Daddy was right. As soon as this healthy wind died, he loaded his carpenter's tools into our '28 model Buick sedan and

In the foreground, Henry Ewing hand paddles the prototype of the canoe, preparing to ram Ted Bollier in *Barnacle Bill*, the improved model with hose-protected edges and some sort of paddle or pole. Behind him is George Ewing in the bobtailed, rear-submersible with a kayak paddle. In the background is a non-combatant Alden Smith with his non-bird-hunter pointer, Floppy, riding in the super model with the slanted ends, designed for combat. Mercedes, Texas —1934.

headed for town, ready to grab his share of the insurance-financed repair work that would give us the best income we'd had since the '29 crash. Now that was good for at least one man.

Along with this, however, that old storm tossed in something for the boys as well, at least for those Anglos around Mercedes where I lived. It scattered sheets of corrugated iron from barn roofs and sheds all over creation, maybe a half-dozen for every boy I knew, and started an activity that was still flourishing when I left the Lower Rio Grande Valley nearly four years later—tin canoeing.

During the Great Depression, the valley boys' life revolved around the irrigation canals. We didn't play ball except at school because the equipment cost too much, and swimming in the canals took no store-bought equipment at all—not even bathing suits or cut-off pants unless sisters came along, which was seldom. Besides the swimming games, we fished, made mud slides, had mud fights, floated on inner tubes, paddled on logs and scrap lumber like surfers, made rope swings on the rare large willows that overhung the banks in a few spots, climbed and bent the young willows to the ground, and built hiding places in the cattails. All these games were fun, but seemed terribly unsophisticated once we had made the canoes.

I'm not sure who first saw the possibilities in those sheets of tin, but my fifteen-year-old brother, Henry, got the credit for the invention in our neighborhood. He took a two-by-ten-foot piece of roofing iron (dozens from Avant's dairy barn had landed in our cornfield and orchard), hammered the corrugations flat in the middle and on the ends, smeared a couple of short one-by-two sticks with asphalt roofing compound, folded the ends of the sheet up around the sticks, and nailed them tight enough to be waterproof. Then he spread the middle apart about thirteen inches with two more sticks, and he had a canoe.

It was challenging success, for though the canoe was easy to make and carry, was costless (everything but the asphalt compound was considered trash, and a can of it was in nearly every barn or garage), and was maintenance-free, its round bottom, low sides, and narrow breadth made it difficult to keep afloat. If one side tilted down more than a couple of inches, water poured in and the boat headed for the bottom. It took some practice to learn to navigate one.

Henry mastered his in a very few tries, and the metal's minimum drag allowed him, paddling with his hands, to skim across the Main Canal faster than the best swimmers among us. Within days, there were half a dozen similar boats built from eight-, ten-, and twelve-foot sheets of roofing iron, and a new wet sport was born .

The equipment developed rapidly. Not seats, because since we didn't know that real canoeists kneeled, we sat flat on the bottom. Because the canoe's width was slightly more than that of the canoeist's pelvis, and that organ was about six inches lower than the water's surface, the boat could be easily propelled by hand, and many continued to use this system. But some dreamed of greater speed and tried paddles made of scrap planks tapered with a handaxe. Oars were discussed, but the sides of the vehicle were too flimsy for oarlocks. Then someone tacked a wood shingle to the end of a broomstick to produce the epitome of propulsion—the kayak paddle. You couldn't improve on that.

The paddles, though, intensified another problem—the sharp edges of the metal sides. We had had some trouble with cuts when we carried or launched the boats and let the gunwales slip through our hands and when we swam underwater dragging the swamped vessels ashore and hit our toes on the edges. Now, with paddles, in the excitement of the race or the battle we were lacerating our thumbs and wrists on careless downstrokes. Pain has probably mothered about as many inventions as necessity. The offspring this time was a piece of worn-out garden hose split lengthwise, put over the edge, and wired to the metal through holes punched with an ice pick.

Since the canoes were under the less-than-transparent canal water almost as much as they were on top of it, the next improvement was a marker system. This was before the days of plastic bottles, so the commonest marker was a half-gallon, watertight syrup bucket attached to the bow stick with eight or ten feet of fishing line. Even the Main Canal was seldom over seven feet deep (not counting the foot of mud at the bottom), and the float would surface and mark the canoe's resting place. One or two of the more affluent boys would use twenty feet or so of quarter-inch rope. They could then swim ashore with the float and stand on the bank to pull their canoes to the surface. The rest of us thought this method less than challenging, almost effeminate. When we went home, we stored our boats on the bottom of the canal, hiding the floats in the cattails or tying the string to an underwater stem.

Later improvements waited for the development of the sport. At first, just managing to stay afloat and negotiate a way across the seventy-five-foot-wide Main Canal was enough. Making a more manageable and attractive vehicle that displayed neater workmanship and might even have a name (like *Barnacle Bill*) on the bow brought added prestige. A few adventurers dreamed up canoe trips, paddling a half-mile or so up to the highway bridge, only to discover the anticlimactic drudgery of paddling back. These boats were toys, not transportation. It was easier and faster to walk along the bank, not paddle, and swimming across the canal usually kept you as dry as canoeing. Canoes were as useful for travel as a rubber gun was for rabbit hunting. I don't even recall anyone trying to fish from one of these ducking machines.

There were some contests of skill among the canoeists, such as riding double (sometimes successful in the ten- or twelve-footers) or standing up (mostly unsuccessful). Next came informal racing—forwards, backwards, and involving turns—and since racing *was* unofficiated, it quickly evolved into the most popular, but nameless, sport—ramming, capsizing, and ducking. The rules were simple: get your opponent into the water and his canoe under it without using hands, paddle, or teeth on the canoeist. Only the boat could be touched.

Since capsizing by hand might cut your fingers or tilt your own canoe over, ramming was by far the most popular mode of attack. This produced a triumph of aggressive engineering design—the slanted bow and stern. Boys with access to tin snips cut a deep V in the ends of the sheet of steel when the canoe was being made, and when the sides were folded up and attached to the sticks, the resulting slant would not only increase speed potential but also allow the destroyer to be driven up on the opponent's vessel, forcing it under.

These were boys' toys. My memory (labeled "male chauvinist" by my four daughters) cannot dredge up the sight of a single girl in a tin canoe. In fact, in my circle, no one who was mature enough to have dated a girl had any part in the design, manufacture, or operation of the canoes. When Howard Roman (we guessed he was a rich boy) showed up in a vessel that was obviously the product of a well-tooled adult, its ends machine-folded and brass-bradded, its surface lacking wood or asphalt or nail holes, the edge-hose riveted in place, and the crossbars smoothed and, I believe, painted, we—not outwardly, but deep within our souls—excluded him as being as unorthodox as a robed Episcopalian in a Baptist camp meeting. He, of course, was also of the rope-float group.

As the smallest and youngest of our coterie, I introduced one more design feature that gained only limited acceptance. Using a piece of tin less than five feet long, I nailed the back end to a seven-by-ten-inch board, making what looked like a half-canoe that would hold up my seventy or so pounds. If I jammed my feet as far as they would comfortably go into the pointed nose, my rear would be about ten inches from the stern, and with my hands or my double paddle, I could maneuver that little cockleshell like a water bug on a puddle's surface. If I got cornered and saw that I was going to be rammed, I could merely lean back, and the vessel would become a stern-first submarine. It was so small I could carry it swimming underwater to shore where I would re-embark and return to the armada. Incidentally, I do not recall anyone who could re-enter one of these canoes from the water. Since my tactical submersion was purposed and self-induced, I could not be credited with either lack of skill or defeat in battle. It was merely an evasive movement.

I don't know how long tin canoeing continued. Since I recall no Hispanics in canoes, maybe it was an Anglo activity that declined with the ethnic change in that region. But by the time I moved away from the valley fifty years ago, it had already been handed down from my brother's generation to mine (five years younger), and we were educating and bequeathing our equipment to a still younger group. I doubt that homemade tin canoes still ply the waters of the Main Canal, for forecast hurricanes probably can't raise the roofs as they used to, and things like Little League invaded during the Fifties and laid upon the kids the responsibility of fulfilling parents' frustrations and increased the involvement of adults—the very thing we tried to avoid. But galvanized steel lasts a long time when cut off from air, and my guess is that if the canal is ever drained, there will still be some rusty scraps of bent corrugated roofing deep in the mud, maybe even one with *Barnacle Bill* lettered on it.

◆ That is the best of floating, making your own boat and paddling about on the water and crashing into other boats, like a real navy in battle. That is glory! Younger children are reduced to smaller boats and to vicarious sailing o'er the bounding main. But that is no mean feat either. Building a floater requires some imagination. I watched children floating and sailing magnolia leaves on Village Creek one summer afternoon. They got large dried magnolia leaves and stuck on smaller leaves, held in blobs of mud, as sails and cast them out into the flow. They pressed captive insects into ship's service and sent fleets down the creek into the river and ultimately, I'm sure, out to sea to populate new worlds—or maybe to live like the Swiss family Robinson on a desert island. It was great adventure.

Arthur Smith of Gary made pine-bark boats: "We would take a piece of bark off a pine about as big as your hand. You would take your pocket knife and whittle a point on the front and a square tail for the back. We would punch a little hole in the middle of the boat. Then get a leaf and stick it in the hole and it acted like your sail" (*Loblolly* 6, no. 4 [1979], p. 40).

Children are still making sailboats out of anything that will float—styrofoam plates with soda-straw masts or corks with toothpick masts. Patricia Hurley sent in a sailboat made out of a bar of Ivory soap and one made raft-like of tongue depressors. Eldridge Harper's folded-paper sailboat requires a skill in construction that is almost extinct. More mobile, however, is the traditional rubber-band-powered motorboat. Lee Haile tells the history of rubber bands and how they are put into use in the motorboat:

Paddle Boats
by
Lee Haile

When Columbus came to the New World in 1492, the South American Indians he met were already playing with rubber balls that they had made. In 1736, French explorer Charles de la Condamine brought samples back with him to Europe. In 1770, an English scientist discovered that a hardened piece of latex would erase a pencil mark if you rubbed hard enough. That is where the term *rubber* came from. The Indians around the Amazon River were making rubber bottles by putting layers of latex on clay molds and breaking out the clay after the rubber had dried. By the end of the century, there had developed a good trade of rubber boots and bottles between South America and Europe. In the 1830s, another Englishman invented rubber bands by simply cutting up a rubber bottle into rings. This invention opened a whole new era in toy making. Rubber bands were soon being used on toys as a power source (Henderson and Wilkerson, 102).

One popular rubber-band-powered toy is the paddle boat. For this toy you need a thin board about ten inches long and four inches wide. This is just a rough figure. The best size to use is whatever you can find handy. Cut a U-shaped notch out of one end. If you use the ten-inch board, your notch should be about three inches deep. Now get another, smaller piece of board that will fit into the notch that you made. It should be about four inches long. Take your rubber band and stretch it over the two prongs of the U-shaped end. Stick the little board

Lee Haile's
paddle boat
(Karen Haile).

in the middle of the rubber band. Twist the little board and wind the rubber band up. Put it in the water and let her go. If the boat pulls backward instead of pushing forward, you have wound your paddle backward.

You can make a much better boat if you use two nails about three inches long. Nail the nails pointing up near the end of the two prongs, like two little flagpoles. Stretch the rubber band over the ends of the nails and put your paddle board in. Make sure the paddle will go into the water only a little way. You can move the rubber band up and down on the nails to make it right. This will make the boat go faster and with less dipping.

IV

Stilts and Stick Horses

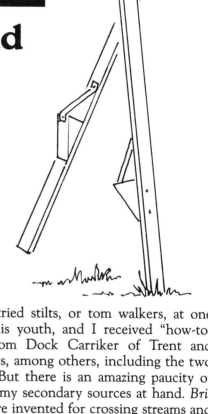

Just about everybody tried stilts, or tom walkers, at one stage or another of his youth, and I received "how-to-build-stilts" papers from Dock Carriker of Trent and Molly Brown of Nacogdoches, among others, including the two contributors quoted below. But there is an amazing paucity of information on stilts among my secondary sources at hand. *Britannica* tells us that stilts were invented for crossing streams and marshes in the European low countries. Stilts were a practical response to a continual problem, and they were used as naturally for wading as painters and sheetrock hangers use stilts nowadays to facilitate their work. During some long dry spell the children pulled stilts into their realms of play, and stilts have since become a universally popular plaything, as well as props for circus clowns and other tom-walking showmen. Incidentally, I never heard them called "tom walkers" until I was grown, and look as I might, I could not find the derivation of that term. The word *stilt* derives from a medieval word for "crutch" or "wooden leg," which makes good enough sense.

I do not remember who built my first pair of stilts. I do remember that the stilts I built in aftertimes were continually coming loose, in spite of my strapping the footrests to the pole with the strongest pieces of harness leather I could lay my hands on. I was always over-nailing and splitting boards. And a good illustration of *awkward* is losing your balance on a pair of stilts and trying to get back on the ground without whapping yourself up the side of the head with a stilt pole. In spite of which—or perhaps because of which—stilt racing was at one time a regular occurrence at BYPU parties in Palestine.

I was eight years old when our new house was finished in 1941. It was on that patch of land that Daddy had first sharecropped and then bought into Nolan County. It was right at the crest of Marguarita Hill, near Eskota Road.

The lumber scraps lay in a pile near the new cistern. Daddy pulled out a couple of boards about one inch by two, and about four feet long. "I'll make something for you like I used to play with when I was a kid." I waited patiently while he dug through the pile again. "Gotta have somethin' for your feet to rest on." He came up with two blocks about five inches long. He nailed one on the broad side of each board about ten inches from one end so they stuck out on the long boards.

"Get my leather." I hurried to the dining room closet and brought out the cowhide, carefully rolled and fastened with an old belt. Daddy pulled out his pocketknife and handed me one edge of the leather. I already knew how to hold it so that the newly cut part would be held steady, but loose enough not to put the blade in a bind. Smooth as silk, he cut two strips about three-fourths of an inch wide and fourteen inches long.

"This will serve as a brace." He nailed one end of the leather to the bottom of each foot piece and pulled the leather up to the long board and nailed it in place. "Gotta pull it tight, else the leather will stretch from your weight."

Daddy held the free end of the long boards. He turned the foot pieces toward each other, placed first one foot then the other on them, then walked across the yard, nearly a foot off the ground! Daddy had made my first pair of stilts.

When I started making them for myself, I soon learned that old bed slats were just the right size.

My long-term goal was to make a new set each week, making them taller and taller each time. I had every intention of becoming the female version of the "Tall Man" in the circus, towering high above the crowd, eliciting "OOH's" and "AAH's" from an appreciative audience.

I had not taken into account that there were no bed slats that long.

A Career with the Circus
by
Bettye Martin McRae

Alice McRae on bed-slat stilts (Betty Seaman).

We knew the word *stilts* in Edinburg in the spring of 1930, but we called them tom walkers. My daddy was a builder, he always had scrap lumber around the house. He probably showed my brother Henry, who was twelve years old at the time I was seven, how to make the things, but I remember that we made these on our own, cutting the triangular blocks and nailing through the uprights into them. The straps were usually made of pieces of old belts or harness leather, but cotton sash cord could be used. The straps, we thought, would keep the blocks from pulling free

Tom Walkers
by
George W. Ewing

Henry Ewing (nearly 12) and George Ewing (about 7) in Edinburg, Texas, early 1930s, on homemade tom walkers (George Ewing).

of the nails, and were also handy in mud—we could lift with our feet. Henry soon learned to tuck his stilt handles under his belt and free his hands. I never had the courage to do this. My foot pieces were about three feet off the ground; my brother's were about four and a half. The next pair he made so tall that he had to climb on the front porch roof to get on them—probably close to eight feet from the ground to his foot.

Tin-Can Stilts
by
Elton Miles

Before we were ready for stick stilts, we walked on stilts we made of inverted empty tin cans and wire. As a six-year-old I made them for myself in Gatesville, Texas, in the 1920s. As a father in the Fifties and Sixties at Alpine, Texas, I showed my own small children how to make them. They were overjoyed.

Tin-can stilts are made by punching a hole on each side of two empty cans, barely above the bottom. Half-gallon cans are best. For handles, a loop of wire is passed through the holes of each can and twisted securely inside. Then a child stands on the cans and walks, holding them firmly against his feet by means of the wire loops.

For the first time, a youngster can walk tall without the fear of falling.

◆ Natalie Ornish as a child in Galveston made Carnation-can stilts with the added convenience of straps that went over the shoulders. Even simpler than the tin-can stilts, but closer to the ground, are what Carrol Daniels of Nacogdoches calls "space shoes." Space shoes are made from empty aluminum Coke cans. When the child steps in the middle of a can, its ends hook up and attach themselves to the shoe. These make a fine clatter and are cheap and easy to make.

Both stilts and stick horses are walkers and incorporate the user's legs and feet in the process of play. Almost as necessary as legs is imagination, particularly so in the use of stick horses. A boy on stilts can imagine his dominance because of his height or imagine he is the tall man in the circus, but the imagination has to be on full power when a child throws a leg over a mop handle and hi-hos Silver. I watched my grandson once as he started out with a decent enough three-foot stick for a horse. He eventually rode (and broke) that horse down to a nub of a stick that was as horse-like to him as the original stick had been. I personally preferred old brooms with binder-twine reins through the straw. Now that *looked* like a horse! So did Kim Brooks's horse made out of a mop handle and her brother's tube socks. They stuffed the sock and painted on a horse face with magic markers and rode the range in style.

I trust [the author says to me in a September 1987 letter] you will not forget the "stick horse"—not a hobby horse or a rocking horse or the horse's head on a dowel, but a real stick horse made from the "seenie weed" of our Texas prairies and open grazing lands. Its smooth, straight offshoot is broken away at the root. All leaves are removed except for a handsome spray at one end—for a tail, of course, and to leave a splendid trail in the dust. A length of string is looped in a half-hitch about the leaf-less end for a bridle and reins, and one is ready to mount and ride the range after herds of cattle or wild horses, or flee at a smart gallop from the sheriff's posse. There is no play horse like a Texas stick horse. He's cheap, expendable, and has never thrown a rider.

"Seenie Weed" Horses
by
Josephine M. Smith

In a boy's life, the years between five and eight seem to be the years suited to the stick horse. One day there dawned on me the idea of establishing a cavvy of stick horses. There were plenty of small chinaberry limbs available. Across the alley from our back acre was a clump of fishing-pole cane, and I discovered that these too made excellent steeds, though they tended to split between joints when stepped on. The oak trees didn't have

A Cavvy of Stick Horses
by
Charlie Oden

Stick horse race (Richard Orton).

much to offer in the way of useful horses. Nor did broom handles. Of course, the chinaberry and cane poles had to be selected for quality and appeal, then trimmed suitably and cut to length.

At first, older siblings would cut notches for the string bridle at the "head" end of the stick. There were no heads such as are found on store-bought stick horses. Later I was able to do this chore. The members of our family were trucker farmers who grew turnip and mustard and collard greens to be pulled and washed and bunched by the dozen bunches. Each bunch was tied with four quick wraps of string, so there was plenty of string available for making bridles and reins for stick horses. By doubling a piece of string about eighteen inches long, thrusting the thumb and forefinger through the loop thus formed by the bend, then catching the doubled string with thumb and forefinger and pulling it through the bend, a noose was formed, which was slipped onto the stick horse's head and tightened into the notch.

For some unknown and unboyish reason, I never left my stick horses scattered about but kept them lined up together, side by side, down by the old well. At one time there must have been between fifteen and twenty of these fine critters, and I recall experiencing a sense of satisfaction on those occasions when I surveyed the remuda. There were favorites among the horse herd, but I rode each one some, feeling that somehow I was obliged to use what I had and feeling that somehow it was wrong to have possessions that I didn't use. I never traded horses with anyone, but that may have been because I seldom had other kids with whom to play, and the idea just didn't come to mind.

The natural way of riding one of these *caballos* is a hopping run with the trunk of the rider's body turned slightly to the right as he lays on the quirt with the right hand. For this reason, riding stick horses really impeded playing cowboys and Indians and cops and robbers; a boy just can't run as fast astride a stick horse as he can without one. I might have ridden stick horses to play at herding cattle, but the main use of them seems to have been burning off energy by just straddling one and running around the place at a full hopping gallop while yelling so loudly that Mother would say, "Go down behind the barn to ride your horse, son."

I suppose Momma finally burned the remuda under the washpot when she decided that I had outgrown stick horses.

◆ On December 12, 1984, the Reverend Frank Walker interviewed Royal Clinton "Red" Stoner on the Big Tree Ranch by the Frio River near Concan, Texas. Royal vividly remembered his stick horses of seventy years earlier:

Royal Clinton Stoner: Our main playthings were stick horses which we'd whittle out. Everyone of us had our own favorite. Mike [Michael L. Stoner, Royal's brother and owner of the hundred-plus-year-old Big Tree Ranch] had a cedar stick. Glorious Red Cloud, he called him. He came to a bad end. Liked to broke Mike's heart. That was what Dad picked up one time to kill a skunk with, and he broke the stick horse doing it.

I remember I got a sotol stick one day and I decided I wanted a paint horse. And I got some persimmons, and I made a black horse out of him. Then I took my pocketknife, and I made a paint horse out of him by whittling spots on it. Boy, I was all fixed up, and I went to riding that horse.

I don't remember having a name for it. Mother probably had some kind of name for it and me, both, by the time she finished washing those pants with that persimmon on them. And Margaret had a sotol that somebody had brought, one of these Mexican herders from out in the mountains, but it came up here and dropped down and back out, just a perfect neck on him and everything. And that was her pride and joy. That really was the best one any of us had.

Margaret Stoner McLean [Mrs. Malcolm D. McLean of Arlington, commenting on the interview in a September 1987 letter]: Red has correctly remembered that Mike's cedar stick horse was named Glorious Red Cloud. I recall that was a name suggested from stories our mother used to tell of the fine horses owned by Stoner relatives who lived in the Kentucky area of Lexington-Paris-Mt. Sterling.

None of us recall the name of Red's horse, which was made from a soft wood sotol stick. It took the persimmon juice extremely well, and the ever present pocketknife made it an easy job to turn the horse into a paint.

My horse, as Red has noted, was also made of sotol. This was indeed a wonderful horse! The sotol stick had grown perfectly straight for some three or more feet; then something in nature caused it to make a gentle curve up, to form a graceful neck of some ten inches, before again curving out to form a lovely head. Either the Mexican goatherd or my father had

Glorious Red Cloud and Others
by
Royal Clinton Stoner and Margaret Stoner McLean

Small boy adjusting
inner-tube chaps
with bottle-cap
conchos, fashioned
by Elton Miles.
Broom-type stick
horse looking on.

carefully trimmed and smoothed the stick before giving it to
me. I believe there were even notches made so that a bridle
could be attached. Such a horse certain deserved a worthy
name: I called him Stonewall Jackson!

◆ Texas's most famous stick horse was one built by Roddy
Reynolds of Putnam, near Cisco in Callahan County (see the
Houston Post, February 27, 1966). Roddy was twelve in 1960
when he built a stick horse named Gold Dust to celebrate
the hundredth anniversary of the Pony Express. On a family
vacation in New Mexico he left Gold Dust at a Route 66 road-
side park with a note asking travelers to give his stick horse a
lift, in order to celebrate and emulate the Pony Express. Travelers eventually carried Gold Dust all over the world before he
got lost somewhere in the outback of Australia. The Aussies,
embarrassed by the disappearance, sent Roddy a stick kanga-
roo. It was friendly and it was appreciated, but it just wasn't the
same.

V

Weapons

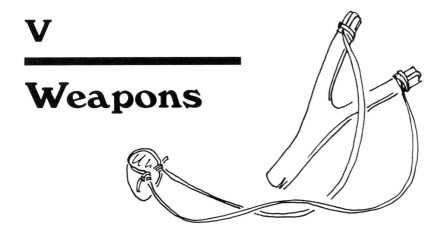

Robert Ardrey has a chapter in *African Genesis* that he calls "The Bad Weather Animal." He is talking about man, of course, and is discussing that period in man's evolution when he began using hunting tools—weapons. It was during the drouth of the Pliocene, according to modern archaeological conclusions, that our primate ancestor became a meat eater. The command came from the natural selector, Ardrey says in almost mystical tones: "Kill, and eat meat, or die!" So man left his browsing on fruits and nuts and roots and bugs and hefted some handy sticks and stones and began to fatten himself on the animals that heretofore he had foraged with.

Arthur C. Clarke took that chapter and created the first book of *2001 Space Odyssey*, although Moonwatcher, the protagonist, receives his command from the mysterious crystal monolith, rather than from some genetic mutation. The result is the same; Moonwatcher becomes the hunter and ultimately the warrior. There is this great scene in the movie adaptation of the novel when Moonwatcher begins wielding a club-sized thigh bone and starts banging around and feeling the power he gets with this new tool, this weapon.

Moonwatcher's progeny unto this very day are hunters and warriors, weapons users. And weapons using begins early for some young warriors and hunters. Whether the cause be genes or conditioning or both, young males begin wielding and throwing early on in their lives, and the toys they make and use are practice weapons for their maturity.

Store-bought cap pistols and battery-powered zap guns— along with a well-aimed index finger, a well-flung rock, or a well-swung stick—constitute early childhood uses of weaponry. New constructions come later, in the Neolithic and Bronze Ages of maturation, when the weapons users have developed the

Mexican *Nigasura*, or slingshot, made of wire wrapped with plastic-coated wire (Joe Graham).

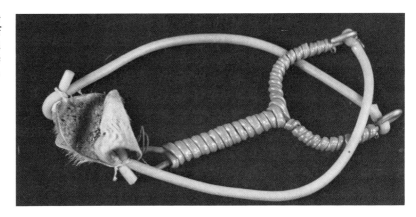

dexterity to use simple tools. Then the hand-flung projectile is not enough. They want the reality of contact, of propelling an object for both distance and accuracy and striking a victim, or at least a target. And all of this shooting and flinging is as natural to many modern Texas kids as spearing the rolling hoop was for Wichita Indian children playing along the banks of the Red River two hundred years ago.

Ten- to twelve-year-olds in Palestine were regularly armed with niggershooters two generations ago. We called them by that name thoughtlessly, without consideration of the implications of the term and without any thought of shooting black people with them. And if my memory serves me right, the black kids that we played with at the old practice field by The Creek called them niggershooters too. It is a term that is presently, properly, and universally eschewed, and I shall hereafter refer to that toy weapon as a slingshot, knowing full well what a true slingshot is, as I shall later describe.

Please allow me to digress for a paragraph to discuss Palestine's old practice field (and playground) along The Creek (if The Creek had a name, I never heard it) because it represents, I believe, that universal phenomenon in the territorial imperative, a neutral ground. It was the one area in town that was in neither black nor white territory and thus constituted a place of games for youths of both races. Playing racially integrated stick-ball or football or having a rubber-gun battle with black kids along The Creek boundary was comfortable and natural. I remember one black kid getting mad because he didn't get to pitch or something and taking his ball and going home. Everybody—black and white—got mad at him and called him bad names as he crossed The Creek and went home. And the black kids were a lot harder on him than we were.

To return to slingshots—

Several of us during one spring and summer went through a slingshot phase. We had slingshots of all sizes and makes and for all occasions. We had slingshots with forked-stick handles, less practical slingshots that we sawed out of boards using a coping saw, and small stiff-wired-handled slingshots that were slung with rubber bands and were concealed about our persons for surreptitious use in study hall. We never looked at a tree without sizing it out for slingshot stocks. We rummaged through the trash barrels behind filling stations looking for old inner tubes made of red rubber, the mark of highest elasticity. We scavenged the junk at mechanics' shops for ball bearings for ammunition and sampled the criminal excitement of stealing glassy marbles at Woolworth's. We stashed our regulars in our lockers when school began but kept ourselves ever-ready with our miniature concealed pocket slingshots. Most of the time we carried them in our hip pockets, but if action was imminent and rocks and targets were handy we hung them around our necks. I probably still have a scar on the chin from momentarily hanging my neck-dangling slingshot on a barbed-wire fence as I crawled through it. When the slingshot finally let go of the wire and whapped me in the chin, it gained revenge for every dumb beast that I had carelessly shot in my ramblings.

Building a slingshot for this article was a pleasure, and I have recaptured the old thrill of pulling down on a transient cat or chicken. I have, also and unfortunately, lost my aim. The stock is of cherry laurel, and you will notice that the stock is not a symmetrical Y. Stocks seldom are; branches don't fork that way. In fact, one fork—the main branch—will always be larger than the other and will require shaving down to match its mate. The fact that the handle will always angle off is an advantage also. One slings the stock so that it will be comfortable to the grip, and the angle helps. I was informed that red, stretchy inner tubes were no more, so I resorted to a longitudinal slice out of a bicycle tube. It has the stretch but not the strength of the old reds. Pockets were traditionally made out of old shoe tongues; one wasn't readily available to me, but some scrap leather was.

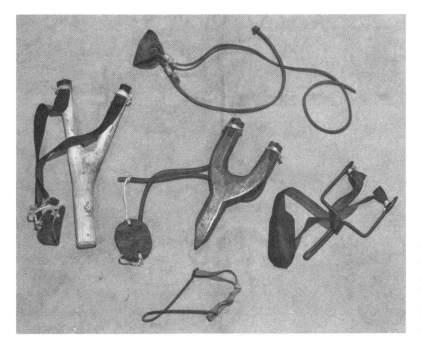

Traditional slingshot, (top); cherry laurel slingshot, WWII slingshot, TP&L ground wire slingshot (left to right); pocket derringer (bottom).

Nylon string was a decided improvement over vintage cotton cord, and I secured my knots with a drop of Elmer's Glue, another boon to modern builders. The finished product works beautifully and was built in an hour, more or less. I carried it to school one morning and let my friends get the feel of it. Needless to say, they were envious.

The second-sized slingshot pictured on page 47 is one I cut out of a piece of wood when the U.S.S. *Harkness* was in Majuro on its way to Okinawa in WW II. That it is still rattling around among my effects reveals something about character, I imagine. Whatever the flaws may be, it was available for re-slinging, and for illustration's sake I used surgical tubing, which has great elasticity but lacks the sturdy class of the traditional weapon. To complete the set, I made a third slingshot of TP&L ground wire, and a fourth pocket-derringer model out of #10 guy wire. All in all, I should say this is a formidable arsenal of slingshots. You slingshot users do remember, I am sure, that you could always use your fingers as the slingshot stock and a regular rubber band for the slings, whistling a rolled-paper projectile at a retreating derriere with considerable accuracy. As a footnote, lizard-hunting students with whom I used to associate used slingshots armed with marshmallows to stun their prey.

I conclude with a true slingshot, the kind with which David slew Goliath and the kind with which Ayla became so proficient in Jean Auel's *Clan of the Cave Bear*. Periodically some boy would show up with a real slingshot, but I never knew anyone who was good with the weapon. The method of launching the shot is simple enough in theory. You wrap the end of the long thong around the base of the index finger, hold the end of the short thong between the thumb and the tip of the index finger, whirl, and release. The shot flies off at a tangent to the whirled circle, and if released at the exactly correct moment, the shot will hit a designated target. Calculating the proper time to achieve the proper tangent requires a mind comfortable with advanced calculus, which I fortunately flunked in order to become an English teacher. This time around, I was finally able to release somewhere within a planned ninety-degree arc, so Goliath has nothing to worry about from me.

Rubber Guns
by
Tom Breedlove

A well-known fact of physics is that a stretched rubber band suddenly released at one end will fly through the air causing various amounts of pain when it contacts exposed flesh. This phenomenon was the basis for the rubber gun. The following descriptions are based on personal experience during the late Thirties and early Forties and were common in South Texas. I am sure various modifications evolved in other parts of the state. A boy needed a rubber gun to join in the summertime neighborhood mayhem known as "Rubber Gun Fights." Three basic items were needed for a rubber gun: a board, preferably a 1 × 4, at least two feet long and cut into the shape of a long-barreled

Lee Haile teaching the firing of the multiple-shot rubber gun (Karen Haile).

pistol; an old inner tube; and a clothespin, one of the modern type with a spring.

The inner tubes were the raw material for rubber bands, most commonly called ammunition. Prior to WWII these were readily accessible around any filling station, but as the war wore on they became more and more precious due to rationing. They came in two colors, red and black. However, there was no color or, for that matter, brand preference. A tube from a blown-out tire was preferred over a worn tube, which tended to break at worn spots, or over a patched tube, in which the elasticity—we called it "the stretch"—was reduced by a patch.

The tube was cut into rubber bands approximately one-half-inch wide. Many a mother's sewing scissors were dulled in this operation. One tube would supply countless rubber bands. One cut until blisters appeared or until anticipation of the coming fight overcame logistical prudence.

The clothespin was disassembled, and one stick was attached to the back of the grip of the pistol with a few loops of a rubber band. The spring and remaining stick were fitted back into their original positions and were wrapped with the remainder of the rubber band, giving the clothespin a stronger hold. [Editor's note: An alternative method of attaching the clothespin is simply to hold the clothespin against the butt of the gun and loop the stretched rubber band around it and the gun butt as many times as possible, stacking the loops from the coil spring out to the jaws.]

Loading was accomplished by looping one end of the rubber band over the end of the muzzle and stretching and twisting it back over the top of the barrel to the grip, so that a fold would be held in the clothespin.

[Editor's note: A basic difference of opinion arose on the matter of loading. As an old rubber-gunner, I maintain that the rubber band is folded and inserted into the jaws of the clothespin as the first step. Then one holds the jaws tight on the band with his right hand while he stretches the band down and over the end of the muzzle with his left hand. It is next to impossible, not to mention dangerous, to pull a rubber band the length of a long barrel and *then* insert the folded end into the clothespin. Try it. To substantiate my position, I asked several aged rubber-gunners in the English department to load a long-barreled gun, and those that remembered, loaded the clothespin end first. I say this in spite of Mr. Breedlove's support by his wife and the president of the Freer Chamber of Commerce. I am reminded of Swift's Big Endians and Little Endians, for some reason.]

This simple loading procedure was fraught with hazards. Long barrels and thin or worn rubber bands were not compatible. Too frequently the elastic limits were exceeded, causing the ammunition to break and fly back on exposed anatomy. This resulted in a rather large red welt and thus secured one's opponent's objective. (Only those with an active death wish attempted to load a three-foot barrel.) Add to this that in actual combat, reloading was attempted in all-out retreat. Ninety-five percent of the wounds in rubber gun fights were self-inflicted.

Folk art was incorporated in the South Texas gun in the form of a crescent cut in the muzzle. Theoretically this was to hold the rubber band more securely; it didn't, but peer pressure mandated it or else "you will shoot yourself."

Modifications of the basic model were common. Most changes were ornamental, notches being the most frequent adornment. However, vivid still is the memory of my first encounter with the infamous Triple Shooter.

After ducking a poorly timed shot by a new opponent, I was closing in for the kill when to my utter amazement he raised his "empty" gun and let me have two shots to the head at close range. This cultural shock was akin to that of the Indian when introduced to Colt's revolving pistol.

At Kool-Aid break I was allowed to see but not hold my assassin's prize possession. His gun had clothespins attached to each side of the grip as well as the rear.

Not wanting to be left behind in this new-found technology, I soon assembled my own Triple Shooter. After several losing encounters with this advanced armament, I realized that shots must be fired in reverse order of loading or else the gun "jammed." If I stopped to think I was dead. The Triple Shooter has the same length barrel as the single shot. The model made for the illustration here was scaled to fit my particular rubber band.

Another variation was the machine gun. This was more of a rifle than a pistol in design and did not use a clothespin. Notches were cut in a barrel starting about eighteen inches from the muzzle and about one inch apart as far back as one thought a good rubber band would stretch—usually two inches further than one

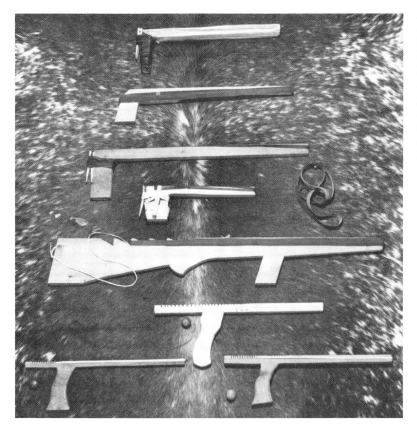

Top to bottom: Molly Brown's double shooter, Fred Rodewald's flip pistol, the editor's standard rubber gun, Tom Breedlove's triple shooter, editor's machine gun, three assault pistols by Lee Haile.

actually would. A string was attached in front of the first notch and was laid back over the notches, extending approximately a foot beyond the last notch. The rubber bands were looped from the muzzle to the notches with the string beneath the rubbers. Firing was accomplished by lifting the string. It was awesome. An accomplished machine gunner could fire one shot at a time, if he was cool. The problem was that in South Texas summers, in the middle of a rubber gun fight, no one was cool. This weapon tended to resemble a shotgun, wreaking havoc on anyone in front of the blast but leaving the gunner unprotected for the inevitable counterattack. Reloading was best accomplished in the privacy of one's own home.

The best part of rubber gun fights was the complete absence of any rules. It was total war. Prisoners were shot several times and with unbounded glee. Shooting in the back not only was fair but also was the safest shot.

Various defensive tactics were employed. Shields of garbage-can lids, cardboard, and wood were common. These not only warded off shots but also were very handy when tempers flared and the victim used his empty gun as a club or hurled a dirt clod.

Modern technology of synthetic rubber, tubeless tires, and electric dryers have caused the extinction of the rubber guns of my youth. Yes, some toy makers at craft fairs offer a simulated version of this artifact. This modern variation is designed to sting, not hurt. That takes away all the fun.

The Multi-Shot Flip Pistol

by

George W. Ewing

The multi-shot flip pistol replaced the clothespin rubber gun in the groups I shot with in Edinburg and Mercedes, 1929–36. My father was a building contractor and master carpenter, so we always had access to tools and scrap lumber, and we cut our rubber guns out of 1 × 4's.

We used the old natural rubber from the inner tubes bought for our Model A Fords, unless we could locate a special purple tube that I think was for the skinny-tired Model T. When we cut a one-half-inch band from that four-inch-diameter tube, it took strong boy fingers to stretch the band on one of these pistols (it was almost unbreakable), and it could make a red spot on an arm at eight or ten feet.

Firing a flip pistol was faster than firing the clothespin model, and certainly getting ready for the next shot took only a fraction of the time required for the older type. By 1931 the best gunmen had all gone to the crisscross method of loading, in which six or seven rubber bands were loaded. The bands were crisscrossed on the butt of the gun for easier access, and firing was like the fanning of a Colt .45. The right thumb held the loaded band on a bevel that was cut at the top of the butt while the left thumb was rolling the next band up to the bevel for firing. As soon as the right thumb fired the first rubber band, the second was rolled up into place for firing. A boy could fire six shots as fast as he could roll and load his gun.

On a draw-and-shoot, face-to-face duel, the clothespin gun had the same advantage over the flip gun that the double-action, self-cocking revolver had over the thumb-cocked or fanned single-action—but we didn't fight that way. Ours were the sneak-and-shoot gunfights, with the loaded weapons in hand, probably a more authentic imitation of the Western battles than what we saw on Saturday at the picture show.

I said the gun "replaced" the clothespin model; that's not quite accurate. We still continued to make the inferior weapon for the little boys and beginners, including people like my sister, who insisted on joining in sometimes (after all, she *could* chin thirteen times), but we flip-gunners definitely had a condescending attitude toward such, especially as we popped the enemy four times while they were trying to reload their guns.

The flip gun also had the advantage over the pull-string repeating rifle in that every rubber was stretched the same—the maximum that we found practical. As my brother got older, I think some of his pistols reached over twenty inches long. If the rubber could be stretched longer, it would shoot harder, but it was also harder to roll and hold.

Variation of the Flip Gun

by

Fred Rodewald

On our rubber guns—in Brownsville in the 1940s—the top of the grip was at a right angle to the barrel (rather than at a 45-degree bevel), with the edge at the top of the grip sanded down or carved to prevent the bands from hanging when we fired them. Our guns were from four- to six-shot "repeaters." We loaded from the end of the barrel back and would hang the first band at an angle over the left corner of the top of the handle. The next band would go over the first, except it would be hung at an angle over the right corner. The third band went over the first band, except it would be a little higher on the handle. The fourth would follow the second and so on. Though loading this way was a delicate operation, firing the bands from a single corner of the handle was fast and easy and gave the gun a hair trigger. (The band was being pushed over only one obstacle—either the left corner or the right corner—rather than over two corners of the handle top.) Holding the gun in his right hand, a shooter could, with simple pushes of his right thumb, quickly unload his four to six bands. This ease of firing made it possible for a dexterous shooter to become a formidable "two-gun man."

Prickly-Pear Darts and Spear Grass
by
Ruth Semrau

Each new generation of children in the brush country of South Texas invents prickly-pear darts, a seasonal weapon. In the center of a big, bright-yellow prickly-pear blossom is found a perfect little torpedo-shaped structure, the fleshy pistil, attached at the bottom by a short neck. You can carefully reach in and snap this off, watching out for bees and bugs and thorns. Break off one of the large, dry spines and push the blunt end of the spine into the blunt end of the pistil—voila, a dart. Make a few more for a stockpile and then go looking for a target. If you find when you go poking into your blossom that the pistil is gone, then watch out! Someone may be aiming for you.

In Collin County, another natural dart game is played with something called spear grass. Whereas the prickly-pear darts are a finite resource—how many you can make depends on how many pear bushes with blossoms you can find—the supply of spear grass is huge while it lasts. This grass grows in thick round clumps, the seeds being borne at the tips of slender stems, each one a tiny spear eight to ten inches long. Bothersome little hairs grow on the seed hull, spoiling aim and retarding speed, and must be licked off. Any other method of removal is considered inefficient and unacceptable as part of the ritual of preparation. This occasionally causes spear-grass-in-the-tongue and lots of spitting. Another slightly more serious side effect occurs when the spear is accidently inhaled and sticks in the back of the throat, causing the victim to gag, cough, and flap his arms. If the young soldier can't get the thing out himself, nor can a fellow soldier, then a mom must be appealed to. This is a last resort, as the mom will always be annoyed, at the very least. She will pass this annoyance (or worse) along to the sufferer by saying things like, "Can't you leave that stuff alone? I told you this would happen." Sometimes she will try to enact a taboo, but this is rarely effective. The spear grass fights go underground. If all goes well, an arsenal of spear grass to last all day can be laid down. Most fellows take a pelting in good part, guarding their personal clumps of ammo or setting traps around them. It is generally not thought wise to shoot at girls. It is simply not their idea of fun to be stung by tiny darts, and they will often get mad, run off, and tell. Speargrass fighting too is a seasonal activity and like the bluebonnets can be enjoyed for only a few weeks a year. If it lasted any longer it might pall.

A third game involving homemade weapons is of more recent vintage. If it is called anything, it might be called pen-gun, and it is played almost exclusively in the schoolroom. A cheap ball-point pen and a coat hanger are the raw materials. You remove the innards from the pen, leaving a hollow cylinder with holes at either end and a small hole along the shaft. This latter hole must be closed—wrapping with tape is best. Cut your wire about three inches longer than the pen shaft, leaving enough for an individually shaped handle at the end. Wad the end of your wire with paper, sliding it up and down the inside of the shaft until you've got it moving easily but without space for air to leak through. The best spit wads are made with toilet paper, but if that is not available, notebook paper will do, chewed to the right consistency. No teacher can be allowed to observe any chewing, or the player so caught will be "out." When the spit wad is ready, the gun is loaded on the narrow end with the ramrod fully extended out of the barrel. The gun can then be fired by forcing the ramrod down the barrel—the accumulating pressure will expel the spit wad with a good deal of force. The resulting "Pop!" can be heard all over the classroom, but if the teacher happens not to be looking in the right direction, she usually cannot tell where the sound is coming from. From her point of view, the kid who is pretending to have heard nothing is often the culprit, but it is never safe to accuse without more conclusive evidence than this, and the kids know it too.

You will have noticed that this game has an added depth of complexity in that it is played not only kid versus kid but also kid versus teacher. The student's objective is to continue the game, scoring as many coups as possible. The teacher's objective is to shut it down. Recently a group of teachers brought in the principal as artillery for their side, in the interest of their own sanity. The response of the kids was to make more pen-guns to compensate for the increased confiscations. This little war can go on for a long time, since the odds, for once, are with the student if he doesn't get too careless. The last time this game was played at my school, it finally died because the kids got tired of it and went on to something else. There must be a lesson in that somewhere.

Blood-weed Javelins
by
Ben Myers

When I was growing up on the edge of Sherman in north Texas, we poor boys didn't have store-bought toys to play with. So we made do by playing with readily available things, like frogs and snakes—and blood-weed javelins.

In the fall of the year the "blood-weeds" died and got very hard, almost as hard as wood. It was fun to pull them out of the ground and have team fights with them. The blood-weed grew about six to seven feet high, but the root system was shallow. We would pull them out of the sand, down by the creek, and shake off the dirt around the taproot. This made a fine six- or seven-foot javelin. The dead leaves and stems left on the top of the old weed would make it sail true, like an arrow.

We would choose up sides and allow about fifteen minutes for each side to gather enough good javelins for ammunition for the coming face-off. Usually each boy would get about a dozen javelins. Most boys would also get a tin sign or piece of heavy pasteboard to put under his belt as a breastplate. The taproot of the blood-weed wasn't likely to penetrate through the ribs. However, we found that the stomach was too soft, and a heavy blood-weed thrown forty or fifty feet through the air could do real damage. We didn't bother about eye protection; our theory was that anyone could see the arrows coming and duck his head. One of the boys did manage to get an aviator cap with goggles, thinking this was a positive step forward. However, he soon found that this restricted his view somewhat, because he was taking more hits. The real experts learned to duck fast and often, because a javlin hit hurt something fierce. A direct hit, many times, required first aid.

Usually one guy acted as the umpire to score the major shots. A hit on a limb was only a wound. A major hit on the body trunk was considered a kill. However, most players were adept at turning quickly to receive only a glancing blow. This was termed a wound.

Both sides usually had about the same weapons. To win, a team had to develop a strategy that would knock out the top javelin-throwers on the other team as early as possible. You could usually dodge even the hardest javelin-thrower if you were looking at him when he threw the javelin. However, a team would set up a cross-fire with several members who would spread out, each throwing at the "head knocker" on the other side.

This may seem like a very savage game. However, poor boys like us didn't have footballs, or softballs and bats, and this was just a good game for letting off steam. It was a very energy-demanding pastime, and actually it was a good way to develop teamwork.

When anyone got really hurt, everybody got involved in getting him some first aid, just as boys playing sandlot ball would do. Luckily no one got an eye put out or any other wounds that were not recoverable.

Elderberry Blowguns
by Howard Peacock

Blowgun battles required chinaberries for ammunition. Guns were made by cutting a one-inch-thick, straight elderberry stalk to a length of eight or ten inches. The pulpy center was reamed out with a stick. A plunger was made by trimming a piece of hardwood branch that had been divided into a rod section and a handle section. The rod part was cut to fit the inside of the elderberry barrel, about one inch shorter than the barrel to allow for two chinaberries. The handle of the rod was sized to fit the user's hand, and a small piece of cloth was wrapped around the tip of the rod to maximize compression. To load the gun, a chinaberry was placed into the rear of the barrel and pushed by the plunger to the other end. A second chinaberry was then loaded into the rear of the elderberry barrel. The gun would now be ready to fire. The tip of the plunger was fitted against the second berry. The plunger was rammed forward. Compression created by the second berry being thrust through the barrel caused the first berry to explode from the other end. To reload, another chinaberry was inserted into the breech.

"The longer the barrel, the better the aim" was a principle of blowgun battles. But ten inches was about the longest practical length. The rules of the game included no shooting at the eyes, and if hit, or if hit first in a two-gun standoff, a player was out of action. A well-made blowgun would make a loud slap when fired and raise a welt on the skin of an "enemy" at fifteen feet.

Alder Shrub Popgun
by
A. L. Miles

The popgun was a popular homemade toy when I was growing up in the early 1900s, mostly on the Leon River in Coryell County. It was made from an alder shrub, which grew in the river bottom. There were two kinds of alder. The one we used had a thick, wooden branch with a soft and spongy pith center about one-fourth inch in diameter, while the overall diameter was an inch to an inch and a fourth. The popgun was cut usually six to nine inches long.

Removing the pith was not difficult. I formed an instrument out of heavy, smooth wire hammered flat at one end and filed sharp and to about the width of the thickness of the pith. Then I twisted the wire into the pith and hollowed out the tube. After that, I whittled a plunger to fit the hollow of the alder.

You got into business by chewing two wads of paper, one for each end of the popgun. Having stuck the wet paper wads in each end of the popgun, you took the plunger and quickly pushed one paper wad toward the other end. You would hear a "pop" as the compressed air in front of the back wad blew out the front wad.

Spoke Gun
by
Russel H. Goodyear

Back in the late 1940s and early 1950s, growing up as young boys in the Brinkley, Arkansas, area, my friends and I used to make a pistol from bicycle spokes. We would take a bicycle spoke and bend it into a pistol shape. Then we would take a .22-caliber rat-shot shell and extract the BBs and the powder. We put a few grains of powder into the spoke base and then rammed a BB down on top of it. When we held the "gun" and twisted the spoke base, the pressure that built up would eventually ignite the powder and expel the BB with a "pop."

The Clothespin or Match Gun

Lee Haile: The clothespin or match gun cannot be very old in origin because the steel-spring clothespin that it is made from is not very old. This probably accounts for the fact that I have not been able to find a reference to this toy in literature. My father-in-law played with them when he was young in the Thirties and Forties. He called it a match gun because they shot flaming kitchen matches from them. V. V. Turner from Gause, Texas, called it the same name and used it in the same way. We never shot matches out of ours, and if anyone else around did I am

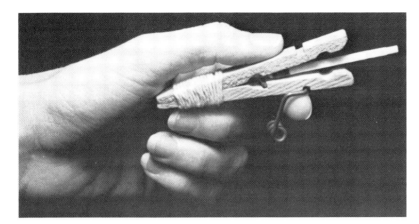

Elton Miles's clothespin or match gun.

sure that with my early-developing pyro tendencies I would have picked up on it in a hurry.

During a battle we always kept a good supply of small rocks or BBs. Sometimes we carved little grooves in the two wooden parts of the gun to give the BBs a barrel to shoot out of. We had teams and we had shoot-outs. We had duels of the three-steps-turn-and-fire type. Sometimes we just shot at targets or chickens or dogs or cats. The clothespin gun does not shoot very hard and is relatively safe, unless you get shot in the eye.

Elton Miles: To make a match gun, take the two wooden clips of the clothespin apart by removing the spring. Inside both wooden clips are semi-circular indentations to accommodate the coiled portion of the spring. With a knife, convert one of these indentations into a notch, so that the forward side of the notch is perpendicular to the straight back of the wooden clip. With tape or string, tightly bind the handle ends of the clips together so that the jaws of the clothespin remain open. The taped end is the butt end of the match gun; the open end is the barrel. Position the spring on the bottom of the gun with the lower L in its original slot and the upper L resting on the inside of the lower jaw. The spring now becomes the trigger.

Cock the gun by forcing the inside L back into the new-cut notch. An extra clothespin clip makes a good cocking stick. If you are shooting a match, force the match, head first, into the barrel of the gun so that it is held tightly in place just ahead of the cocked L. When the trigger is pulled, the firing-pin L pops out of the sear and strikes the match head, sending it out in a flaming arc. If you are shooting a BB or small rock, you do the same thing; that is, you position the projectile in the barrel of the gun just ahead of the firing pin. When the trigger is pulled, the shot is fired.

Harry Miles, a match-gun shooter of the Fifties who made a test model for this publication, noted that the metal springs of recently made clothespins were weaker than those of his time. It is ever thus!

◆ Another weapon popular among youngsters when wooden thread spools were common was the spool pistol, or pea shooter,

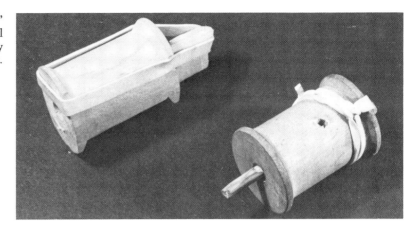

"Cotton" Leatherwood's spool pistol (left) and Molly Brown's pea shooter.

Gayla Sanders's needle dart.

as contributed by "Cotton" Leatherwood, formerly of Victoria. It was a simple machine, easily concealed about the person. It consisted of a spool with a plunger that was attached with rubber bands. The spool could be loaded with a pea and cocked, ready for firing. A simple flick of the finger would fire the pea with force and some accuracy. Lacking spools, soda straws made good BB blowguns, as did a tightly rolled piece of notebook paper loaded with a cone-shaped, pin-tipped projectile. Patricia Hurley sent in the latter weapon, as well as a miniature bow and arrow in which the bow was a bobby pin strung with thread and the arrow was a match with a needle stuck in the end. Deadly!

Various kinds of darts were sent in by contributors. They were sailed at a target more often than at a victim. The needle dart was a popular item, and a description was sent in by Gayla McLain Sanders. It consisted of a match stick with the head cut off and a needle inserted for a point. The opposite end was split about a half inch and folded paper vanes were inserted. Lee Haile sent in a corn-cob dart that had the shucks folded back for the vanes and a twenty-penny nail in the other end for a point.

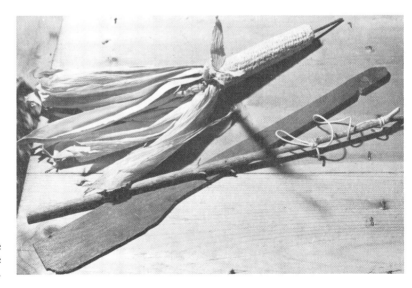

Corn-cob dart by Lee Haile and shingle dart by Joseph Jones.

Shingle dart
(Karen Haile).

It would stick in a wall if it were thrown hard enough. Lee and Joseph Jones both sent in shingle darts that would make good weapons as well as toys. The butt end of a one-inch-wide piece of shingle is sharpened to a point, and a tail is whittled at the thin end. A launching notch is cut three or four inches from the point. The launcher is a whippy stick about fifteen inches long with a twenty-inch string tied on the little end and with a knot tied at the end of the string. The knot is hooked into the launching notch, and the dart is held by the tail with the right hand while tension is exerted with the stick in the left hand. The tail is released, and the launcher whips the dart up, up, and away. You could raise a welt on a body with this weapon, in case you are interested.

Of a slightly different nature, more like grenades, corn stalks with dirt balled around the roots made formidable throwing weapons. A full revolution of the body before the release was the usual method with big stalks. In a drouthy year, less energy was required. Engaging in a corn-stalk war required that continual attention be paid to one's adversaries, and developed considerable agility among the participants. Dan Moore told Ken Davis of a refinement of this weapon. He and his friends made clay mud balls and put them on the end of a stick and whirled them at targets.

Along the line of grenade battles—and consistent with a chapter on weapons—a six-year-old peer and I discovered a large crate of old eggs in my uncle's cellar (he had a general merchandise store in Allison, Texas) and spent one glorious, hilarious afternoon pelting each other with them. The incident was so outrageous and we smelled so unbelievably bad that we were not even punished. In spite of the obvious evidence, our elders could not believe that we could possibly do anything as stupid as throw old—very old!—eggs at each other. Moral: Do not take your eyes off a six-year-old boy, even for a minute, when any kind of weapon is available.

VI
DOLLS

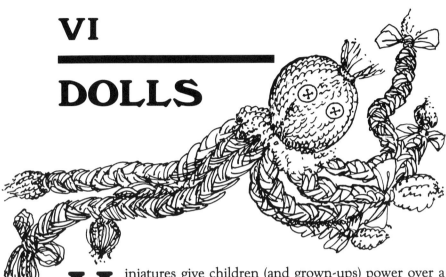

Miniatures give children (and grown-ups) power over a life small enough and contained enough to give them a feeling of control. Dolls fall under this category. They are usually soft, small, cuddly creations that can be held and rocked and talked to and played with—and they do what you want them to. When they cry, it is only because you want them to so that you can pretend to be changing them or feeding them. And unlike a real baby, dolls stop crying when you get tired of hearing them. Dolls are manageable toys that satisfy the maternal instincts of little girls and, I suppose, although I haven't thought much about this, the paternal instincts of young boys. Lauren Tijerina of Paris illustrates an interesting twist on this point: "The little girl is the mommy and the doll is her baby. The little girl gets to make all the rules and acts just as her own mother would not, for she knows when she is grown up and has her own children she will not be as strict as her own mother is."

I had a doll that I cherished in my childhood and that my mother still keeps in a cedar chest among other mellowed memories. It was a black baby with overalls, and I had it before I knew there were black people or recognized any differences in skin tone. From my own experience, however, there are two types of miniature people: dolls, which are played with as babies and are practice items for later parenting; and miniature people, which are used as tractor drivers and horse riders and which act as grown-ups pursuing purposeful, grown-up activities. All children play with the latter type of toy, along with equal-size trains and cars and houses—all in a miniaturized world. It is a world that the child, like a creator god, makes for his own pleasure and recreation, separating the dry land from the ocean waters, and night from day. It is a world that he can use to his own desires, building what he wishes and destroying what he tires of. It is a

Mammy doll by Edna Mae Baucom (1943) with yarn octopus (Betty Seaman).

power that the child loses when he returns to the actual-size world—and when he grows up.

Dolls Generally

by Joyce Roach

A Lantern in Her Hand by Bess Streeter Aldrich speaks of a frontier child who used a stick, an ordinary dead tree branch, for a doll. Early peoples of the forests shaped rushes, reeds, straw, and husks into figures identified by anthropologists as dolls. Small, crude, clay figures representing male and female, dug up in the dry desert country, are sometimes called dolls by archaeologists. Although branch, rush, or clay imitations of human figures might not satisfy our notions of suitable items for the play of little girls and, sometimes, of little boys, dolls—like beauty—seem to be in the eye of the beholder; a doll by any other name would smell as sweet; a doll is a doll is a doll. Of all children's toys, dolls are familiar playthings the world over and leave each individual with a general notion so that we all know what we mean when we say *doll*. A doll is a small imitation of a person, often a baby.

We are nearly certain too that we know the purpose of dolls and doll play. Dolls served, intentionally or not, as teaching toys. Little pioneer girls coming from whatever socioeconomic or ethnic background practiced mothering-wifing-family skills. Native American and Mexican children did the same.

Dolls crafted by the folk on the frontier were varied. Roughly made dolls fashioned from all kinds of natural materials were plentiful. Corn husks and cobs, pinecones, straw, acorns or other nuts, sticks, feathers, and grasses were handy. None of the materials were soft or gave much reason for cuddling the dolls. Rough dolls may not always have been held closely, but rather they were looked at, carried in a basket, or posed on a shelf along with other dolls of like composition. Often such dolls did not have arms or legs, but some did. Examples indicate that putting features on the rough dolls was not terribly important. Some had clothes made from natural goods, such as corn husks, or from actual cloth; some did not. Other native products such as gourds, dried and cleaned out, found use as sturdy storage places for dolly items.

Wooden figures, also referred to as dolls, were crafted to represent not babies but men, women, and children of all ages. Features and clothes were usually painted on, and there were fewer moving parts. Such dolls might include representations of Santa Claus or other special religious or ethnic figures. These dolls were not designed to be cuddled but rather to be manipulated by hand or to be looked at. Doll-like figures were also crafted from wooden clothespins, the type without wire springs. Wooden thread spools were strung together to make doll figures or were used alone for tiny furnishings. Some wooden dolls went far beyond the single-block variety. Germans, particularly

World War I nurse and walking doll, made from cone-shaped thread spool (Betty Seaman).

Ada Harper's
clothespin dolls.

remembered as master carvers, made dolls with jointed limbs.
Carpenter skills were put to use in making ancillary items connected with dolls—doll beds, houses, buggies, chairs, and furnishings of any kind.

The most satisfying dolls, at least in the minds of us
mother-types, were made entirely of cloth. Many varieties exist.
On the most basic level are those made of handkerchiefs or a
single piece of material. Babies in a blanket, made by folding and
rolling a handkerchief to form the babies and using another fold
of the same cloth for cover, are an abstract representation. Another example of a handkerchief doll uses only one piece of
cloth to fashion head, bonnet, and body. Arms are merely knots
on two ends. The rest of the material makes the dress. The head
of the doll is stuffed with cotton or perhaps a large nut. Other
cloth dolls range from faceless, flat representations, sometimes
with yarn hair, to the carefully detailed rag dolls, complete with
rounded limbs and embroidered features on the faces. Such dolls
often have clothes—pantaloons, shoes, dresses, and bonnets—
that demonstrate fine needle craftsmanship. Dolls with braided

Furniture for
clothespin dolls (left)
and paper cut-out
furniture (right) by
Ada Harper.

bodies, made from old socks and sculptured from worn-out quilts and clothing, are more examples of the type. Handkerchiefs, flour sacks, and discarded clothes provided materials for covers and wrappings for the dolls.

It would be wrong to dismiss the idea that elaborate dolls with china heads and arms and feet did not exist or count as folk items on the early frontier. Granted, such dolls were treasures, without a doubt. Heads might be ordered from catalogues or brought along in the family wagon, as might an entire doll made of china, bisque, porcelain, or even papier-mache. Catalogues, incidentally, were available as early as 1896 from Sears and Roebuck; and the book, from the beginning, offered toys. Catalogues featuring dolls were well known in Europe from the early 1800s.

Neither were all dolls representations of the Anglo settlers. Enough examples exist to verify that all races made or had dolls appropriate to their culture, and there was probably an exchange of ideas and samples. Some of the most popular rag dolls were black. Plantation life in the slave South provided examples that might easily have made the trip to Texas. Black dolls for little white children were not likely provided to teach tolerance or brotherhood but might have given a kind of artificial contact sometimes forbidden in real life. And they were nonthreatening.

One last category of doll deserves mention: paper dolls. Paper dolls, along with paper clothes, were early creations of the toy trade, and no doubt some of them were brought along in wagons rolling toward Texas. Further, if paper could be found, children or parents could make their own dolls. Paper products, such as cardboard boxes, held the paper dolls, served as beds for other kinds of dolls, and could be stacked to make a house or rooms, provided a child could get a box, so valuable were they.

Psychologists have long recognized the therapeutic value of playing with dolls. Dolls serve as a medium through which a child can act out situations in life. Children playing with paper dolls use sound effects, such as clicking noises with their tongues to approximate sounds made in walking. In addition to sound effects, little girls sometimes sing, make up conversations between the dolls, give audible explanations about their movements ("now we're going in the living room"), and explain about life or the peculiarities or problems of their world. Usually family-oriented, the dialogue may serve the same function as using puppets: the speakers say through the mouth of the paper dolls things they might not say themselves. It has been observed that paper doll play is often a more private kind of play. That frontier folk recognized the therapeutic value of paper dolls, or any kind of dolls, is speculative.

Playing with dolls of any kind seems to combine the values of therapy, learning, and pleasure without the child's being aware of any of the processes. The modern Barbie doll, complete with most-attractive body parts, may have something to teach little girls about expectations and roles in the modern world. Boy dolls too have entered the public arena with Barbie. Now made of rubber, plastic, and synthetic fabrics in addition to existing materials, there are dolls that cry, wet, talk, walk, sing, ask questions, couple, and give birth. The multimillion-dollar doll business—which grew from a doll as a small imitation of a person, often a baby—is a major factor in the economy of the world. It is bewildering enough to make me think that a stick in a basket is dear and sweet indeed.

◆ Soft cloth dolls were the most common dolls made and played with. Handkerchief dolls, made by mothers to keep children quiet during long sermons, are described by Jovita F. Lopez of San Antonio: "A single baby is made by rolling both sides of the handkerchief toward the middle, then turning the handkerchief over and rolling only one side toward the middle and tucking in the sides to form the head. Eyes and mouth are made with a pencil. To make twins, roll a handkerchief from two sides toward the middle; turn it over and roll the two edges or rolls toward the middle of the two side rolls. Cover over with side edges to form the cradle for the twins."

Elizabeth Stuart, a student at Texas Tech, tells of her grandmother's dolls made from discarded cloth: "Granny would take three rags, one large and two small. She would wrap the two smaller rags inside the middle of the larger rag and tie a string toward the top of the bundle. This would make the head. The rest of the larger rag would hang loose for the body and the dress. She would make several of these dolls so that they could have tea parties." Mrs. W. F. Barnett of Nacogdoches tells of tying off stuffed pieces of quilting material for the head and body and rolling and tying pieces for the arms and legs. The limbs were safety-pinned onto the body, and facial features were added with charcoal. Ruben Villareal describes dolls that Mexican women made for their daughters out of old cotton stockings

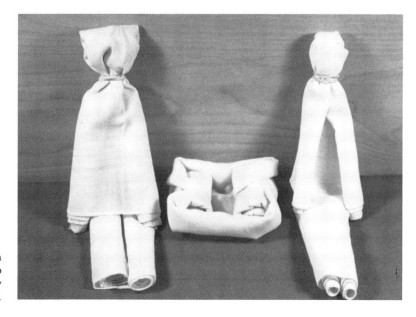

Handkerchief man and wife with two babes in a cradle by Jovita Lopez.

stuffed with rags. They embroidered faces on these stocking dolls with colored thread. That's called "makin' do."

I suppose that all little girls, at one time or another, had dolls. The dolls were their make-believe babies that they cuddled and rocked and fed and washed while their imaginations ran free, making them real mothers for a time. Eventually they grew tired and put the dolls back in bed, if the doll was lucky enough to have one, or in her own box, or the toy box. My grandmother made my first doll—a rag doll—while I was still an infant. As I grew older, I felt she needed a name. After all, didn't I have a name? After much thought, as well as suggestions from others in the family, I named her Rosa Betsy Lina, after a play-party song, and even yet, she is Rosa Betsy Lina! She is eighteen inches tall and was made from medium-weight sturdy cotton material. Two identical pieces of the white material were stitched together, allowing sufficient material so that her feet were made to turn at right angles at the heel. Being of an artistic nature, grandmother drew a realistic face with pen and ink on the front of the doll's head. The thing that pleased me most was the slipcover she made for the doll's head, also with a face drawn on it, so that

A Rag Doll
by
Dorris Y. Tull

Rag dolls by
Maybelle Jarvis (1960)
(Betty Seaman).

when she became dirty from sharing too many tea parties with me, as well as from general wear and tear, the slipcover with the face and a necklace drawn on it could be taken off and washed. It was almost like getting a new doll! In my imagination, her soft mitten-like hands patted my face and held countless cups of cambric tea. Her dress was like the blue-and-white checked dresses I wore, decorated in red scalloped trim around the neck, along the edge of the short sleeves, and across the top of the miniature pocket. I had many other dolls, china-headed dolls and bisque dolls imported from Germany, but none could take the place of Rosa Betsy Lina.

◆ Inventive and imaginative children made dolls out of anything at hand. Ruben Villareal describes a Mexican spool doll: "One type of doll is made with many spools. A large spool is used for the head. Smaller spools are strung out with string to make the body, arms, and legs. Facial features are painted on the large spool head." Miriam Lowrance of Alpine and her friends made short-lived dolls from poppies, which grew in abundance around Gainesville in the 1920s and 1930s. Sandra Nelson of Paris Junior College made dolls out of soda-pop bottles and panty hose. Ada Phipps Harper relates: "When I was small, my grandmother gave me a straight clothespin and several neckties.

Stick doll (center) by Alice McRae (1984). She wrapped a stick with yarn, leaving tufts for the skirt. The Jingle Bell Jack and Jill were made by gathering the edges of four-inch circles of fabric scraps, stringing them on thread to make body, arms and legs, and adding bells for hands and feet (Betty Seaman).

BLADE OF GRASS

POPPY

REVERSE PETALS DOWNWARD

TIE BLADE OF GRASS AS SASH. INSERT GRASS STEM FOR ARMS. ONE PIECE SLID ALL THE WAY THROUGH.

FLOWER DOLL
Miriam Lowrance and other girls made short-lived dolls from poppies, which grew in abundance at Sherman (and elsewhere) in the 1920s and 1930s. Because of narcotics regulation, poppies are scarcely anywhere now to be found. (Drawing and directions by Miriam Lowrance)

I cut dresses for the clothespin doll out of the part of the tie that fits under the shirt collar." Patricia A. Hurley of El Paso collected descriptions of folk toys in 1969 and found dolls made of potatoes, of egg cartons, and of leaves and twigs tied into doll shapes with grass. And dolls made of corn husks:

Corn Husk Dolls

Floyd Martin [as told to Bettye Martin McRae]: I used to help my sisters make some of their dolls. We lived on a farm near Trent in Taylor County. It must have been about 1918, when I was twelve years old, that I made my first one.

Wait till it's corn shucking time. Choose an ear that has a long clump of silk still hanging on and a husk still nice and green. Shuck the ear, being careful not to tear the husk or leaves. Carefully pull the silk off in one bunch and set it aside for the hair.

Take the inside, lighter-colored leaves, or some old ones that have turned brown, to form the head, arms, and legs. Fold one of those over a wad of cotton about one inch in diameter and tie to form a kind of ball for the head. Don't trim the ends that are left. These will form the neck and will tie on to the arms and legs. Now set that aside till later.

Roll up three or four brown leaves and trim both ends, making the roll about four or five inches long, to form the arms. Tie with strong twine about half an inch from the cut ends to form hands.

Now take the head and pull the loose ends down over the center of the arms and roll and tie again, still leaving loose the ends of the "neck" to tie the legs to.

Next make two rolls of five or six brown leaves each and tie like the arms. These will be fastened to the loose ends of the "neck" and will form the legs, completing the body.

For a girl doll, make hair from the silk, handling it carefully. A bunch can be glued onto either side of the top of her head and can hang loose or be plaited into braids. Next, make a dress by tucking and tieing some green leaves over the body. Be creative. A cape can be fashioned from green leaves and even a

Corn-husk doll and
various stages in
the making by
Bettye McRae
(Betty Seaman).

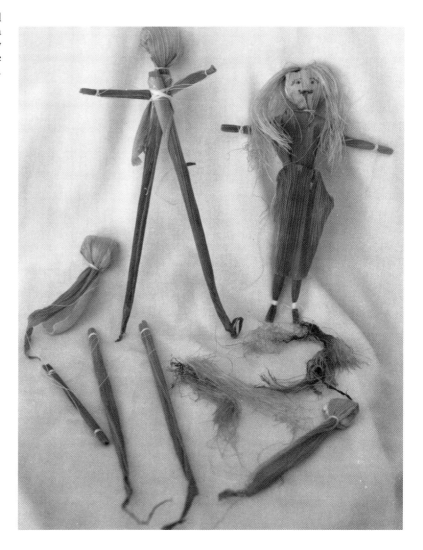

Cornstalk horse by
Elizabeth Wallace.

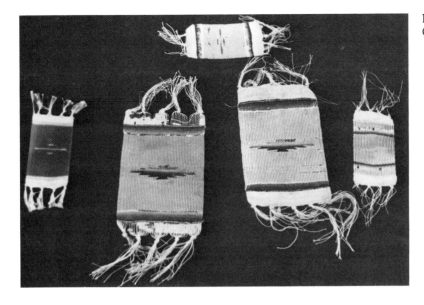

Doll *Serapes* (Joe Graham).

bonnet and apron. Those green clothes will turn brown after a few days, so you might want to make them from scraps out of Ma's quilt-making fabric, if she'll allow it.

For a boy doll, short hair can be made by glueing silk onto the head, then cutting it. Make him trousers, shirt, and maybe even a hat and some cruppers.

You can make a whole family of corn husk dolls that way, just making smaller ones for the kids.

Thomas E. Willis: My father describes corn husk dolls that he saw carried by impoverished black youngsters when he was young. He says they were made by stripping the ear of its kernels, and then tying the shucks together at the stalk end of the ear, bunching them to form a rounded head. Faces were drawn on the shucks. The corn silk was used for hair. Tying pieces of the husk (pulled over to the side) provided arms for these dolls. The remaining husks formed the clothing for the doll.

Paper Dolls

Ada Phipps Harper: Paper dolls were printed in America as early as the 1870s. It was not necessary to purchase commercially made dolls. When I was a little girl, *Pictorial Review Magazine* printed a Dolly Dingle paper doll in each issue. Little girls eagerly awaited the arrival of each issue. (Grace Drayton, who also created the Campbell Kids, was the artist.) A bakery included a paper doll with a loaf of bread. You can bet I lobbied for that brand of bread as long as the advertising scheme lasted. I had another doll that was used to advertise Camel cigarettes. The company slogan was, "I'd walk a mile for a Camel." The doll was drawn in profile and was constructed to make it appear to be walking. Also, free fashion plates could be picked up in the piece-goods departments of stores. Fashion plates, along with the Sears catalogue, became a wonderful source of paper dolls for me.

Paper dolls, late
1930s vintage.

Gayla McLain Sanders: I spent many hours playing paper dolls with cutouts from the Sears catalogue. I was allowed to use the family's one pair of scissors for this, a ten-inch pair of mule shears kept finely honed. I would choose the ladies and men who were illustrated with their full figure showing, cut them out very carefully, and place them between the pages of the catalogue to store them. I chose children and babies. I chose outfits for dress-up and for work and put them together with a mother and a father or a girl and a boy. My imagination carried them to parties and on dates and to play with the toys I saw in the catalogue. I learned to fold paper and make chairs my dolls could sit in and beds they could sleep on.

Thomas E. Willis: Little girls during the Depression used to make paper dolls by cutting out pictures in the Sears and Roebuck catalogue, my mother tells me. Pasting these on cardboard, my mother was able to make them stiff enough to stand. Tabs were cut along with pictures of clothing and were bent over the figures at the shoulders to hold them in place. She assures me that only old catalogues were used for this—for to use the latest issue would have resulted in a spanking from her elders.

**Cardboard
Walking
Dolls
by
Elton Miles**

When the notion struck us, we youngsters made cardboard walking dolls in Gatesville in the late 1920s. We did not know that they were of a pattern called "Dutch Doll." In sharing time with my girl cousins, I played paper dolls and enjoyed it. We never included our walking dolls among our catalogue cutout characters.

From cardboard we cut a Dutch Doll figure about seven or eight inches tall, without feet. This plump doll, in profile, was all sunbonnet and blousy Mother Hubbard, always facing to our left. On her side we drew a simple, hanging arm with a line to denote a mitten-like hand. Another line separated bonnet from dress. We colored in the fabric designs with crayolas.

Next, from a disc of cardboard the size of a fruit jar lid we cut out her feet. Each of her four feet, with ankles, projected from the center of the disc, and the result resembled a fat swastika. We then colored the Oxford-like shoes and the stockings.

With a short, two-prong paper brad (or whatever would do) we attached the foot cutout to the blank side of the doll so that in her standing position only one foot could be seen projecting below her skirt hem. She was ready to take a walk.

We held the doll upright, foot on the floor or on a table-top, and moved her lightly forward or backward. Never more than two of the revolving feet moved out at the same time, giving the appearance that her legs were in action. She walked more readily on a rug or a tablecloth than on a hard surface. Also, she performed more efficiently if the toe of her shoe sole was slightly curved.

After considerable walking, the doll's ankles would bend, crease, and become useless. We then traced the worn-out foot attachment onto cardboard and cut out a new one.

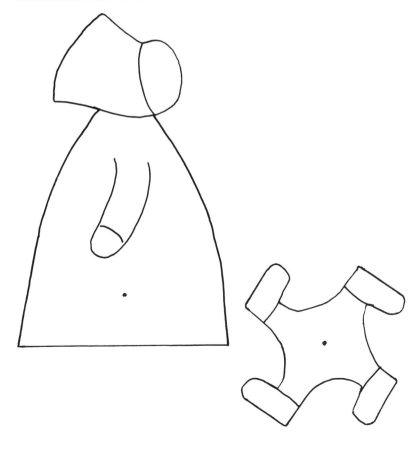

Elton Miles's Walking
Doll (4¼" × 6¾").

Yahoo Doll
by
Pamela Lynn Palmer

To make a yahoo doll, draw a face on a spool, and glue on pieces of crepe paper for hair. Hair can be cut and curled, if desired.

Cut about eighteen-inch-long pieces from two streamers of different colors for legs. Cut the eighteen-inch pieces in half, lengthwise. Place two strips, one of each color, at right angles, and glue together.

Begin "weaving" by folding the strip that is on the bottom over the glued ends, then alternate colors until you reach the end. Pull the woven strips open (like pulling a "Slinky" open), and glue the finished ends together. Clip off any excess paper at the end.

Cut fifteen-inch strips of two colors of crepe paper streamer for arms, and repeat same steps as for legs.

Using a pipe cleaner, attach arms to legs at the middle of each, then thread the end of the pipe cleaner through the spool head. Make a hook or knot in the pipe cleaner so that it won't slip out of the spool.

Cut hands and feet from paper, and glue to the ends of arms and legs.

Matchbox Wagon and Broom-Straw Dolls
by
Thelma Nalley Parks

When I was about five years old (in the 1920s) my mother was quite ill. We lived for a while near Fair Park in Dallas. I became creative at making my own entertainment. I found two empty matchboxes. I used one box for a bed of a wagon, and from a top I made a cover. I "glued" it all together with mesquite gum wax from the sap of a nearby tree. To make a "Daddy" doll, I found a small stick with a forked branch. I used a pin and made holes in the soft stick and used broom straws for arms and hands. I frayed each end of the broom-straw arms to make hands. I used scraps from the quilt box to make his pants. In similar fashion, I made "Mama" and "Baby" and made frilly bonnets for them. Off to church my little family went in their covered wagon—the full length of the room. Here's how the family sang my favorite hymn: "At the cross, at the cross where I first saw the sight, and the birds saw my heart roll away. It was there by my side I received my face and now I am happy all the day."

Depression Porcelain
by
Anita Conlee

My mother, Juanita May Clendennen, grew up on the banks of Keechi Creek in Palo Pinto County, Texas, just outside the little town of Graford. Born in 1925, she and her brothers did not really realize that they were living through the Depression. As long as there was a rope hanging from a tree limb overlooking the creek, they could always entertain themselves. No wonder she could swim like a duck before she was five years old.

But one of her most memorable toys was a beautiful doll she received on her sixth birthday. It had dark eyes that looked like agates, much like her own eyes. And it had beautiful long black hair. It touched a feminine chord in her being that she had not recognized before. But her mother offered a stern warning when she presented Mother with the doll. Never was she to leave the doll outside, not in the sun and not in the rain, but particularly not in the sun.

Soon the tomboy was beckoning to Mother again, and the day was too warm and sunny not to take a dip in the creek. Her beautiful doll with the stunning porcelain face was simply left on the bank in a sunny spot. After an hour or so of swimming, Mother returned to find her doll a totally different toy. The porcelain face had swollen and blistered, and when she picked the doll up, eyes and hair and face just kind of oozed into one.

Mother still recalls the memory a little wistfully and calls it Depression porcelain.

Shoe Box Dollhouses
by
Jewel Irwin Shankles

A favorite summertime activity was to make shoe box doll-houses. During the late Twenties and early Thirties, I made one each summer. Small doors were cut, leaving one edge attached so that they could swing open. Windows were cut out, sometimes with strips left or glued back to form panes. Cellophane made the window glass. From the Sears catalogue, one could use the slick wallpaper samples for the linoleum floors and other wall-paper to paper the walls. Bits of cloth were used for window curtains. Some girls used a box for each separate room. Furniture could be made of smaller boxes.

The paper doll families came from old Sears, Montgomery Ward, or Chicago mail-order catalogues. There was always a father, a mother, a boy, a girl, and a baby, although the baby was usually large in relation to the rest of the family because there were no small babies in the catalogue. If you were careful, however, you could find a baby the right size with all arms and legs showing! By being especially observant, one could find the same sizes and poses and cut dresses from some pictures so that the dolls could have a change of clothing.

After several days, when all was ready, each dollhouse and doll family lived in a different corner of the room and there was "visiting."

Older cousins showed us their carefully made clay furniture with the drawers and designs etched on. We were not allowed to touch. Can you imagine the hours of time and trials to get clay solids three-by-three-by-four inches to dry straight and without cracks? Of course we couldn't touch.

It must have been about 1929 when I received a white wooden doll bed with a mattress and a beautiful china baby doll wrapped in a doll blanket made of flannel exactly like my mother-made nightgown. It had a crocheted edging in yellow to match some of the nursery-rhyme characters in the print. I know that Daddy sawed and made the little bed in his barn workshop on some cold winter afternoons before I came in from school. At the same time Mama was busy cutting and sewing the scraps into squares for the blanket before crocheting the yellow edging. Love makes lovely presents and memories!

Ernestine Sewell's
Indian dolls.

The Dolls' Repertory Company

by Marguerite Nixon

In an old hatbox in the attic a troupe of dolls is waiting for a curtain call. They have not performed in four decades, and forty years have had an eroding effect. The arms of the second-leading man hang loosely at his side, the elastic cord that held them having given way. The leading lady has lost a toe on her right foot. And the celluloid dog has a dent in his side. But the leading man is as stalwart and handsome as ever, and the ingenue still wears the painted blue bow in her blond china curls.

The doll children have fared much better, probably because they were tiny enough to hide in the corner under feathers, scraps of faded satin and velvet, and pieces of cotton used in making wigs.

They used to perform every Saturday morning. Mary, my best friend from down the street, and I set the stage on either her front porch or mine and let the dramas roll. Our props were shoe boxes, candy boxes, painted cardboard, and anything that seemed useable, snatched from wastepaper baskets and purloined from bedroom and kitchen.

Our favorite productions were fairy tales. At least we were familiar with them and performed them with a reasonable degree of accuracy. "Sleeping Beauty" was a favorite.

The leading lady was put to sleep in a cookie tin. Mary manipulated the prince as he fought his way through a forest of painted cardboard. She held him by his heels as he planted a glassy kiss on the heroine's equally unyielding lips, and I, standing in for the beauty, said in dulcet tones, "Oh, my prince charming, you have come at last to awaken me. Let us fly away together and live happily ever after."

"Little Red Riding Hood" was a natural for drama. We had a furry rabbit left over from some Easter basket, and with a bonnet that I contrived and two paper fangs pasted to his upper lip, he did nicely as the wolf. A piece of red velvet tied around the ingenue, and a basket made from a thimble and strapped to her arm, made Little Red Riding Hood totally believable as I tripped her daintily along the path to her horrendous encounter.

"Hansel and Gretel" was a delight. We whispered and whined dolefully and jiggled the dolls up and down in their terror, and Mary said plaintively for Gretel, "Oh, I am so frightened." And I intoned in a deep voice, "I'll get you out of this, " for Hansel. We did in the wicked witch by shoving her under a small flowerpot, which substituted for an oven.

Every Saturday afternoon we went to a picture show, and movies added to our repertoire. *The Hunchback of Notre Dame* held plenty of dramatic high points. We had a little fat, short doll for whom it was difficult to find suitable rolls, but with a wad of cotton wrapped in a scrap of cloth and attached to his back he was perfect for Quasimodo. We stood him on two coffee cans, representing the cathedral, while Esmerelda simpered below.

In one particular movie, a vamp with lots of kohl around her eyes fascinated me, and I insisted on carrying out this role. We made a black turban with a fake pearl bead stitched to the front for the leading lady, and a long black satin dress completed the costume. But it was difficult to make a stiff-legged doll slink or glide across the stage. I settled on giving her a slight twist from side to side as she approached the hero.

I was saying as seductively as I knew how, "I love you; I love you," when Mary said in exasperation, "Oh, for pete's sake, can't you think of anything else to say?" I immediately said, "Darling, meet me tonight when it's dark. You'll know me; I'll be wearing Perfume of the Nile."

Whereupon Mary promptly fell over laughing and hooted, "Perfume of the Nile!"

I was indignant. "Well, I didn't laugh when you were playing Esmerelda and kept saying, "Save me. Save me!"

"I'm going home," she said.

"No you're not until you help me pick up all this stuff. You know how Mama is."

The classics were not left unscathed. Shakespeare, Victor Hugo, and a few others must have shuddered on their celestial planes when Saturday mornings approached. Our rendition of *King Lear* led to a small tragedy of our own. Our schoolteacher, in trying to put across a lesson in filial obedience, had told us the story of King Lear. Naturally, we tackled it the following Saturday.

As the old king (the leading man with a cotton wig) was walking up and down bemoaning the ingratitude of his children, Mary got carried away with her improvisations and struck him a blow with our one pair of scissors. King Lear's gold-painted crown flew across the porch, and his head went rolling after.

Mary began to cry. I knew her father had chastised her the day before for some infraction of house rules, and in her desire to get even she had used too much force on father Lear.

"I've killed him!" she wailed. "He's dead!"

He certainly was as far as his usefulness to us was concerned. There was nothing to do but to acquire somehow another boy doll before the following weekend. Neither of us had any money. We were given twenty-five cents each Saturday afternoon—fifteen cents for the matinee and ten cents for refreshments. We were also given ten cents each Sunday morning to deposit in the collection plate at Sunday school.

Our plan developed. We would save our popcorn and ice cream cone money, which was certainly starving for art's sake, and we would simply not give our donation to God. This totaled forty cents, which, if we were lucky, would suffice.

Monday, after school, we were off down Beaumont's Pearl Street to Kress's. Kress's had a counter of assorted china dolls ranging in price from ten to fifty cents. It was a delightful counter. We pondered the selection until the saleslady walked away, saying wearily, "Call me if you ever decide."

We finally selected another leading man—pricetag thirty-five cents and no tax—and took turns carrying him home. He turned out to be an exceptional actor and quite easy to fit into the trousers we made before the next performance.

But remorse set in. "What we did was a sin," I said reluctantly, "not giving the church the money."

"Yes, it was," Mary finally admitted after some consideration. "We'll have to do something to make up for it. That's what people do when they sin."

It was my turn to ponder. "We could not go to the picture show next Saturday and give them that money."

Child and hand-
made doll in
matching dresses by
Mary Lou Van
Buskirk (Jared
Satterwhite).

"I'm not going to miss *Phantom of the Opera*," Mary flatly declared.

With great relief I agreed. It was too much to ask of anyone. We finally hit on the next most disagreeable thing we knew. We would practice our piano lessons for the next five days without fussing about it. The penance would be hard, but we felt redeemed.

We were totally absorbed when we played, oblivious to sound and people, and we both jumped when my oldest sister, who had been surreptitiously listening and watching, suddenly snorted, "You all are so silly. Besides, you're too big to be playing with dolls anyway."

After that we took to playing in one of the bedrooms with the door closed and a handmade sign tied to the doorknob, with the words PRIVATE, KEEP OUT written in crayons on it.

But one Saturday morning we didn't get out the hatbox; we strolled over to the schoolyard to watch the big boys of the sixth grade practice baseball. And then we joined the dramatic club, where we could give vent to our well-honed acting talents, to the dismay of the grammar teacher who rehearsed the members every Saturday morning when a production was in the offing.

So many Saturdays disappeared into years. And Mary and I were grown-ups.

But sometimes at night I hear small sounds in the attic, like tiny china feet tapping across the floor, and I listen. And I know that somehow the troupe of dolls has gotten out of the hatbox, and in the moonlight from the dormer window they are performing for the shadows of two little girls sitting cross-legged on the floor, applauding.

VII

Toy Box

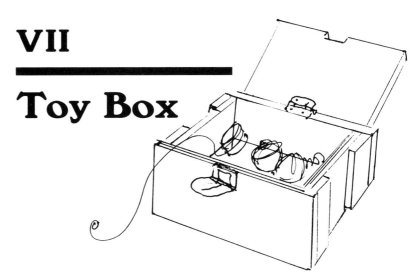

ee Haile sent in a box of toys that he had made and used at the Texas Folklife Festival in San Antonio. The box contained tops, yo-yos, flying-floating-and-rolling toys, zizzers, whizzers, and zoozers, among other things. This chapter is a box of miscellaneous toys that are still popular items—some in memory rather than in actuality—but that are not widespread enough to make a chapter by themselves. And these are the sorts of things you would toss in the toy box and slide under the bed after the children leave—most of them. I also included toys that would not fit in elsewhere.

The button buzzer is among the most common toys in the world. Lee says of it: "When I was young we called it a whizzer, and because of the sound it made it is also called a buzz saw. South American Indians called it a *mou-mou*. It was depicted in paintings on ancient Greek vases. It is also an Eskimo toy (Henderson and Wilkerson, 60). Whatever it is called, it is always made of two things: a string and a circular disk, commonly a large button. The string is threaded through the opposing holes of the button, making a loop with the button or disk in the center. The button is whirled, which winds the string and takes up slack. The hands are stretched out, which unwinds the string, but the momentum of the button winds it again— the process continues, the hands accordioning in and out, the buzzer spinning fast enough to hum." Dorris Tull and Jewel Shankles also sent in buzzers. The pleasure of simple buzzing could be increased, I was told, by spinning the toy in a girl's hair. Ralph Miller sent in a deadly model made from a jaggedly cut tin-can lid that not only hummed noticeably but also would cut paper like a true buzz saw.

Hog and cow bladders used as swim floats and as balls to play with were once popular items. W. E. Souchek and Bettye

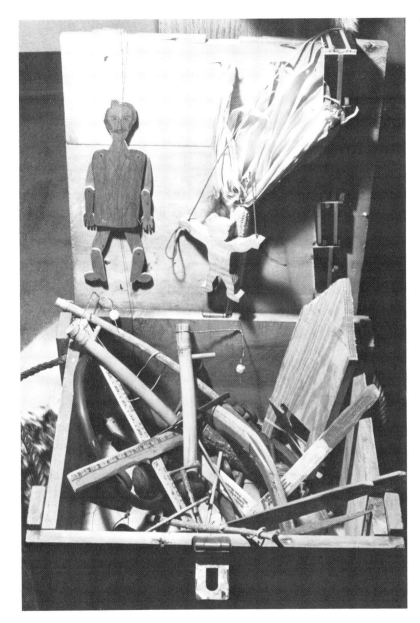

Lee's toy box.

Button buzzer
(Karen Haile).

Tops from Lee's
toy box.

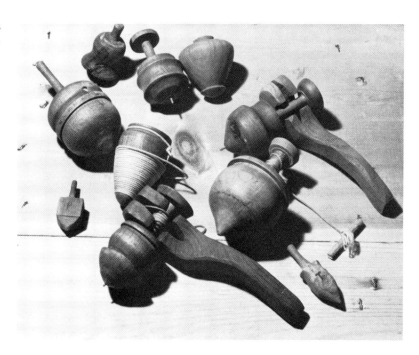

McRae discussed the naturalness and simplicity of turning this anatomical part into a toy. Then I received a firsthand description of the process from Jo Lee Anderson, a student at Paris High School: "My grandfather took me to a meat packing plant and bought me a cow bladder, which is not pretty to look at. It smells bad and it has fat attached to it. The worst thing is that you have to get your mouth close to the organ to blow it up. It's a floppy, slimey, balloon-like organ that has a hole in the end of it. It really does expand when inflated. We used a piece of garden hose inserted into the bladder to blow it up. The cow bladder is the folksiest kind of toy I've ever been exposed to." I imagine that the traditional folk process of handing down toys made of cow bladders collapsed in her family's line.

Toyful Noises

I started to refer to this entry as "Musical Instruments." Then I remembered that a lot of toyful noises are not meant to be musical, if *musical* denotes making controlled sounds in an ordered manner. That definition precludes bull-roarers and dumb bulls and Elton Miles's balloon-scrap nose blower, in which a tag end of a busted balloon was blown while a handkerchief was held to the nose. It made a satisfyingly disgusting sound that effectively grossed out young girls and parents.

Part of qualifying for childhood required learning to blow fists tunefully and to whistle through fingers. In fist blowing, the right-hand fingers are grouped and the left hand is cupped over them. This leaves the two thumbs together as the mouthpiece. Tonal variation is achieved by raising and lowering the fingers of the left hand. In finger whistling, the tips of two fingers are placed beneath the upturned tongue. Air properly blown through the fingers produces an excruciatingly shrill whistle. In the same vein is whistling by blowing a blade of grass or a leaf. The blade is held vertically between both hands' second and third thumb joints and is blown across. The sound is musical, and the tone can be controlled by opening and closing the hands. To illustrate the seriousness of this musical art form, Australians have national contests for eucalyptus leaf blowers, and I myself have heard a flawless "Stars and Stripes Forever" blown on a eucalyptus leaf. Bettye McRae reminded us of acorn-cup whistles, and Glenn Lowrance and Ralph Miller sent in great, piercing whistles made from a piece of folded tin with opposing holes. One step away from the skilled activities described above is the kazoo effect one can get from a comb folded in tissue paper or a toilet paper roll with a piece of wax paper rubber-banded to the sounding end.

More sophisticated are the various types of slide and stop whistles. I watched Ronnie Wolfe of Timpson cut and construct a slip-bark whistle out of a pecan branch (hickory is good too) in less than five minutes. These can be made only in the spring when the sap is rising and the bark is slipping. Tonal variation is controlled by the movement of the free-moving endpiece. The willow whistle (from A. L. Miles) is constructed in much the same way but has only one pitch. Whistles and flutes with finger stops are made from straws, feather quills, squash stems (from Lee Haile), and pumpkin vines (from Ruben Villareal). For simplicity of design and moderate tone control, I recommend Molly Brown's bamboo-joint pipes. A simple slice down the side produces a vibrator whose tone depends on the length and diameter of the joint. A small joint—three inches long and a quarter of an inch in diameter—makes a great squealer, sounding like a wounded rabbit.

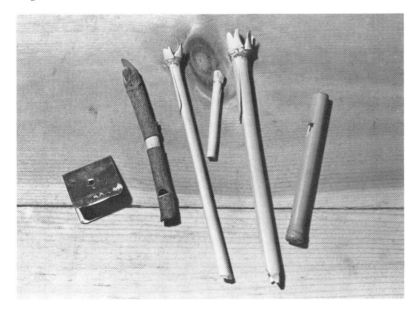

Home-made whistles and chanters. The smallest split-bamboo chanter can be used as a game squealer to call up coyotes and bobcats.

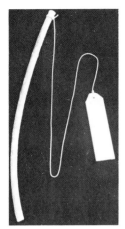

Haile's bull roarer
(Karen Haile).

Myths degenerate into children's tales, and religious articles become toys. The bull-roarer, the voice of the gods for many aboriginal folk, is an easily constructed plaything for children. Haile's basic model consists of an eighteen-inch stick handle, a two-foot line, and a small, flat piece of wood, about two inches by six inches, for the roarer. Dimensions are not critical, and the tone of the roar varies with the size of the roarer. The whirling of the flat piece as it is rapidly swung about the head causes the roaring sound.

I heard my first dumb bull at a night camp on an East Texas fox hunt. The sound was sufficiently startling coming from the wood's darkness away from the campfires that there was a momentary pause in all conversations. "What the hell was that?" was answered by "That's some damn fool with a dumb bull." The "damn fool" later showed up with his machine, a hollow log with a hide covering one end and a waxed string coming out of the center of the hide. The perpetrator, now the center of interested attention, could make all sorts of moaning-groaning sounds by sliding his thumb and forefinger along the string.

And as long as we are on waxed strings, let us not forget the tin-can telephone (from Carrol Daniels), which does not make music but does transmit sound. It is a simple toy and I am surprised that Alexander Graham Bell didn't invent it. Attach two tin cans (waxed paper cups will also work) with a long waxed string connected to the bottom of each can. Keep the string tight between the cans, talk into the empty end of the can, and the voice will be heard at the other end. We tried this in an eighth-grade science class, and I am pleased to say that it worked even then.

Whirligigs and Fluttermills
by
A. L. Miles

The whirligig is a plaything my father, Roman Miles, showed me how to make when I was a boy. This was in Coryell County in the early 1900s. Made of wood, it resembles a bow drill and might be a form of that tool. It consists of a wooden disk fixed rigidly on a round, verticle shaft that is turned by a string wound around the shaft and attached to each end of a pump lever fitted loosely onto the shaft. The shaft was about one inch in diameter, and the disk was at least six inches in diameter to furnish momentum that keeps the apparatus going. The pump lever is parabolic in shape, with each end whittled for tying the string and for providing handholds. String is run from each end of the pump lever to a nail on top of the shaft and is tied in these three places. After turning the shaft several times to wind the string around it, thus drawing the lever upward, you push down on the lever with both hands. The shaft and disk spin rapidly, and the momentum generated by the disk winds the string up again, repeatedly elevating the pump lever.

I also used to make a water-driven fluttermill with pulleys and belt-driven spool attachments. The fluttermill was a four-paddle wheel mounted on a main shaft, which rested on forked sticks set up in swift-running water. Attaching pulleys served no purpose except for achieving much-increased speed by driving a smaller pulley by a string belt from the larger one.

Joe Jones's steam-powered fluttermill.

◆ A. L. Miles's fluttermill is an exercise in pure physical science, as is a similar machine sent in by Joseph Jones. Instead of waterpower, Joe's machine is run by steampower. It consists of an airtight can with a small hole punched in one end at the top for steam to issue from and to turn a paddle wheel mounted on a wire holder. Pulleys possibly could be mounted on the paddle wheel shaft to turn little fans—or something.

We are talking educational toys here, experimental playthings that could lead to discovery. Mr. Bristow, in this great Palestine eighth-grade general science class I was telling you about, in a momentary mental lapse discussed the properties of explosives and casually mentioned that black powder was made from equal parts of sulphur, charcoal, and saltpetre. I availed myself of all three equal parts, mixed them thoroughly, and flashed the powder with a match, to my immense satisfaction. I went one step further and built a passable gun out of iron pipe. I put the powder in the pipe, tamped it with wadding, poured in a good tablespoonful of BBs, tamped them with wadding, lashed the gun down to a sawhorse, and pointed it at the side of our very old and dry garage. I lit the fuse, fled the scene, and witnessed from a distance the successful firing. Soon thereafter I went in the house for dinner. During the meal my father got up to investigate "a crackling noise" he heard out back and quickly returned with the information that the garage was in full flame. After the panic and the firemen and the realization that with hot BBs and smoldering wadding I had burned down a garage and a storeroom and my clubhouse, my main concern was whether or not Dad was going to let me go to the shoot-'em-up that Saturday afternoon. Bless his heart, he did.

A result of that same science class was an arc lamp I tried to make from carbon poles taken out of flashlight batteries. I nearly arced Mother out of her rocking chair. But then, she should have been paying attention to what I was doing.

Kraft Cheese Propeller
by
Roy E. Cain

When I was a child in rural Bastrop County in the late 1930s, the youngsters in that area enjoyed making what we called "propellers." These were made from Kraft Cheese boxes, which were about $5 \times 5 \times 12$ inches. Each end was a 5×5 square of pine about a half-inch thick. The bottom, sides, and top were strips of pine lath, with about a half an inch between the laths. Four of these were cut to a length of about six or seven inches. These became the blades of the propeller, and one of the 5×5 squares became the hub. We whittled indentions in each side of the square so that the blades would be angled properly. We made a small hole in the center of the square and then attached it to the end of a length of broomstick (about ten inches long) with a nail with a diameter slightly smaller than the hole. The nail then served as the axis of the propeller. We cut a slot in the other end of the length of broomstick and inserted part of one of the laths in the slot to act as a vane to keep the propeller facing into the wind. We usually mounted the propeller—the name we gave the entire toy—on the top of a fence post with a nail through the center of the broomstick so that the device could swivel to face the wind. These toys usually lasted a month or two before the wind and rain caused them to come apart.

The Whoopee Stick

The whoopee stick—also called a whistle stick, gee-haw whimmy diddle, liar's stick, etc.—certainly deserves recognition as a popular folk toy. Lee called it a whoopee stick and sent in building instructions. Roy Whitmire, who won second prize at the World Whimmy Diddle Contest putting one through its paces, sent in his prize stick for display and illustration. It is a limb ten inches long and three-eighths of an inch in diameter, with a slight pistol-grip curve for the handle and a carved two-inch propeller on the opposite end. In the first five inches behind the propeller Roy cut notches about a third of the way through the stick. When one vigorously *and properly* rubs these notches with another stick, the propeller will spin. When the user whistles, yells "whoopee," or commands "gee" or "haw," the propeller will stop and then reverse its direction of spin until the next command is given. It is a truly wonderful toy that must be governed with skill and understanding.

Equally wonderful and simple and ridiculous is a belt-hanger stick sent in by Tom Laramey. The stick is four inches long and a half-inch in diameter with a slanted notch cut into the last half-inch of the stick. A belt can be hung in the notch, and the opposite end will balance on the tip of your finger with the stick parallel to the ground, seemingly defying all rules of gravity. I recommend it for attracting attention and for eliciting outrageous "scientific" explanations.

Tom Laramey's belt hanger.

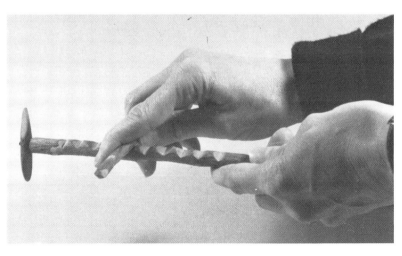

Whoopee stick.

To be sure I had missed nothing, I turned Lee's toy box upside down and poured the contents out all over my office floor. There lay a previously unnoticed flipper dinger—and a diabolo—and several cups and balls—and some yo-yos. This particular flipper dinger (not to be confused with the whimmy diddle) consists of a nine-inch bamboo joint with a small quarter-inch, hollow bamboo reed inserted near the joint end. Beyond the joint a piece of wire is wrapped and twisted to form a one-inch loop poised directly over the small bamboo vent. The purpose of flipper-dinger play is to blow a small ball with a wire hook in it so that the hook will catch on the overhanging wire loop. Believe me, it ain't easy.

The diabolo is a part of our heritage from the Far East and is an hourglass-shaped piece of wood that is spun and flipped on a string tied to two sticks. Yo-yos, a part of the same Eastern heritage and once used as a lethal weapon in the Philippines (Fraser, 15), are a well-known toy in Western culture, having gone in and out of fad-dom since the eighteenth century. Wooden yo-yos are not in fashion at this particular time and are very difficult to find in stores.

The cup and ball, still a popular toy in Mexico, is presently out of fashion in the States but has been present in Western culture since the times of classical Greece. Captain Cook found Hawaiians playing with the cup and ball, and early explorers found American Indians and Eskimos playing with it and with a ring and stick, the object of which was the same: the development of hand-eye coordination (Provenzo, 195). As Lee describes it: "The toy consisted of a small cup with a handle below it and a ball tied to the handle with a length of string. The object of

The Bottom of Lee Haile's Toy Box

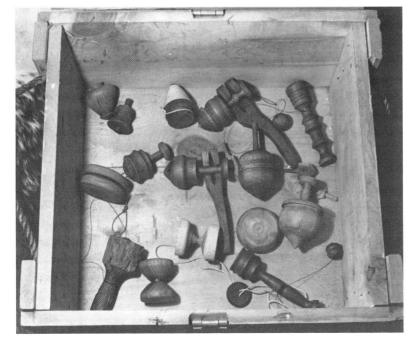

The bottom of Lee's toy box.

Flipper dinger
(Karen Haile).

Diabolos and
yo-yos from Lee's
toy box.

the game is to swing the ball out and up and catch it in the cup. The smaller the cup and the larger the ball, the more difficult is the game."

Also in the toy box, now on the floor, was an escalating bear with strings going through his outstretched paws and reaching up to a frame hung from a high place. As one pulls on the strings alternately, the bear climbs the lines to the top. Similar— but different—is the jointed plywood dancing man. You hold him up by a string attached to his head and jerk on a string that is attached to his joints, and he jumps and swings around in a most diverting manner.

I am impressed with Lee's toy box, even the remainders.

Cups and balls from Lee's toy box.

Climbing bear (Karen Haile).

A cigar box of
treasures.

Imported Cuban Seed Wrapper And Filler
Made in Tampa

**Playground
Toys**

None of these would go into a toy box, but by necessity they had
to go in this chapter. The toys are not really "playground" toys,
but they are *like* playground toys. That is, they are home-style
versions of playground slides, swings, seesaws, and merry-go-
rounds. All a kid has to have is the idea, and if he is inventive
enough he can make something that will work. For instance, on
a Ferris wheel I rode in upper Burma, where there was no power
source, Burmese boys monkeyed up the frame till they overbal-
anced us and started the wheel turning. After that they climbed
and found the counterbalance, and a couple of guys on the
ground kept us spinning quite smoothly.

A merry-go-round is simpler than a Ferris wheels because
the axis is parallel to the ground and reachable and therefore
easily spinable. Ada Harper tells about a buggy-wheel model that
was extant at least three generations ago. The axle was driven
into the ground leaving the buggy wheel several feet above the
ground. The rider sat clinging to the wheel, and the partner
kept it spinning.

The flying jenny was built on a similar principle, according
to James Biggar. An available stump or a set post with a spindle
was the fulcrum, and a long pole or plank was centered on the
spindle. Boys, or very active girls, mounted each end, and co-
horts set them to spinning. The flying jenny not only went
around in circles like a merry-go-round but also seesawed at the
same time. This made for an exciting ride, if one could stay with
it, but was an instrument of destruction to anyone stepping
within its whirling radius or hanging a leg under the end of the
pole.

Bettye Martin McRae: "When I was five years old in 1938, Daddy made me a merry-go-round designed to seat two people. Growing up in the country, six miles east of Sweetwater, I had few playmates, so I spent many an hour spinning alone on that thing till I got dizzy. Then I would reverse and spin it back the other way to unwind.

"To make it, Daddy found an old Model-T axle with one good wheel left on it. Next, he got out his post-hole digger and buried the other end until about eighteen inches stuck out of the ground. Then he centered a twelve-foot 2×12 on the wheel and bolted it down. He fired up his forge and welded two T-shaped handles out of some old pipe for each end. Finally, he bolted on the handles and painted the whole thing barn-red.

"I remember one time when cousins Janelle, Buddy, and Christine were all visiting at once. We had two kids on each end, facing across the handles. Buddy pushed until he got it going real fast and then he jumped on. Daddy had it balanced so well that it would just keep turning with the momentum built up."

The traditional homemade seesaw consists of any kind of board that is handy and that is long enough to be balanced across a sawhorse, or any other fulcrum of the proper height. Jack C. Phipps sent in a seesaw variant called a jumping board, for which "the Isbell girls" used a ten-foot 2×12 across a log: "Using a log as a fulcrum, the two of them would position themselves and alternately catapult each other about three feet into the air. Their coordination and balance in continuing the activity in swing time for several minutes was outstanding. Each ascent was made with arms outstretched and with an exhilarating scream. Since shorts and slacks were then unheard of as women's wear, the descent was made with arms hard pressed to sides to prevent skirts from flying up and exposing bloomers."

Slides are harder to come by. In East Texas, red clay banks sloping down to creeks and rivers can be formed and splashed to make an exciting slide. One of the greatest pastimes at the Texas Folklife Festival is sliding down the berms on a piece of cardboard. Hills covered with pine straw make good slides, as do haystacks. I have seen few cellar doors that one could slide down, despite the verse in the song recommending such a pastime. Folk slides can't be made, as can a buggy-wheel merry-go-round or a jumping board. Probably the fear of terminal splinters has stopped the creation of homemade slides.

Swings, on the other hand, are everywhere. The most popular model seems to be the tire swing because of the many ways a child can mount one and still swing or be swung. My favorite swing was a tow sack filled with rags and tied to a pecan limb near the back porch launching platform. The most exciting swing I ever had was a large knotted rope that hung from a tree perched on a high bank of the Trinity River. If one swung far enough out and released at the proper time, he could hit a current in the river's bend that would take him under and across and would shoot him out almost on the other bank. And if I had ever caught my sons doing that I would have worn them out.

Young lady on the ever popular tire swing.

VIII

Playhouses, Clubhouses, and Tree Houses

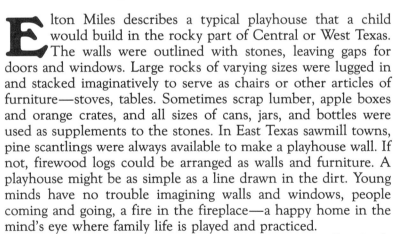

Elton Miles describes a typical playhouse that a child would build in the rocky part of Central or West Texas. The walls were outlined with stones, leaving gaps for doors and windows. Large rocks of varying sizes were lugged in and stacked imaginatively to serve as chairs or other articles of furniture—stoves, tables. Sometimes scrap lumber, apple boxes and orange crates, and all sizes of cans, jars, and bottles were used as supplements to the stones. In East Texas sawmill towns, pine scantlings were always available to make a playhouse wall. If not, firewood logs could be arranged as walls and furniture. A playhouse might be as simple as a line drawn in the dirt. Young minds have no trouble imagining walls and windows, people coming and going, a fire in the fireplace—a happy home in the mind's eye where family life is played and practiced.

Jewel Irwin Shankles from Deep East Texas recalls: "Little girls built outdoor playhouses by laying off rooms under trees, using small branches or stove wood to mark the walls. One was very careful to walk through the open spaces left for doors. Each little girl built her own playhouse. After furnishing it, the girls played at visiting back and forth, perhaps taking their stick dolls with them. Broken bits of pottery could be used for dishes on the stump tables.

"Ma's pale-green glass fruit jars had gray metal screw caps with white glass liners. After a few seasons of canning, the zinc lids deteriorated. By being very careful one could remove the little white liners and make perfect little plates to set on the stump table along with twig knives and forks. Large acorn cups made fine cups for the table. Bits of bark served for other serving pieces. Chips from the woodpile made very good platters. Imagination supplied the rest."

This urge to build and have a home, a place of one's own, a hideout or clubhouse, is called the territorial imperative. It is a genetic command that boys and girls are born with, to a greater or lesser degree, and a drive that causes man and his animal kinfolk to seek and control enough space to guarantee their survival.

Another genetic drive, the urge of males to bond together, is responsible for the millions of clubhouses that adolescent males build and deny females entrance to, except in specific cases. Frank Lassiter and I set out one Saturday morning to dig a dugout clubhouse in his backyard, but his mother shut down the operation before we were able to dig deep enough to create a hazard—or a clubhouse. The two Jacks and I dug a cave in a sand cliff on The Creek in Palestine and disguised the front with branches stuck in the ground. We went there regularly and stealthily, looking over our shoulders to see that we were not being followed. We hid out in this wilderness a half-block off Sycamore street and smoked grapevine and coffee and ultimately Kite tobacco in homemade corncob pipes. We kept our valuables and things that we stole on shelves scraped out in the back of the cave or buried in fruit jars in the sand floor. Looking back I can see that this is the way Hole-in-the-Wall gangs begin. During one stage of adolescence we had clubhouses—in backs of garages, in packing crates, in trees—scattered all over the north side of Palestine. Secret whistles identified us to each other and kept out pushy girls and uninitiated boys.

The finest clubhouses, however, were tree houses where we could climb up and pull the rope up after us and thus guarantee our privacy and exclusivity. From the heights of a good tree house one could have a separated, godlike view of the world without being touched by the troubles that were usually a part of it. A tree house is a boy's ultimate hideout. Kevin Hinzman of North Texas State University looks back on tree houses of his youth and recommends the following procedure for building: "Wire, tie, and nail extra-long fence posts to the supporting limbs to serve as the tree house platform. Onto this, nail a cattle panel covered with plywood. For walls, it is best to use four-foot-high hog wire. Leafy branches can be inserted into the hog wire to give the walls the appearance of something out of a Tarzan movie. The roof can also be made of branches crossed and lashed down with twine." That sounds like a great tree house to me, except a boy would normally get his tail in a crack if he used a cattle panel as the floor of his tree house.

Hitch Your Wagon to a Tree House
by David Sharpe

"As for me, so safe and so full of peace did this sweet spot seem, that I could but think that if we were to build a home on top of these high trees, I could find it in my heart to spend the rest of my life here."

The Swiss Family Robinson

When I was little my brother and I had a tree house in the backyard of our parents' home in Austin, Texas. Our father helped us to build it. Correction: our father built it; my brother and I held the nails. When the tree house was finished it was a grand sight, perched four feet off the ground in a cedar tree overlooking a creek. Looking up from the creek bank towards the house, high among the trees, one would think of those old German castles along the Rhine. It had wooden floors, walls, and roof, a five-foot doorway, and three windows. Along a large bough outside the door an open platform extended like the deck of a ship; indeed, in a good breeze the house would gently rock and creak like a ship tossing on the ocean waves.

My brother and I spent many happy hours in the tree house playing together, or with our friends, or even alone. Some of my best memories are those times when I played Davy Crockett at the Alamo by myself. I pretended the tree house was the famous

Dressed in coonskin caps and Davy Crockett frontier clothes, and looking bad, David Sharpe (left) and his brother Ernest reenact a bloody Indian battle in their tree house for a newspaper photographer in 1956. The tree house was built by the boys and their father, but mostly their father. Depending on the day the boys were playing, their tree house was a western fort, a ship, a look-out's nest for traffic along a nearby creek, a King Arthur castle, and a private space to retreat to.

mission chapel, and I was the last surviving Texan left standing to defend the Alamo against the onslaught of five thousand enemy soldiers. I can't tell you how many times I gloriously died, ending up draped over a tree limb, killed by a stray bullet or run through by a bayonet. Life was good in the trees.

The old tree house, like the "one-hoss shay," is gone now. Time took its inexorable toll, and our house, which we had innocently thought would last forever, began to rot and collapse and eventually had to be taken down. The only evidence of its existence are some black-and-white photographs of the two of us standing on the deck looking fierce and mean in coonskin caps and frontier clothes.

I hadn't thought of those days and experiences for a long time until recently when walking about my neighborhood I noticed three tree houses in various yards. It occurred to me that a series of tree house photographs might make an interesting photographic essay. After all, everyone growing up has either built or dreamed of building a house in the trees, like the Swiss Family Robinson. So, I started taking photographs in my neighborhood and talking to the kids about their tree houses. From them I got leads to more houses, and in a couple of months I had managed to locate and take pictures of over fifteen tree houses in Austin. Although they weren't on every corner, I was surprised how many there were. It reminded me of a cartoon I had seen once. In a big tree are four jerry-built tree houses guarded by a pair of tough-looking kids. Down below, an exterminator serviceman wearing a white coat is speaking to a woman: "Well, you've got quite an infestation here, ma'am . . . I can't promise anything, but I imagine I can knock out some of the bigger nests."

Each house was different, just as each tree was different. Each house had its own unique features that made it an expression of the child's personality. Some were almost palatial, while others were crude, two-by-four constructions. A couple had trapdoors in the floor for secret entrances and exits. On top of one the roof was built extra strong so that the kids could climb out and get a real bird's-eye view.

A surprising number belonged to little girls; no longer are tree houses strictly a male domain. Naturally, these tree houses had a feminine touch. Inside one girl's tree house were a table, a play stove, some chairs, and a carpet that a neighbor had given away. Hardly a place one would see in *Architectural Digest*, but the interior had a rough domestic charm.

Outside two houses the owners had tied ropes to tree limbs and attached baskets to raise and lower provisions and, in one instance, the family dog, although the dog didn't seem to relish the riding in the basket. Evidently, dogs and tree houses don't mix. One person told me that as a young boy he fell from his tree house ladder and broke his arm trying to carry the dog down. Finally, one house had a very special exit—a monster slide shooting down to the ground. Just thinking of the ride down makes the mind reel.

It's not much to look at, but as far as Austinites Teo Willcott (left) and his friend Peter Todd are concerned it's a tree house. Teo and Peter's primitive tree house was one of those rare instances where the owners conceived and built the tree house by themselves without any family help. It was built in 1983. Most of the time, the boys said, they used the tree house to "mess around." On occasion, Peter would haul up his portable TV, and the boys would watch old "Star Trek" episodes. (David Sharpe)

What Travis (left) and Marshall Roderick enjoyed most about their tree house was shooting at passing joggers with their waterguns. Fall and Spring were usually favorite times for playing in the tree house, which they helped their father build. (David Sharpe)

Willy (top) and Benny Morrison have done a little bit of everything in their tree house. They've played guns; they've spent the night in it with a friend; and they even tried to get their dog up in it, but the dog declined the offer. The tree house has a canvas roof. It was built by the boys' folks. (David Sharpe)

One could almost live permanently in the tree house of Ian Harris (left) and Chanda Waulters. Inside, it has a bed and electricity; outside, the roof can be an observation deck. The roof is reached through a secret opening from inside. Built so high up, this tree house is a real eagle's nest. (David Sharpe)

What makes Brent Bunge's tree house unique is that it was built completely on the ground and then lifted up into the tree. At least, that was the plan devised by Brent, his two brothers, and their father. However, a funny thing happened on the way up: the house fell to the ground and broke apart. Perseverance prevailed, and on the second attempt the tree house was successfully lifted into place. (David Sharpe)

Zac (top) and Buster Hanna built their tree house with the help of a friend. It took them two weeks. The house is over three years old and very sturdy; it has three windows and a trap door to the roof. The boys have camped out in it a couple of times. (David Sharpe)

One thing I learned was that it is a rare tree house built by kids alone. Usually, they are constructed with the help of an adult in the family, usually the children's father, grandfather, or uncle. Tree houses for children are by their nature a family-bonding project. The grandfathers of one little girl drove to Austin and combined their efforts to build in ten days an extravagant tree house that would have qualified for honorable display at San Simeon.

One little girl who knew her own mind drew up ambitious plans for the tree house of her dreams, presented it to her uncle, a contractor, and asked him to get bids on building it. Her uncle simplified the design and built the tree house himself, saying, "That kind of initiative has to be rewarded." Then there were the three young brothers and their father who decided to build a tree house completely on the ground and then lift it up into the tree, like prefab housing. However, the plan suffered a minor setback when the house fell as it was being lifted and crashed to the ground "flatter than a pancake." Eventually, it was nailed together and, on the second attempt, successfully hoisted into place.

Nowdays, you can find listings in the telephone book of specialists in building slick-looking tree houses, or "play structures." I'm sure they're better looking, but somehow I feel that participating in the building of one's own tree house is an important rite. Of course, business may have found a ripe and uncharted area to claim. For the kids' sake, though, I wish the area would remain uncharted.

What trees make good tree houses? Usually, the biggest and sturdiest tree in the nearest front- or backyard. In Central Texas that usually means a cedar, an elm, an oak, or a hackberry tree. Any one of these would serve as a reliable base for a tree house. The tree doesn't have to be large. A child is a natural romantic, and any tree can easily become a mountain, and the house in it a castle. Nor does it matter how high in the tree the house is. Most of the ones I saw in Austin were from four to six feet off the ground, but one was about twenty to twenty-five feet above the ground—a real eagle's nest.

Concerning the actual construction, one purist builder stressed that a tree house should never be nailed to a tree. The reason, he explained to me as we stood in his tree house one Saturday morning, is that a tree is "dynamic," still growing. If a tree house is nailed to it, the tree's growth will eventually cause the house to slowly split apart. No doubt that's true. But surely the process is so slow that by the time the house begins to break up, its owner will already be in college. Kids grow faster than trees.

After the tree houses are built, what do the kids do up in their houses in the air? The answers brought back memories. "Camp out . . . play guns, army . . . watch 'Star Trek' reruns (on a portable TV) . . . picnic . . . look over the neighbors' rooftops . . . play kitchen . . . spend the night out with a friend—that was 'spooky' . . . shoot at joggers with water guns . . . meditate . . . oh, mess around." On hot summer days my brother and I and friends would stage serious water balloon battles in and around our tree house. They must have been quite a show. By the end, everyone involved was drenched to the bone. The only dry people around were my mother and sister who would usually sit in lawn chairs and, like Roman generals on a hill, observe the watery spectacle from a safe distance. On a quieter note, Brent Bunge of Austin spoke nostalgically about his tree house experiences: "I'd like to read a book in it and sip a glass of tea. The wind would blow the pages, and I'd doze off, wake up and read again, and doze off." What an empty grocery sack on the floor is to a playful cat, a tree house is to a young boy or girl. Its possibilities are endless.

However, the span of a child's interest in tree houses is not endless—it's only temporary. Like childhood itself, the affair a child has with a tree house is ephemeral, quick, and over before you know it. At the most, children use and play in tree houses for a couple of years, and then, like a toy bear or a doll that was once a constant companion, the tree house is gradually abandoned. Bunge reflected: "There was a special aura about the tree house for two years. Then we stored fertilizer in it for a while." The purpose may disappear, but the memories remain, bright and strong. And sometimes the house stands long after its owners have outgrown it. Too big to put in the family scrapbook, it is also too important to dismantle and throw away. Brent and his brothers, Brian and Bruce, have all grown up and have no more use for a tree house. And yet, today, Brent's tree house still sits in a tree where every afternoon the setting sun hits it and casts its shadow over the family's backyard.

Misty McNairs must have been the only 4-year old in Austin to have a tree house that resembled a little Alpine Swiss chalet. Misty has long since outgrown the tree house built by her grandfather, but the picturesque little house still sits in the giant oak in the yard of Misty's grandparents. Her grandmother says one of these days she intends to give the tree house a new coat of paint and repair the steps leading up to it. (David Sharpe)

Now, some may believe that tree houses and their signifi-
cance fall pretty low in the general scheme of things. Tree
houses certainly don't have any practical value. Children don't
live in tree houses, as our early ancestors lived in trees. By all
accounts, tree houses are pretty frivolous. But if they are, then
you might as well say that circuses are frivolous, and that reading
Treasure Island is not important, and that lying on a blanket
outside at night to gaze at the stars is a waste of time. Tree
houses are important. More than wooden boards nailed to a tree,
a tree house is an aerial stage on which to act out childhood
fantasies and independence. Moreover, it's a place where one
can temporarily escape the omnipresent parental eye and be
alone with one's own thoughts or with one's own friends. Tree
houses matter, just as kids matter.

To adults, Ralph Waldo Emerson once said, "Hitch your
wagon to a star." To kids, I say, "Hitch your wagon to a tree
house." For as long as there are kids and tree houses, there will
be no shortage of fun and good times. Like stars, tree houses
can spark the imagination and keep the world from becoming a
dull place.

Part Two
─────────
Folk Games

Games are forms of individual or team competition, played to a decision according to agreed-upon rules. Games are voluntary and nonproductive, and people play them because they want to, not because survival depends on it. They are also played in their own territories with their own characters, outside the struggles of everyday realities. "Folk" games are those traditional games passed along informally from one playground to another. Games are played when people have leisure time, and because children have more leisure time than the adults who work to support them, they are the ones we turn to when we are looking for games.

In spite of television and organizations, children still play games. They might not be playing as many games as they used to (I could find no marble shooters or players of knife or top games in my classes), but on lightly supervised playgrounds in grammar schools children are still playing Red Rover and Wolf Over the River. And when two or three are gathered together and a hill is handy they naturally fall into King of the Mountain. At Sunday school parties they play musical chairs, and picnickers play Pop the Whip. On Friday nights girls still give parties at their houses and play Spin the Bottle or Charades or Hide-and-Seek. And they play clapping games and chant jump-rope rhymes and count out "One potato, two potato, three potato, four . . ." Games are still played because they satisfy the need of individuals to be together in groups at the same time as they are pecking for dominance and competing for territory.

Organized playing and playgrounds have cut down considerably on free and easy childhood play. Adults are everywhere, seeing that rules are adhered to and that everybody gets to play and that children improve their skills and themselves through play. Children become performers playing the game for adults and not for each other. This is not the spirit in which folk games are played. That folk-game spirit can best be found among a bunch of kids playing stickball or One-eyed Cat in a vacant lot or playing Horse at basketball hoops nailed to a garage. These kids make ground rules as they go, they stop playing when something better or more pressing comes along, and if one of them doesn't like the way the game is going, he will take his ball and go home. They can't do that in Little League.

IX
Guessing and Gambling

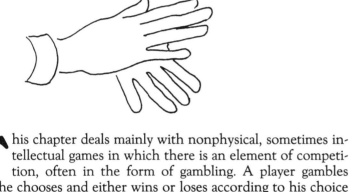

This chapter deals mainly with nonphysical, sometimes intellectual games in which there is an element of competition, often in the form of gambling. A player gambles when he chooses and either wins or loses according to his choice or when he participates in a random choosing and either wins or loses by chance. Real gambling took place when Bryon Rhodes and his grade-school friends bet candy on caterpillars racing along strings (from Ken Davis). Elton Miles reminded us of the general popularity of gambling on license-plate poker (similar to dollar-bill serial-number poker) as played by high-school students: "Those poker hands were formed of digits only, as were the license plates in the 1930s. Zero was the lowest 'card,' with One standing for the Ace. In Alpine in the 1980s young people play the game combining letters with numbers. A, K, Q, and J are the Ace, King, Queen, and Jack; O's are wild and can therefore stand for ten. A one can be an Ace or can stand at face value." That is true gambling, particularly if something is bet on the outcome.

Counting out is a form of gambling. One lines up or gets in the ring to be counted, realizing that chance controls—or is supposed to control—whether or not he will be chosen. He is gambling on being or not being It. Being It can be good *or* bad, however, depending on the game. Sometimes It is the center of attention and will be controlling the game, as in Jack in the Box and Fruit Basket, Turn Over; sometimes It has to play pigtail or be the target in

Counting Out!

Dodge Ball. Whatever the case, counting out is one of child-hood's means of inclusion and exclusion and is an attempt at choosing fairly, although everybody remembers how counting out could be made selective by a cunning counter. And we remember how racially or ethnically discriminating counting out could be, in Texas the Jews and blacks being the main targets.

> Acka backa soda cracker,
> Acka backa boo,
> Acka backa soda cracker,
> Out goes *you!*
> (Ada Phipps Harper and William Stokes)

Or the anti-Semitic or anti-Hibernian version, both now fortu-nately quite rare:

> If your papa chews tobacco
> He's a dirty *Jew!*
> (or)
> He's an Irish *stew!*

Most of the counting-out rhymes involved counting, tap-ping, or slapping fists ("potatoes") and were prolonged because of the enjoyment of the counting rhyme and ritual and because of the excitement of the selection process, the gambling. The fear of being counted out versus the hope of remaining within the body of the group is based on the human being's desire to be a part of the surviving social group.

> Eeny meeny miny moe,
> Catch a feller [happily changed from "nigger"] by the toe.
> If he hollers make him pay
> Fifty dollars every day!
> [One could be "out" or It on *day,* or the counting could continue.]
> You old dirty dishrag,
> You get *out!*

> Pease porridge hot, pease porridge cold,
> Pease porridge in the pot nine days old.
> Some like 'em hot; some like 'em cold;
> Some like 'em in the pot nine days *old!*

Potato counting was an elaborate selector, with all partici-pants standing in a circle, fists out to be tapped on each word, with a fist counted out on *more.* The last fist in was either the winner or the loser, depending on what the group was selecting for.

> One potato, two potato, three potato, four;
> Five potato, six potato, seven potato *more.*

> Bubble gum, bubble gum in a dish;
> How many pieces do you wish?

The last person pointed to, on *wish,* says a number. The counter counts out persons until he arrives at the stated number, then says, "You are not it, you dirty, dirty dishrag, ugly you!" People are selected out, until the remaining one becomes It. (Shari Wolfe of Paris Junior College)

Sometimes William Trembletoe was used by itself, counting out on *none* or concluding with an "O-U-T out goes he!" Sometimes it was prolonged with Wire, Briar.

William, William Trembletoe
He's a good fisherman,
Catches hens,
Puts them in pens,
Some lay eggs,
Some lay *none!*
 (or)
O-U-T out goes *he!*

Or it could be concluded:

Wire, briar, limber-lock
Three geese in a flock.
One flew east; one flew west;
One flew over the cuckoo's nest.
O-U-T spells out goes he!
(Ada Phipps Harper and Dorris Yates Tull)

In a game that was often played with William Trembletoe, the child that was counted out, or that was chosen It, runs away some distance from the other players, who are sitting in a ring. He stands aside while the counter gives names of animals to the children in the circle. Then he calls to the one who is It:

Counter: When are you coming home?
It: Tomorrow afternoon.
Counter: What are you going to bring?
It: A tablespoon and an old raccoon.
Counter: Which had you rather come home on—a bear, wolf, panther, etc.?

It names an animal, and the one who bears that name goes out and brings him home on his back.

Counter to the animal carrier: What have you got there?
Carrier: A bundle of ticks and some old dry sticks.
Counter: Shake him till he spits (which he does).
Counter to the rider: Would you rather lie down on a bed of thorns or a bed of feathers?

If the rider says he wants a thorn bed, his carrier lays him down very gently. If he says he wants a feather bed, he is shaken off very roughly. So ends the game. (Ida B. Hall)

Paper, Rock, and Scissors

Paper, Rock, and Scissors is also a counting-out game, but it is usually used to choose between two people. Or it can be played as a gambling game, with the loser getting whapped on the back

Paper, Rock, and
Scissors (Richard S.
Orton).

of the hand. Two kids sitting or standing face each other. The left hand is held out, palm up, and the right hand is made into a fist. The players strike their fists against their palms simultaneously three times. On the third time, they make the sign for paper with a flat hand, rock with a fist, or scissors with extended index and middle fingers. Paper covers stone, scissors cut paper, and stone crushes scissors. That is, if you have paper you can beat rock but lose to scissors. Rock beats scissors but loses to paper. And scissors beats paper but loses to rock. Martin Beversdorf of Paris High School, who grew up in the Philippines and later lived in Japan as an exchange student, reports that PRS is played in Asia and is called Jan-ken-po. My Chinese friend Li Bo calls it Shitou Jianzi Bu. It is a popular game worldwide and is centuries old. (Pam Palmer, Benjamin Capps, Steve Marchbanks of Texas Tech, Shawna Cook of Paris High School)

Hully Gull A favorite fireside gambling game with the children of several generations was Hully Gull. Any nut, corn kernel, or other small object could be used. Each player began with the same number of nuts. Our favorite kind each fall was the small shiny chinquapins just after we picked them from their prickly dried burrs, although small native pecans were all right. The first player holds a secret number of pebbles in his closed hands. He extends his fists to the second player, who responds, "Hully Gull!" The first player then says, "Hand full." The second asks, "How many?" The first answers, "Guess." If the second player guesses correctly, he gets to keep all the nuts. If the second player is wrong, he must give the first player the difference between those in hand and the number guessed. The second player then becomes the caller. They play until someone wins all the markers. (Frances Vaughan to Kenneth Davis, Jewel Irwin Shankles, Ida Hall, Ada Phipps Harper, Dorris Yates Tull)

Rock School was a sitting-on-the-steps game, indoors or out. Players began by sitting on the bottom step. The "teacher" held her hands behind her back with a small rock in one hand. She would present her closed fists to each "pupil" on the step, saying, "Which hand do you choose?" The pupil would indicate which fist he thought the rock was in. If the pupil was correct, he moved up one step. The first pupil to ascend and then descend the flight of steps won the game and became the teacher.

Rock School
by
Ada Phipps
Harper

Spin the Bottle requires only an empty bottle and a circle of alternating boys and girls. The object of the game is to spin the bottle on its side in the middle of the circle (it is like a roulette wheel) and hope that it will land on that special person. This game is played by fifth graders, more or less, and each player must have lips able to make that "perfect pucker."

Spin the
Bottle

To begin the game a player reaches over and gives the bottle a spin and watches as it whirls to a stop with its top pointing to a player of the opposite sex. The spinner must then lean across the circle and kiss that person for one second. If the bottle points to a person of the same sex, then he gets to spin again. After the kiss, it becomes the kissee's turn to spin. (Chris Ann Morrow of Paris High School, Gayla McLain Sanders)

Spin the Bottle
(Richard S. Orton).

◆ Somehow I don't remember the kissing part of Spin the Bottle. What else could we have done—gone walking? No, that would have diminished the number of players. Maybe we did kiss but I have forgotten. Pitiful!

Here is more socially sanctioned gambling: the first being a lottery, the second roulette, with the people going 'round and 'round instead of a wheel:

Candy Drawings and Cake Walks
by
Rebecca Radde

In the fall of 1919, I lived in Nacogdoches County between Chireno and Etoile. I was only nine years old, but I had a sister just turned sixteen and eligible to attend gatherings of young people. So our parents took us to a number of night parties, always in a rural area. The whole family attended.

The host family bought several boxes of stick candy, maybe three or four kinds: red-stripe peppermint, yellow-stripe lemon, pink sugar stick, yellow sugar stick, etc. On a table at one side of a room sat a box with an opening just large enough to put a hand in. The candy was dumped into this box and mixed. As the guests entered, each man or boy who planned to participate signed his name on a register and paid a fee, which was supposed to cover the cost of the candy drawing.

When all the neighbors and visitors had arrived, a man began calling names, beginning with the first signature. This youth chose a young lady as his partner, and they approached the box. She thrust her hand into the box and drew a piece of candy. The boy did likewise. If the two candies did not match, they both continued to draw until they drew two pieces alike. Then this couple retired, and the caller shouted another name. The process was repeated until all the candy was gone. It was expected that the men choose a different girl each time.

At the end of the drawing, a cake walk was held. Couples were lined up outside the house, and at a given signal they began walking slowly around the house, holding hands. It was usually dark. Unless there was a moon, the only light would be the kerosene lamps shining through the windows. When the second signal was given (usually a single gunshot fired in the air), everybody stopped. When the leader came out, he revealed a secret mark that he had placed on the house earlier. The couple closest to it received the cake. In a large crowd, there might be several cakes to be walked.

I do not remember any purpose for the cake walk except that it gave the couples a chance to be in the dark with each other.

I Spy
by
Dorris Yates Tull

At the end of the day, when I had grown tired of my hoard of toys and when my dolls didn't respond to my questions, my grandmother might play a game of I Spy with me.

"I spy something blue," she said.

"Is it my doll's dress?" I asked. With a smile on her face she shook her head. I had not guessed what she was spying.

"Is it the book on the table?"

"No. Guess again. It is made of wool."

"I know," I said in excitement. "It's your fascinator."

"That's right. Now it is your turn."

I looked around the room trying to decide what I would ask Grandmother. After some thought, I said, "I spy something white."

Grandmother looked around the room. "Is it my dress?"

"No," I said in glee that she had not guessed right. "It is in your chair."

"But I am in my chair. What could it be?" she asked as she looked around her.

"It is round," I said.

"I know. It is my ball of knitting thread."

And so the game went on from one object to another, each of us taking a turn until one or the other grew tired of playing.

Packing Grandma's Trunk was a circle game played indoors. All participants formed a circle with their chairs and faced the center of the room. The first participant said, "In Grandma's trunk I found an afghan"—or any item beginning with A. The next person in line said, "In Grandma's trunk I found an afghan and a napkin"—using the last letter of the first word and adding a new word starting with that letter. The third person would repeat what the second person did, and each person continued the process in his turn around the circle. If someone failed to come up with his word or if he was unable to repeat all the items in order up to him he was dropped from the game.

An easier version of the game has the first person put in an item beginning with A, the second person an item starting with B, and so on around the circle with the alphabet. It is much easier to recall the list if you can come down the ABC's and stay in alphabetical order.

In another circle game, Hole in the Bottom of the Sea, the game starter reads out the sentence "There was a flea on a hair on a wart on a frog on a knot on a limb on a log in a hole in the bottom of the sea." The first person to begin the circle says, "There was a hole in the bottom of the sea." The second person begins with "There was a log" and adds "in a hole in the bottom of the sea." The third person begins "There was a limb" and adds "on a log in a hole in the bottom of the sea." Each person in turn adds the next item in the phrase and repeats the whole phrase. Anyone who misses is dropped from the game.

Indoor Circle Games
by
Gayla McLain Sanders

A voice calls, "Wollen Stimmchen spielen!" ("Let's play Voicelet!"), and immediately all the young German-Texan players scamper about seeking hands to clasp to form a circle. Usually the child suggesting the game will be It, the blindfolded interrogator with a stick who occupies the center of the circle. With an important air he takes his place, and after the players have spun around him a time or two, he pokes about with his stick trying to locate a victim. Having "spiked" one, he demands, "Stimmchen!" ("Little

Voicelet
by
Julia Estill

voice!"). Usually the response comes in a mousey squeak or a basso profundo, and the one in the center tries to identify the voice. If he is a good guesser, the one identified takes his place in the center and the game continues.

Texas Grunt   A variant of Voicelet is called Texas Grunt. Children join hands in a circle and march around It, who stands blindfolded in the center. It holds a stick with which he strikes the ground as a signal for the marching to stop. Then It walks straight ahead till he touches a child. The touched child has to give a grunt. If It guesses the name of the child giving the grunt, the two exchange places, and the grunter becomes It. If It fails to guess correctly, the game continues until he makes a correct guess. The fun comes when the grunting child tries to mimic another person. (Ida Hall)

Blindman's Bluff   Elwin Brownlee tells of his mother's playing Blindman's Bluff [traditionally called and spelled *buff*] at the Dollarhide Union 76 Camp some thirty miles east of Kermit. Only girls were allowed to play the game because there was no way of knowing where one player would touch another. The girls formed a circle around a blindfolded It. The girls in the circle ran and danced around It, trying to get her attention but trying not to get caught. When It finally did catch someone in the circle, she had to identify her by touch. If she did, It was free and the identified girl had to take her place. If she did not guess who the girl was, she continued as It. The winner was the last one caught. (Elwin Brownlee to Kenneth Davis)

Boogie in the Dark   Joanie Preston's Boogie in the Dark, unlike Mrs. Brownlee's Blind Man's Bluff, is a game that allows participation by both sexes and is not overly concerned about the problems involved in touching. Instead of It being blindfolded, the game is played in the black dark and nobody can see anybody. A strategy frequently employed by It is to stretch out his arms and move toward a corner, herding all before him. Once It touches a player, the player must stand still. In some versions of Boogie in the Dark, It must not move his hand from the place he first touched the player. There are both advantages and disadvantages to that rule. In other versions, It is allowed to tactually check the tagged player to ascertain his or her identity. Whether or not this promotes groping depends on the quality of the players. If It succeeds in identifying his captive, the captive becomes It for the next game. (Joanie Preston of Paris Junior College)

Seven-Up   Seven-Up is an ideal game for a classroom. First, the teacher chooses seven members of the class to start the game. These seven come to the front of the room and stand. Then the teacher says, "Heads down, thumbs up!" The members of the class put their heads on their arms, shut their eyes, and raise one thumb. The chosen seven then pass among the students, and each one folds down the thumb of one classmate. Then the seven return to the front of the room, and the teacher calls out, "Seven up, stand up." When this command is given, the class sits up straight, and the seven who were tagged stand up. The teacher then calls on each one of the tagged to identify his tagger. If a student cannot guess correctly, he must sit down. If he guesses the identity of his tagger, he takes the tagger's place up front. It is considered proper for the tagger to give a tactile clue to his identity by the way he or she folds down the thumb. All is revealed before the next game is started. (Jason Davis of Paris Junior College, Melissa Wilson of Texas Tech)

Killer
by
Lori Phillips
of Paris High
School

At least ten players sit in a circle, Indian-style. A card dealer hands out a card to each player, and among the cards is one joker. The killer in the game is the one who receives the joker. Now everybody is looking at everybody, the killer looking for his victim and the players looking for the killer before he strikes. The killer's weapon is a wink. The trick is getting a shot without getting caught. The killer finally catches a player's eye, and he winks. The victim counts to three slowly to give the killer a chance to look away and then falls over and says, "I'm dead!" The game continues with the killer stalking another victim and successfully killing him. There is the off chance that the killer will get everybody without getting caught. Also, if somebody accuses the wrong person of being the killer, the accuser is out of the game. But usually as the number of players decreases the chance of catching the killer making a hit with a deadly wink increases and murder will out!

◆ The purpose of the following games is to trick players, making them do something wrong or silly or making them laugh, in spite of a penalty put on laughing.

Jack-in-the-
Box
by
Tammy
Thompson
of Texas Tech

My great-aunt described a few games she played when she was a kid. One of these games was called Jack-in-the-Box. First the children pick one person to be the leader. The rest of the children form a circle. The leader yells, "Jack-in-the-Box," and the kids must squat quickly. Then the leader yells, "Jack-out-of-the-Box," and the children must stand up. The leader can try to trick the children by saying the words quickly or slowly or by repeating the same phrase twice. The first person to mess up is disqualified. The last person left becomes the leader. Obviously this game takes a great deal of concentration, and the children must listen very closely.

Fruit Basket,
Turn Over
by
Tammy
Thompson
of Texas Tech

Another game that interested my great-aunt when she was a child was the game Fruit Basket, Turn Over. The activity needed at least three or four people. The children would sit in a circle and would choose one child to be It; he would stand in the middle of the circle. The child that was It would give each child the name of a fruit. Then he would yell out one of the names three times, such as "Apple, apple, apple!" If the child given the name "apple" did not stand up before It was finished shouting, then he became It. If the child did stand up before the caller was finished, then he could sit back down, and the game would continue. My great-aunt says, "If you are It, it was a good idea not to pick names of fruit like banana or papaya, because they are very hard to say three times fast!"

Old Mother Hubbard
by
Ida Hall

Children sit in a row. The leader, beginning with the first child, addresses each, one at a time:

> Leader: Old Mother Hubbard's dead.
> Child: How did she die?
> Leader: Blind in one eye. (Child shuts one eye.)
>   And mouth all awry. (Child twists mouth out of shape.)

The leader continues with each child in the same manner, and all say the same words and imitate the first child's gestures. When the leader has finished, all children are sitting with one eye closed and mouths twisted—and trying to keep from laughing. Whoever loses his face or laughs is out of the game.

Grandmother Humbum
by
Ida Hall

The leader stands facing a group of children and begins the following dialogue:

> Leader: Grandmother Humbum sent me to you, sir.
> Group: What for to do, sir?
> Leader: To beat one hammer as I do, sir.

He begins hammering with one fist while the group imitates him. Then he leaves and returns. He could be sawing or imitating any other action or group of actions that would create a humorous pantomiming situation.

> Leader: Grandmother Humbum sent me to you, sir.
> Group: What for to do, sir?
> Leader: To beat two hammers as I do, sir.

He begins hammering with two fists while the group imitates. He leaves and returns.

> Leader: Grandmother Humbum sent me to you, sir.
> Group: What for to do, sir?
> Leader: To beat three hammers as I do, sir.

He begins to nod his head up and down while still beating both fists, the group imitating him. He leaves and returns.

> Leader: Grandmother Humbum sent me to you, sir.
> Group: What for to do, sir?
> Leader: To beat four hammers as I do, sir.

He begins stamping a foot while still wagging his head and hammering his fists, the group following his lead. He leaves and returns.

> Leader: Grandmother Humbum sent me to you, sir.
> Group: What for to do, sir?
> Leader: To beat five hammers as I do, sir.

He then stamps both feet while still moving other members of his body as before. While the group of children continues to imitate him, the leader quietly steals away and does not return, thus leaving the group in a ridiculous position. Or he could stand and watch them until they begin laughing at the ridiculousness of the scene. A variant of this game is called Wag-Wag.

A ring game popular in Fredericksburg during its early colonial days was Esel, Lass Dich Hoeren. The players, impersonating animals, sit in a circle with ultra-sober mien, while the ringmaster and the donkey, chosen by their fellows, occupy the center. The ringmaster in a dominant voice commands, "Esel, lass dich hoeren!" The donkey then brays loud and long, while the ringmaster watches closely for grins on the faces of those seated in the circle. If any one of them smiles, laughs, or even shows his teeth, he must pay a forfeit or take the place of the donkey.

Esel, Lass Dich Hoeren, or Donkey, Let's Hear You
by
Julia Estill

Another laughing game handed down through several generations of children in Gillespie County is Stumm, Stumm wie Buttermilch. A chosen player advances on children sitting on a bench and says the following lines while tapping one of them on the chest:

Stumm, Stumm, wie Buttermilch, or Dumb, Dumb as Buttermilk
by
Julia Estill

> Stumm, stumm, wie Buttermilch!
> Lache nicht; weine nicht;
> Zeich deine, kleine weisze Zaehne nicht.
> (Dumb, dumb as buttermilk!
> Laugh not; weep not;
> Show not your little white teeth.)

The closeness of the laughing leader's face and his thoracic thump will usually provoke a grin on the victim's face. When it does, he is hoisted upon the locked hands of two other players and swung and bounced about as his punishment.

Players sit on the floor or around a table to play Club Fist. They make a pole of fists, each holding the thumb of the hand below his. The leader keeps his right hand free and starts the game when he says to the owner of the top fist, "Want to take it off, knock it off, or let the crows pick it off?" Then the owner of the top fist can remove it, let the leader try to knock it off with one blow from his free hand, or hold on as the leader tries to pinch his hand so hard that he lets go. The same sequence follows

Club Fist
by
Dorris Yates Tull

until there is only one fist left. Then the owner of the last fist and the leader recite the following:

> Leader: Where's the water?
> Fist: The ox drank it.
> Leader: Where's the ox?
> Fist: The butcher killed it.
> Leader: Where's the butcher?
> Fist: The rope hung him.
> Leader: Where's the rope?
> Fist: The rats gnawed it.
> Leader: Where are the rats?
> Fist: The cat caught them.
> Leader: Where's the cat?
> Fist: The gun shot it.
> Leader: Where's the gun?
> Fist: The hammer broke it.
> Leader: Where's the hammer?
> Fist: Behind the door cracking hickory nuts!
> Leader: The first one who grins or shows his teeth gets a hair pulling and a pinch.

At this point all the players try to keep a straight face without smiling or showing their teeth. Eventually all succumb to laughter, and the leader is busy delivering penalties.

Poor Kitty
by
Carrol Daniels

Everyone sits around in a circle, and the "kitty"—It—walks around the circle, crouches in front of someone, and meows. The person in the circle pats the kitty three times, each time saying, "Poor kitty!" If the patter smiles or laughs, he loses and has to take the kitty's place in the next game. The kitty can go through all sorts of caterwauling and facial and body contortions to make the victim laugh.

Treasure Hunts

Treasure hunts can be played several ways, but all call for hiders and seekers to outsmart each other. One kind of treasure hunt is the scavenger hunt, which is frequently the theme of a party. In the scavenger hunt, the party is divided into two teams. Each team is given a list of various objects, such as paper clips, banana peels, a policeman's hat, the mayor's cat (the degree of availability determines the intensity of the hunt), and a designated period of time within which to find the objects. The first group to come back with all the items on the list is the winner and should get prizes.

In another kind of treasure hunt the hider writes a clue, which might be tricky, on a piece of paper and gives it to a player or group of players. This clue should lead to another, then another, until eventually the players find the treasure itself. An example of one clue might be, "It is on top of the world," which could mean that the clue is on a world globe. The hunt is an intellectual exercise for both the writer of the clues and the searchers. (Ann Alcorn of Paris High School)

X

Chasing and Capturing

The games in this chapter are physically competitive. Most require combinations of strength, speed, and agility and are illustrations and sublimations of man's (animal's) eternal struggles for dominance and territory. Most of the following games are adequate outlets for the superabundant energies of junior high schoolers, and are necessary for the survival of their elders.

One-on-one competition for dominance is illustrated by what used to be generically referred to as "Indian wrestling," which takes several forms and is a good illustration of games growing out of young boys' enjoyment of basic violence. Ken Davis wrote us about thumb wrestling. Thumb wrestling can take place in a classroom across an aisle if the participants are quiet about it. Wrestlers hook their four fingers with thumbs up and push their thumbs against one another. The person who forces the other's thumb back is the winner. In a standing game, the winner can force the loser to his knees for absolute submission. One step up was arm wrestling, which has gained popularity among adults in these days. Participants sit across from each other at a table, elbows and forearms together and propped, with hands locked in a grip. The winner is the one who forces his opponent's arm backwards to the table. For added incentive, lighted candles or thumbtacks are sometimes placed in the pinning positions on the table. A third form, which I have not seen in years, is leg

Indian Wrestling and Other Forms of Combat

wrestling. The contestants lie on their backs in opposite directions, hips touching. They raise their inside legs, hook their opponent's leg, and try to flip him up and over. Another form of Indian wrestling involves two players who put their right feet together and opposite, holding right hands, and try to pull each other off balance without losing the position of the right foot.

Ken Davis sent accounts of two more forms of childhood combat never mentioned by Robert Louis Stevenson: rooster fighting and horse wrestling. Rooster fighting is frequently done in a drawn ring or at least within some prescribed bounds. Opponents fold their arms or hook their thumbs in their belts and then slam themselves against each other's shoulders. Arms are supposed to be kept tightly by the sides, and stabbing with elbows is against the rules. The loser is the one who is either

Indian leg wrestling.

Indian wrestling.

Rooster fighting
(left).

One-legged rooster
fighting
(Richard S. Orton).

knocked out of the ring or hollers "calf rope." Horse wrestling, or playing horse, involved a boy with a rider on his back or shoulders. The "horses" maneuvered for position while the riders tried to drag each other off and to the ground. A typical scene was two kids hanging on to each other's necks, parallel to the ground, with both horses pulling in opposite directions. Technically a rider was still in the game if he had both feet still locked about his horse's waist. He might be dragging his head on the ground, but if he could pull back up into position, the battle was still on. Playing horse was a great favorite among young boys and was a notorious spoiler of clothes. (Victor Smith and Porter Robertson to Kenneth Davis)

Some of Ruth Semrau's Paris High School students play similar games on trampolines. The games are called Bootie Boppers (Jeremy Brazzel), Ketchup Maker (Jenatha Garcia), and Alligator (Brady Roberts). Bootie Boppers is similar to rooster fighting except that tripping is allowed. In Ketchup Maker, so named because of the possibilities of spilt blood, everybody begins bouncing, and It must grab one and pin him for five seconds. Alligator is similar, but It is required to down his opposition with the use of his legs only. All these games are enhanced by the continual bouncing of the players and by the fact that the games are played on a vertical as well as a horizontal plane.

Horse wrestling
melee
(Richard S. Orton).

Horse wrestling, or playing horse.

No winners in this game of horse wrestling.

Slap Hands
by
Kendi Hensel
of Paris High
School

Bus trips, football games, parties, and first dates all have one thing in common: they can get boring very fast. One simple remedy for this problem is a game called Slap Hands. It requires no equipment, virtually no space, and is a cinch to learn.

The basic game requires two players, an offense and a defense. The offense, the slapper, places his hands out in front of him palms up. The defense, the slappee, has his hands palms down directly above and lightly touching those of the offense. The object is for the offense to quickly jerk his hands out, turn them over, and slap the back of the defense's hands before the defense can move his hands out of the way. If the offense misses, the roles are reversed, and the slapper becomes the slappee. If contact is made, the game continues.

Creative strategies can be developed to make the game more challenging. For instance, the offense can cross to slap the opponent's opposite hand. The offense can also try to fake the opponent by shaking his hands but not pulling them out from beneath his opponent's.

Variations allow for three or more people to play. For large numbers of people a circle can be formed with the hands out to the sides so that there is a different person on each hand. This is very challenging because one person could have one hand on offense and the other on defense. Or the game can be played with three people, with one person using both hands, but the other two each having only one hand in the game.

A slightly more painful version is called Knuckles. Instead of having the hands spread out in front, the players close their hands into fists. The two players put their fists together head-on. The rest is the same; the offense tries to hit the other's knuckles while the defense tries to get out of the way before that happens.

Gun Fighting

To play Gun Fighting two players, usually boys, with girls as spectators, stand about three feet apart. Player One holds his hands together in front of him in a prayer-like pose. Player Two has his hands flat against his hips where a pair of pistols might be. He looks as if he has his hands on a set of guns. Player Two tries to slap Player One's hands before Player One can move his hands upward toward either shoulder. If Player Two slaps Player One's hands three times, he switches places with him and holds his hands out. The object of the game is to outlast the opponent and thus to prove greater tolerance to pain. Female spectators supposedly are impressed with such macho behavior. (Deborah Parten to Kenneth Davis)

King of the Mountain

King of the Mountain illustrates in pristine terms the struggle to gain the room at the top, to be the dominant male with the best territory. It is a simple game, the only necessity being a hill. In East Texas a pine-straw covered hill is a favorite; in West Texas a sand hill in the Red River breaks is preferred. The ideal hill, as far as I am concerned, is an old sawdust pile from an abandoned sawmill. For one thing, the hill is conical, and the King can stand in one place and defend his territory. For another, sawdust is spongy, and one can roll and fall and bounce and enjoy every tumble of it. But I shall never forget a traveling anecdote of those sawmill days. These boys went off to play King of the Mountain *without telling their parents* and unfortunately went to a sawdust pile that harbored a long smoldering fire in its core. One of the boys, in his struggle for the top, fell through the deceiving crust of the pile and was roasted by the time grown-ups could be fetched to retrieve him. In spite of which, few games could afford the primal satisfaction of King of the Mountain played on a sawdust pile. (Editor, Todd Kassaw to Kenneth Davis)

Pop the Whip   The leader would make a long line of people, holding hands. The leader, usually a physically strong individual, was in charge and set the pace as the line ran. The leader would then change direction, and he could hold with *both* hands, and pop the whip. Because the outer end had to go so much faster to keep up, those in that position, usually the smallest and weakest, were popped off and were out of the game. The leader continued popping until he got down to the one who could not be popped off. He might be the popper for the next game, or number two in line might be it. The consequences of the game, according to Mrs. Victor Smith, often included dislocated shoulders, broken collarbones, and broken arms and wrists. (Mrs. Victor Smith to Kenneth Davis, Dorris Yates Tull)

Red Rover   The favorite arm and wrist breaker was—and still is—Red Rover. Two captains are chosen, and they take turns choosing from the players until each has a side. Both sides line up, holding hands, thirty to fifty feet apart, depending on the vigor and intensity of the players. The leader of one team then calls, "Red Rover, Red Rover, let Robert come over." Robert, who was

Pop the Whip (Richard S. Orton).

called because he is a weenie, runs to break the line where he thinks it is weakest. Unfortunately he misjudges the strength of the grip of the holders and ends up draped across their arms, now a captive of the opposing team. Robert's old team is now the caller, and they call, "Red Rover, Red Rover, let Richard come over." It is a bad call; Richard is little but he is mighty, and he hits a weak link and cracks it in two. Victorious, he takes the two that he broke through and returns with them as his captives back to his team. And it goes on like this until one team is decimated. It is much like primitive tribal warfare, with just a little less bloodshed. The rules vary. Sometimes a successful line breaker is allowed to choose the one he takes back, instead of having to take the broken links. The children select like nature, attacking the weak and choosing the strong. (Rachel Thomas, Kristi Mashburn, and Reisa Swaim of Paris High School, Dan Moore to Ken Davis, Tammy Thompson of Texas Tech, Dorris Yates Tull)

Leap Frog is an ancient game that has probably survived because of its simplicity. One boy (or girl) bends over, hands on knees, and another leaps astraddle over him, touching him only with his hands. The leaper usually takes a step and bends over as a frog to begin the formation of a line of frogs for leapers. Then the player who first went down as the frog leaps over all the

Leap Frog and Variants

Leap Frog.

Leap Frog
(Richard S. Orton).

other frogs and takes his position again as the first down. This time he will stand higher with his hands on his thighs, making the leap more difficult. The next time he might stand straight up with only his head bent. In any one of the leaps, if the leaper touches the frog with his leg or his seat, he is out of the game. The leader, first frog down, calls the play. He might require that every jumper pat the frog on the head as he passes over, or use only one hand for leaping, or clear the frog while whistling "Yankee Doodle."

Backbreak was popular when I was teaching high school at Woodville. Because of the violence involved, authorities never allowed it to be played on the campus, but when I took my classes for an outing on Village Creek, we played backbreak (I was much younger then). Two teams of boys were chosen. Girls were to look on and admire. One boy stood, and the rest of the team hooked on to him, bending over and forming a long line of backs. The first boy on the other team leap-frogged the end man as high as possible, landing as far forward as possible, trying to break the line. If a leaper broke the team's "back" his team won. Leapers kept coming until all were sitting on the opposing team's back. Then they held on to each other and rocked around in an attempt to collapse the other team. If the down team could hold up, it won; if it collapsed, it lost.

One and Over
by James Winfrey

One and Over was a strenuous, athletic game that grew out of traditional Leap Frog. While all boys from about ten years and up played it, One and Over became a spectator sport when practiced by the best high school athletes on the school ground.

The game would start by each competitor doing a flat-footed broad jump from a line drawn on the ground. The winner became the "setter," and the one with the shortest jump had to "go down." The down-boy planted his feet about one foot apart near the line and bent over so he could hold his ankles, being careful to keep his head down and his back level. The setter took a running start, landed on both feet, then springing forward, leap-frogged over the down-boy, landing on both feet. Where his heels landed, he marked for the down-boy to move forward. It was important for the jumper to cup his hands and touch the down-boy on the rib cage as he went over so as not to knock him over.

After the down-boy moved forward, the setter would say whether it was an "over" or "one and over." If declared an over, each contestant would have to make the jump with a running start and a flat-footed leap from the original line and land on both feet. If he landed on one foot or took off past the line (crow-hopped), he was out of the game. If he knocked the down-boy over (rooted him), he had to go down. As I recall, these young athletes could make an "over" of eight or ten feet.

When all contestants had had their try, the setter would set a new mark, which he would usually call a "one and over." This meant that the contestants would take a running one-step jump from the line, land on both feet, then leap over the down-boy. After all had tried the "one and over," the setter would set a new mark and declare whether it was a "one and over" or "two and over." If one of the contestants thought that a declared "one and over" could not be made, he could challenge the setter. If the setter failed, he had to go down. If he made it, the challenger went down. Also, if the setter declared a "two and over" and a challenger made it in one and over, the setter went down and the challenger became the setter.

For Wolf Over the River two captains choose sides, which line up on each side of a line, the "river," forty or fifty feet apart. A person chosen as It, or the "wolf," is in the middle between the lines. When he is ready, he yells, "Wolf over the river! Don't hold hands! Wolf over the river! Catch all you can!" Each team then runs across the field to get to the other team's line and safety. The wolf tries to catch one of the runners as he crosses the field and to hold him long enough to pat him three times on the back. Those he catches stay and help him catch others. The last one caught gets to be the wolf in the next game. (Charlie Oden, Roy Albrecht to Kenneth Davis)

Wolf Over the River

Two children choose sides to divide the group in half. The groups then walk a distance away from each other so that their discussions cannot be heard. Group number one agrees on something to pantomime—picking cotton, climbing a ladder, changing a baby—that will be hard for group number two to guess. Group number one then approaches group number two saying:

Little White House on the Hill
by
Loweda Hogue

Group one: Here we come.
Group two: Where are you from?
Group one: The little white house on the hill.
Group two: What's your trade?
Group one: Lemonade.
Group two: Let's see some if you're not afraid.

The members of group one then start their pantomine, and group two tries to guess exactly what they are doing. If someone in group two can guess, then group one makes a dash back to their base or starting point. If anyone in group two can tag someone in group one, then the tagged person has to go to group two. The groups alternate until there is no one left in one of the groups.

Two leaders, each with a group of children around him, face each other, standing twenty to thirty yards apart. Between the two groups stand two catchers, a bear and a panther, one on each side of the field.

Molly Bride
by
Ida Hall

First Leader: How far to Molly, Molly Bride?
Second Leader: Three score miles and ten.

First Leader: Can I get there by candle light?
Second Leader: Yes, if you run with all your might, for there's a bear on one side and a panther on the other!

Then each leader with his group runs to the opposite side while the bear and the panther try to catch them. Whoever is caught has to become one of the animals that caught him at the next running and try to catch the others. The game ends when all are caught.

Charge!
by
Tony Clark

The game was called Charge!, and at Jacksboro Elementary School in the late 1940s it served as a masculine rite of passage.

The origins of the game already were lost in time when I reached fifth grade and became a participant. Some of my classmates had older brothers who had played it; beyond that, its history was unknown. Charge! made an almost ideal playground game because it required no equipment and had very few rules. Also, any number could play. And best of all, it was forbidden.

As first and second graders, we had passed our recesses placidly on the south side of the old red brick building, blissfully ignorant of a larger world. Then for the next two years we had played on the north side. But with entry into fifth grade, we moved to the seemingly boundless reaches of the west side, which stretched a full city block. It was there that Charge! entered our lives and provided an initiation from childhood.

Early in the fall term, the first game began almost before we knew it. Boundaries had been determined by line of sight, matching up such landmarks as the end post of the softball backstop with a scraggly mesquite bush to create a rectangular "field" perhaps fifty yards long and thirty-five feet wide. The area was all hardpan, having been trampled grassless by generations of pupils. At each end, several boys had made a "goal line" by dragging their heels to make a shallow, dusty rut from sideline to sideline.

We moved with the herd to the east end and stretched out along the wavering line, fifty or sixty boys toeing the mark. A hulking eighth grader stood forlorn in the middle of the field. In an act of bravado, he had volunteered to be It, the lone defender. With hands on knees, he crouched and faced us. Then someone yelled "Charge!" and as other voices echoed the cry, the whole column dashed frantically for the opposite goal.

The defender picked a target from the streaking bodies, got an angle, and tackled the boy cleanly. The rest raced on across the western line, then quickly reassembled facing east. Now two defenders waited, the original It and the boy he had captured. Once more the shrill call of "Charge!" reverberated, and another passage commenced.

So the game progressed. Captured chargers became defenders, so that the ranks of runners gradually diminished as the troops defending swelled. The rule on tackling was the same as in football: a boy was captured when brought to the ground by a defender.

A game ended when the last charger was taken. It was quite an honor to be among the last surviving runners, and from the process we gained a notion of who would be in the backfield in our approaching football years. The very last boy to fall became a temporary hero, and he also earned the right to be It for the next game, which would begin almost immediately.

Charge! would then continue, game after game, through both recesses as well as the "rest" period after lunch. Play was suspended when the school bell rang, to be resumed at the next break from classes. Sometimes boys who had been captured would try to rejoin the chargers in a new session, but peer pressure usually prevented such infractions.

Several strategies were developed, especially by the younger boys. Early in a game, when defenders were few, it was safer to favor the outside lanes, since action tended to concentrate in the middle. Also, although technically everyone was supposed to start running at the same time, it was possible to break a little late, allowing most defenders to engage before one reached the danger zone. However, such tactics were frowned on, and defenders soon would begin to single out chronic violators.

The game fostered defensive techniques as well. For instance, it was natural that smaller boys would be captured early, and they were not very adept at one-on-one tackling. Soon, though, they learned the efficacy of cooperation and began to hunt in packs.

While Charge! instructed the younger players in cunning and survival, it afforded the older boys an arena in which to assert their dawning masculine instincts. They always charged up the middle, relying more on power than fancy footwork to foil defenders. Some would even surrender to early capture simply to have more opportunities to tackle the best runners. The most spectacular collisions occurred when the big guys went head to head. On the other hand, the best players usually exercised restraint in bringing down the small fry. Such rules were not written down or even uttered—they simply evolved.

The season for Charge! was always short-lived, however. It always ended abruptly with an incident serious enough for teachers to notice. Broken bones were rare, but scraped elbows and bloodied noses were common and all too easy to detect. Sometimes too a parent would complain after a boy came home with a shredded shirt or with rips in his new school jeans.

Whatever brought in the authorities, we would know the end had come when we heard the principal's voice rasp over the intercom, informing us that Charge! was an unacceptable activity. Some teachers would feel obligated to add that the game was brutal and ungentlemanly. They had no understanding that these aspects were essential parts of the game's attraction. At any rate, our playground activity was more closely monitored, and the ban on Charge! stuck—for the time being.

The boys in upper grades would occupy themselves shooting basketballs at the outdoor goals, and the younger ones would take up tops and marbles. We might try to bring back Charge!, with simple tag replacing tackling, but it was not the same, and teachers would stop it anyway, being wise enough to know that the harmless version soon would escalate into the real thing.

Typically, we would start playing Charge! soon after the opening of the fall term and would continue until the ax fell. Then, in the spring when the weather warmed and we were bursting with energy, security often grew lax enough for us to revive the game briefly before detection.

Although its days always were numbered, Charge! provided many of us with early lessons in manhood.

Witch, Oh Witch, What Time Is It?
by
Pam Palmer

The person who is It stands about twenty feet from the players, between them and the base, usually a tree or anything handy. The players think of numbers between one and twelve, then call, "Witch, Oh Witch, what time is it?" The witch gives a time, for example, "Six o'clock." Any player who has that number tries to run to base without getting tagged and captured by the witch. Those captured by the witch have to help her catch the other children. The game is over when all have been captured. The last one captured, usually the most vigorous of the players, is the witch for the next game.

Drop the Handkerchief

Some chasing and capturing games did not require literal capturing. A slap on the back, or three pats on top of the head, or snatching a handkerchief out of a pocket served the same purpose. The person tagged was captured, or put out of the game, or caused to be It. Drop the Handkerchief is a tag game that used to be played by young children at B.Y.P.U. (Baptist Young People's Union) parties. The children stand in a circle holding hands. Whoever is chosen as It walks slowly around the circle until he comes to his victim. He then drops a handkerchief behind this person, who picks up the handkerchief and tries to tag the dropper before the dropper can run around the circle and reach the vacancy left by the victim. If the victim fails to catch the dropper, he then becomes It. In some versions, the loser is considered captured and is jailed in the middle of the ring. A variant of this game is called Flying Dutchman, and the rules are the same, but a boy-girl couple becomes It and they drop the handkerchief behind another couple. (Tammy Thompson of Texas Tech, Davie Gibson Tunnell, Lenoir Moore to Kenneth Davis, Jimmie Tuggle to Kenneth Davis)

Red Light, Green Light and Freeze Tag

In Red Light, Green Light a group of players choose an It, who stands far away from the group. The players call out a number between one and ten, which It must count. It shouts, "Green Light!" and begins counting to the designated number while the players are charging down on him. When he reaches the number he shouts, "Red Light!," and all the players must immediately freeze where they are. If It sees anyone moving so much as a muscle after he shouts "Red Light!" that person is out of the

Red Light, Green Light (Richard S. Orton).

game. If a person is able to tag It before he finishes counting, that person gets to be It, and the game is repeated. (John Cobb to Kenneth Davis)

Freeze Tag is a similar game. One person is It, or tagger, and the rest run around within an agreed-upon territory to escape being tagged. Usually there is a home base, but base hugging is not allowed. When It tags a runner, that person must freeze. A frozen player can be thawed if one of his teammates touches him. The last person frozen has to be It for the next game. (Ann Sikes to Kenneth Davis)

Tag Games Slightly Different

Robert Sikes recalled a tag game that he had played as a senior in high school in the 1920s. He called it Cowboys and Indians, and both boys and girls participated. Each player had a sock partially filled with flour. The purpose of the game, much like a melee, was to chase and hit somebody with the sock and leave the "killing" white spot on him. The person hit was dead and out of the game. The winner was the last one alive, naturally. (Robert Sikes to Kenneth Davis)

Of a different generation is TV Tag, which is another general tag game with one person being It and everybody else being fair game. The only way to avoid being tagged is to fall on your knees and shout out a TV show, such as "Leave It to Beaver" or "Gilligan's Island." The hard part to this game is to think of a show that has not been used by yourself or by any of the other players. A repeater automatically becomes It. TV Tag can be made more difficult by designating a specific type of program to be used—game shows, cartoons—or by requiring character names from TV shows. (Shari Wolfe of Paris Junior College)

A game for children who live in the country and have horses is Rags, remembered by John Halsell of Shallowater. The person who is It and on a horse chases the other players, also on horses, and tries to grab rags stuck in their back pockets. The one who loses his rag becomes It and must try to get a rag from another player's pocket. (John Halsell to Kenneth Davis)

Lezlie Ann Cowley sent in this account of a Paris High School tag game, which is certainly worth considering. This sounds like a spinoff of Li'l Abner's Sadie Hawkins Day Chase of a generation ago: "Texas Chase is basically a simple game originated by someone sometime long ago in Texas, of course. There are two teams—the girls and the boys. All the girls are Its, and all the boys are Itees. The girls chase the boys, who in turn run desperately away from them. If a girl happens to grab one of these critters, she must kiss him. The rules fail to give details of where exactly they are to kiss the boys. There is hope for the boy, however; a base waits in the distance for him to cling to. The base can be a pole, tree, slide, or whatever sturdy object is available. There is no limit to the length of time the boys may stay on base. Yet, for some reason, they normally stay there only long enough to catch their breaths."

Marco Polo
by
Lawrence Clayton

A game played at the Wychwood Swimming Pool, a neighborhood enterprise in Abilene, is an old one called Marco Polo. Any number of persons can play. One person, designated It, goes underwater and counts to a number previously agreed on, usually not more than ten. The other players move to new locations to confuse the person who is submerged and who must keep his eyes closed while being It. That player then surfaces and calls out, "Marco." The other players must answer "Polo," thereby revealing their positions by their voices. Then the person designated It, keeping his eyes closed, moves in the direction of the sound of one of the other players and tries to tag the other person. Other players are free to move but must answer "Polo" every time the person who is It calls "Marco." When one of the free players is touched, he or she becomes It, and the game begins again.

Prison Base, or Sheepie in My Pen

Children playing this game divide into two teams standing behind lines twenty or thirty feet apart. Behind each line and team is a drawn circle, which serves as a prison or a sheep pen depending on what the game is called when it is played. Members of the opposing teams line up facing each other and take turns sending a teammate across the field that separates the two groups. The runner tries to cross the other team's line without being tagged. If he is tagged, he is put in the prison, or sheep pen. He can be freed only by a teammate who is able to cross the line without being touched. The game is over when all of one team has been imprisoned, or penned as sheep. (Mrs. Georgia Nelson to Kenneth Davis)

The smaller children, both boys and girls, choose sides for an exciting old German game their grandmothers used to play— Voegel zu verkaufen! (Birds for Sale!).

Voegel zu verkaufen! (Birds for Sale!)
by
Julia Estill

The two most aggressive youngsters in the group become the self-appointed leaders, each of a side. Choosing then begins, the fleetest runners being prime favorites and first selected.

All on the seller's side are given names of birds, who flutter inside a ring drawn on the ground to represent the cage. Close at hand is a similar ring in which the buyers move about restlessly. When the chief buyer approaches the seller's domain, the birds are all aflutter, especially if the visitor is a dapper lad who will pay a lot of coin for a bird of fine plumage. With greetings over, bargaining begins.

"What kinds of birds have you?" queries the customer.

"Sparrows, hawks, red birds, blue birds, yellow birds—any kind you want," replies the salesman proudly.

"I should like a blue bird," promptly answers the customer. And he looks longingly at a flaxen-haired little girl in a blue-checked pinafore with blue bows on her pigtails.

The shrewd salesman, seeing the trend of affairs and sensing a rival for the fair birdie's favor, screws up the price. But even though twenty-five "bucks" is steep, the customer accepts the "challenge" and promptly and resoundingly slaps the out-stretched palm of the salesman twenty-five times, watching, out of the corner of his eye, the dainty bit of fluff about to take wing at the farther end of the aviary. The last dollar paid with a deal of vehemence, the chase is on, the bird stretching her wings and limbs in flight before the sale is quite complete, for she doesn't want to be caught. (Or does she?)

The bargain hunter is soon in hot pursuit, the chase usually ending in capture. And a breathless, bedraggled bluebird comes trailing along, led by a jubilant captor.

If the bird that has been bought is a Texas roadrunner, however, he usually outdistances his pursuer and returns to the cage from whence he came, vociferously welcomed by his fellow fowls who feel that he bears a charmed life, as all Texas roadrunners do.

◆ Rosalinda Gonzalez describes the game Maria Blanca, as it was played on the ranch on the Mexican border where she grew up in the Forties.

The children form a circle holding hands. In the center is a girl, Dona Blanca; outside is a boy, who is Jicotillo, the hornet. All sing:

Maria Blanca
by
Rosalinda Gonzalez

Dona Blanca esta cubierta	The White Lady is covered
Con pilares de oro y plata.	With pillars of gold and silver.
Romperemos un pilar	Let us break down a pillar
Para Ver a Dona Blanca.	To see the White Lady.

Then the circle moves to the right and Dona Blanca sings:

Quien es ese Jicotillo   Who is that Jicotillo
Que anda rondando mi casa?   Hovering around my house?

The boy outside, Jicotillo, answers:

Yo soy, yo soy ese   I am that one, I am that one
Que anda en pos de Dona Blanca. Who is after Dona Blanca.

The pillars are broken with the children letting go of each
other's hands. Jicotillo runs after Dona Blanca. When he catches
her she forfeits her role, and the game continues with another
girl playing Maria Blanca.

**Chickimee
Craney
Crow**
by
Ida B. Hall

Any number of children entered this game. They formed a line
facing the "Old Witch," who sat on the ground. Each child
caught hold of another by the shoulder and, following the
leader, marched around the old witch, chanting a kind of song,
or lilt, as follows:

Chickimee, chickimee, craney crow,
I went to the well to wash my toe.
When I got back, one of my blackeyed chickens was gone.

The line stopped marching, and the following dialogue took
place:

Leader: What time, old witch?
Witch: One o'clock.

They proceeded as before, singing the same song. At the end of
it the leader again asked, "What time?" "Two o'clock," the witch
answered, and the incremental repetition went on until "Five
o'clock." The children then stopped marching, and the witch
pretended to be hunting for something.

Leader: What are you hunting for?
Witch: Darning needle.
Leader: What's the darning needle for?
Witch: To mend my apron.
Leader: What's the apron for?
Witch: To carry in chips.
Leader: What's the chips for?
Witch: To make a fire.
Leader: What's the fire for?
Witch: To roast a chicken.

Each child began sticking out his feet and hands, asking, "Is
this it? Is that it?" The witch kept saying, "No." Finally each
child put his hand to his chest, saying, "Shan't have me!" All the

children then grabbed one another tightly by the shoulders, still standing behind the leader, who tried to fight off the witch. The witch tried to reach around the leader and touch a child. A child so touched was "caught" and had to get out of line to one side, now belonging to the witch. The game continued in this manner until all were caught. If desired, they could begin anew with another leader.

◆   Three Deep, as described by Charlie Oden, is like Musical Chairs and life: there is never enough territory to accommodate all the people. I think Malthus and Ricardo played this game at one time or another.

Three Deep
by
Charlie Oden

About two dozen kids are needed for Three Deep. The players are divided into pairs, and the pairs are then placed in a circle, one member of each pair standing behind the other and each pair standing far enough from the flanking pairs that a player can dash between the pairs and into the circle. When this is done, the circle consists of pairs of kids standing two deep. There must be an additional pair who become It and Catcher and who take up positions on opposite sides of the circle from one another. The game is begun on signal with the Catcher pursuing It around the circle, running counterclockwise. It will suddenly dash into the circle between pairs and stand in front of the pair to his immediate right, thus making that two-deep group into a three-deep group. Since this can't be, the rear member of the two-deep pair becomes It and must run about the circle, outrunning the Catcher or suddenly dashing into the circle between pairs and taking up position as described before. And so goes the game. Should the Catcher catch It, they reverse roles and race around the circle in the opposite direction until the new It is caught or dashes into the inner circle and stands before a player as described above.

London Bridge and Kin

London Bridge as a capture and tug-of-war game is widely popular in many cultures. It is a singing game where children go through an arch, are captured and forced to choose sides, and end the game in a tug-of-war. In London Bridge, two children form the arch bridge, and the others form a line in a circle and walk under the bridge, singing:

> London Bridge is falling down, falling down, falling down;
> London Bridge is falling down, my fair lady.

On "my fair lady" the bridge drops, encircling a player, who is asked whether she wants a gold ring or a silver bracelet. She chooses one and lines up behind the arch-person who has that piece of jewelry as her sign. When all are captured, the two sides have a tug of war to determine the winner.

Davie Gibson Tunnel played Needle's Eye to the same London Bridge rules but with a different song:

London Bridge
(Richard S. Orton).

The needle's eye
That doth supply
The thread that runs so true,
And many a beau
Have I let go
Because I wanted you.

Zieh Durch
by
Julia Estill

Perhaps the most popular of all the games for young children in Fredericksburg was Zieh Durch, a German version of London Bridge. It involves the repair of a broken bridge that is rebuilt and rebroken many times before the game ends.

Marching in single file, the players, each with his arms locked about the waist of the child preceding him, chain-fashion, pass under an archway formed by two youngsters who stand opposite each other with uplifted arms and clasped hands, both having previously selected a piece of jewelry to represent. All the players chant these lines:

Zeih durch, zeih durch,	March along, march along,
Durch die gold'ne Bruecke.	Under the bridge of gold.
Sie ist entzwei; sie ist entzwei,	She's cut in two; she's cut in two,
Wir wollen sie wieder pfluecken.	We'll patch her up to hold.
Mit was? Mit Glass.	With what? With glass.
Mit einerlei, mit zweierlei.	Just one or two old things will do.
Der letzte soll gefangen sein.	We'll catch and keep the last one through.

The child who happens to be underneath the archway when the chant ceases is caught when the "portcullis" falls, and is questioned as to which article of jewelry he prefers—a gold watch or a gold bracelet, for example. Then, his selection made, he scurries to the side he has chosen and clasps the child before him about the waist.

Thus the game continues until the bridge is repaired. Then the tug-of-war begins; and eventually the "archway" is pulled apart only to be rebuilt in the space of a few minutes.

La Puerta Esta Quebrada
by Rosalinda Gonzalez

Another game that was played at the ranch is La Puerta Esta Quebrada (The Door is Broken). This game is played like the English game London Bridge is Falling Down. Two persons, each representing some object (sometimes an orange and a grapefruit), would make an arch with their hands. As the persons in the game went under the arch, they would sing:

La puerta esta quebrada	The door is broken
Ya la van a componer.	It is going to be fixed.
El que pasa ha de pasar,	He who wants to pass should pass,
Y el que no ha de quedar.	And he who does not want to pass shall stay behind.

The following verse that the Mexican children sing to this game was used as part of the above by the ranch children:

A la vibora, vibora	To the serpent, the serpent
De la mar, de la mar,	Of the sea, of the sea,
Por aqui pueden pasar.	Here it can pass by.
La de adelante corre mucho	The one in front runs fast
La de atras se quedara	The one in back will remain
Tras, tras, tras, tras.	Behind, behind, behind, behind.

At the end of the words of the verse, the orange and the grapefruit would lower their arms to catch whoever was passing through at that time. The person caught would then be taken aside and asked in whispers (so that the others would not hear what objects they represented) whether he wanted the orange or the grapefruit. If he chose the orange he would stay behind the person playing the orange, while other rounds through the arch were made to catch more of the players. By the time everyone was caught, each leader would have enough on his side to have a tug-of-war to see who would win the game. Of course, out of preference, one of the leaders would generally have more on his side.

Hide-and-Seek Games

Hide-and-Seek is a classic game, which has provided thrills and excitement for generations of children all over the world for centuries. It is a simple game. Someone is counted out and becomes It. It goes to an agreed-upon home base, hides his eyes, and counts to a hundred while the other players are finding places to hide. At the count of a hundred, It calls, "A bushel of wheat, a bushel of rye, all not ready, answer 'I'" or "A bushel of wheat, a bushel of clover, all not ready can't hide over" or "Here I come with both eyes open." It begins his search. When he sights a hider, he dashes back to touch home base and calls, "One-two-three for Jack." Jack is now caught and out of the game. If, however, It strays too far from home, hiders can make a dash for home and if they beat him can shout, "One-two-three and I'm home free!" The best ploy is to find a hiding place that is so good that It has to give up and shout, "Alley, alley otfree; all that's out can come in free." The It for the next game is chosen in various ways. Sometimes he is the first one in free, or the last, or the first one caught, or the last. Ground rules are either traditional for the neighborhood or made up on the spot.

A simple game of Hide-and-Seek can be enhanced by playing it in the dark, which is what the older kids do at parties. And they also hide in couples, would you believe it, which is how I got started with the girl I've been married to for forty years. Floyd Martin tells about playing Hide-and-Seek on donkeys in thick brush and woods and bailing out of trees on top of each other. They did that where he went to school in Taylor County in 1914; unfortunately we are too civilized for that sort of game nowadays—and donkeys are in short supply. Bill Stokes played a game of Hide-and-Seek they called Gray Wolf in Vernon in the Twenties. The fact that a Gray Wolf was stalking the hiders in the dark added a fearful dimension to the game.

Teddy Diggs contributed Kick the Can, a variation of Hide-and-Seek and Sheep Board Down that was her favorite game as a second-grader in Waco. A large, loud can is placed at home base. During the game, if any one of the players can sneak or streak back to base and kick the can, he frees all of those who have already been caught. The purpose is to kick the can as far as possible so that the escapers will have time to hide again, because

Hide-and-Seek
(Richard S. Orton).

It has to retrieve the can and return it to home base before he can begin his seeking. Kick the Can can go on for a long time and cover an entire neighborhood.

Sheep Board Down
by
Gayla McLain Sanders

Sheep Board Down was a type of Hide-and-Seek. The first shepherd was chosen by drawing straws. A short board was leaned against the house near home base. While the shepherd counted to one hundred all the sheep hid themselves. At the end of the count the shepherd went to look for the sheep. The first one he found had to be the next shepherd, but the shepherd had to first find all the sheep. At any time in the game a sheep could run in and kick the sheep board down, and all the sheep would then be allowed in free, causing the shepherd to have to serve as shepherd again for the next game. I remember playing this game with other children at the home of Jimmy Hamilton, who lived on top of Flowery Mountain.

XI

Sticks and Stones

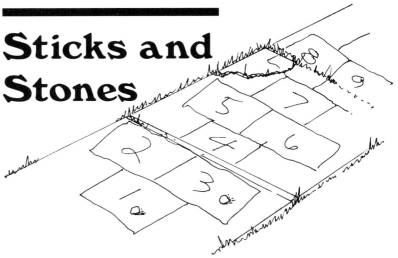

This chapter is about games that are played with "things," with sticks and stones, and bats and balls. Games using marbles, tops, and knives should rightfully be in this chapter, but these categories were so large that those toys and their games required two extra chapters.

First in this chapter are stealing games. Stealing something within the accepted confines of a social game was as much fun to children as stealing horses was to Indians. Greg Wilson describes the ever popular Capture the Flag, a favorite game of large neighborhoods and Boy Scouts for at least three generations.

Capture the Flag
by
Greg Wilson of Paris High School

For weekend warriors the ultimate game is Capture the Flag. It is played best when you have an entire day to play and ten to twenty players. Each player is equipped with six flour bombs before the game begins. Flour bombs are made by tying a handful of flour in a rag.

The players are divided into two teams. Each team has a flag of some sort (a handkerchief tied on a stick will do) which it posts in front of its base or hideout or headquarters. The entire neighborhood may be used as the battleground, or some wooded area, but specific boundaries are decided on before the game begins. After the teams decide on their home bases and plant their flags and post their guards, all players come back together to begin the game.

At a given signal each team sets out in search of the other team's flag. If they encounter "enemies" and can hit them and mark them with their flour grenades, the victims are "dead" and must stay in the same place until a teammate restores them to life and the game by touching them. When they do finally locate their opponent's flag, they have the problem of capturing it without getting hit by the guards. Then they have to get back to their own home base with the flag before they can pronounce themselves the winners. Capture the Flag is accompanied by much shouting and maneuvering and running about and is much fun.

Beware of enemies lurking in trees and behind bushes, and never stop until you get that flag!

◆ J. Russell Kieffer sent in the instructions for Steal the Bacon, which operates on the same principle as Capture the Flag but is not played on as grand a scale.

Each team stands on a line facing its opponent, with about twenty feet between them. Each team member is assigned a number and is instructed to stand diagonally opposite the member of the other team who has the same number. A bandana or handkerchief is placed in the center of the field between the two lines and serves as the "bacon." The leader calls out a number, and the two players with that number run to the center to "steal the bacon." The one who steals the bacon has to return with it to his spot in the line before his opponent tags him. If he makes it, his team receives two points. If he is tagged, the other team receives two points. The first team to reach a set number wins.

Steal the Bacon
by
J. Russell Kieffer of Texas Tech

◆ Stealing Sticks and Stealing Rocks are two games that operate from the same principle and with similar rules, the only difference being in what is stolen. The joy of stealing from an opponent's treasure of sticks or rocks and getting away with it is obvious, as Ida Hall describes Stealing Rocks.

Children are divided into two equal groups and take their places on opposite sides of a line drawn across a playing field. Piles of small rocks, equal in number, are placed equidistant several yards from the center line. These rock piles are bases. It was the purpose of every child on each side to break across the line and touch a rock on the opposite side without being tagged by the enemy. If he can reach the enemy's side without being caught, he can safely bring back a rock to his own side. Enemies cannot tag him as long as he carries a rock in his hand. But if he is tagged before reaching the enemy's pile, he has to stand on the enemy's base until one from his own side can tag him out. The game ends when one side has all the rocks.

Stealing Rocks (and Sticks)
by
Ida Hall

◆ Jacks or Jackstones or Knucklebones is an ancient game going back to Greek and Roman times at least. Earliest forms of the game used sheep knucklebones to toss and catch. Later generations in the Old World and the New used stones instead of bones but played the game in essentially the same way. Dorothy

Howard played typical games of Jackstones, consisting of exercises in agility and manual dexterity, called Onesies, Twosies, Threesies and higher to Over the Stile, Cows Through the Gate, Horses in the Stable, Pigs in the Pen, and Kittens in the Well. Each movement required both hands, with the right hand juggling a stone and the left hand putting the Pigs in the Pen, or whatever was required.

Stump Jack
by
Jewel Irwin Shankles

As a small girl growing up in Deep East Texas, "Warsh Day" was my favorite because Margie came to help Mother and brought her little girl, Essie, who was just my age. So besides the activity, smells, clean clothes blowing on the line, sweet-smelling sheets to sleep on, and fresh stiffly starched dresses, I had a playmate for the day.

I don't remember being aware of color. We were just two little girls playing. And years later, when Essie came back from California and came to see me, we threatened to play our favorite game of Stump Jack on the end of the front porch. Maybe it was originally played on the top of a stump in cleared new-ground, but we always played on the end of the front porch.

First, find five small rocks shaped just right—no sharp edges and not too flat. Take turns. The first player goes until she misses. Hold the jacks (rocks) in one hand. Toss them into the air, quickly turning the hand over and catching the rocks on the back of the same hand. Toss them again; turn the hand and catch them in the palm. Then toss the rocks on the floor. Pick up one to use as the taw. Toss that one into the air and pick up the others one at a time, catching the tossed pebble with the same hand used to pick up the rocks for each series. Then do twos, threes, and fours. Conclude by repeating the first pattern. The object is to be the first to complete the sequence of pickups. When you miss, the next person has a turn. Stump Jack is a lot more fun than jacks played with a ball. And much quicker, too!

◆ Andy Wilson writes about his mother playing Jacks of the usual kind. This game is played with jacks that one purchases at a store along with a rubber ball. Up until recently the jacks were made of metal, were fairly sturdy, and could cause great pain and bloodshed when stepped on. Jacks that I purchased recently were smaller and lighter, and I was informed that some were made of plastic! I would hope not.

Jacks at Recess
by
Andy Wilson of Texas Tech

When my mother was in grade school in the late Forties and early Fifties, a favorite game she and the other girls would play was Jacks. Every recess they would rush outside, find a nice flat smooth piece of concrete sidewalk, and begin their game. The girls would pair off and sit on the sidewalk facing each other. Not everyone would play: some would only stand around as spectators, cheering the more talented players along. And talent it did take, as some of the maneuvers of throwing the ball and collecting the jacks were very intricate.

The pieces for the game would be removed from their little drawstring bag and placed on the sidewalk. The jacks were X-shaped pieces of metal with a perpendicular bar in the center of each. They were lightweight, about the diameter of a penny, and usually grayish in color. Seven jacks were the standard number used in playing. The key to a successful game was a ball that had a good bounce. The ball, about the diameter of a nickel, was made of medium-soft rubber and was usually red in color.

Since each game was a continuance from the previous recess, each girl had to know whose turn it was and at what stage of play they had left off. No time was lost in throwing the little jacks onto the sidewalk in a pattern that would be beneficial to the player as she proceeded with the game. The girls followed a set pattern of play. The first level was regular Jacks, the second level was called Pigs in the Pen, the third level was Eggs in the Basket, and the fourth level, the most difficult, was Around the World.

The first level was played by throwing the ball into the air, picking up one jack, and catching the ball, after its first bounce, in the same hand that held the jack. Each jack was picked up in this manner until all had been removed and placed in front of the player. Then the player threw out the jacks again and proceeded to pick up two jacks at a time until all had been removed. This continued, picking up three jacks at a time, then four, and so on until the player would have to pick up all seven jacks at one time and catch the ball after its first bounce. A player continued to play in the above sequence until she missed the ball, dropped a jack, or didn't pick up the correct number of jacks. Then her opponent was given an opportunity to play, and she continued until she made an error. Each player continued at the point where she was when the previous error was made. For example, if she had missed while attempting to pick up three

Jacks—up to
threesies
(Richard S. Orton).

jacks at one time, then when her turn came again she would begin on the "threes."

As mentioned previously, the jacks were thrown out in a pattern to benefit the player. If the player was attempting to pick up one jack at a time, then the jacks would be thrown out in a wide pattern. If the player was attempting to pick up several jacks at once, then the pattern of throw was grouped closer together.

After completing the first level of play, the player moved on to the second level, Pigs in the Pen. The jacks were thrown, and the player cupped her left hand and placed it palm-side down on the sidewalk. The ball was thrown, and one jack was pushed into the left-hand "pen," and the ball was caught after its first bounce. This continued until all the jacks had been placed in the pen. The jacks were thrown again, and then two jacks were pushed into the pen at one time, then three, and so forth until all seven jacks were pushed into the pen at one time.

The third level of jacks, Eggs in the Basket, was played as follows: the jacks were thrown, and the player cupped her left hand against her body to make the "basket." The ball was thrown, and one jack was picked up and placed in the basket, and the ball was caught after the first bounce. The player continued until all the jacks had been placed in the basket. Then the jacks were thrown again, and two jacks at a time were placed in the basket until they were all removed. The sequence continued until all seven jacks were placed in the basket at one time.

The fourth level of jacks, Around the World, then began. The jacks were thrown, the ball was thrown into the air, one jack was picked up in the right hand, the ball was circled with the right hand holding the jack during the ball's first bounce, and then the ball was caught. This continued until all the jacks had been picked up. Each jack, after making its trip "around the world," was placed in front of the player. As previously explained, the sequence was followed until all seven jacks had been picked up at one time, and had made their circle around the ball and the ball had been caught.

Some of the better players could progress through the third level of jacks before making an error and having to give their opponent a chance. The first player to complete all the levels of play was the winner. As the play was often interrupted by the recess bell, a complete game might take two or three days. Usually the winners of the various games then paired off and began another round of Jacks. If the weather was bad, they moved their Jacks tournament inside.

Jacks were entertaining and fun and also developed good hand and eye coordination, plus good dexterity of the hands. The little girls might not be able to remember their math facts, but they were a whiz when it came to remembering what level of jacks they were previously at the day before. (Jacks games also sent in by Janet Jeffrey, Dorris Yates Tull, Sandra Luna, Deborah Fields of Paris High School)

There is only one way to give some idea of a Hopscotch layout as we played the game in the 1920s in Gatesville and as Lillian Neale played it in Moody. It was played the same way in Alpine in the late 1960s by Rosella Celaya (now Salmon) and is played so now by her small sister in the mid-Eighties. See the drawing of the layout. The square spaces measure probably about twenty inches on each side. We drew this plan with a stick in the dirt, or on a sidewalk with a chalk stub from school or a white chalk rock found on the ground. We never numbered the squares, nor did we have names for the layout itself or for the turning zone.

Two or more can play Hopscotch. The object of the game is to be the first to complete six rounds of hopping on one foot from one square to another, along with properly casting and picking up a rock. Preferably the rock is flat, so that it may be slid without rolling.

This is how you hop the course: First, slide or toss the rock onto square one. Next, hop over square one to square two (beyond the rock), hop on each remaining square in sequence, hop into the turning zone, and turn around. Now hop the same course in reverse, to square two. Still on one foot, bend over and pick up the rock. Hop onto square one and out. Now both feet may touch the ground. Repeat the same procedure, but slide the rock onto square two, then onto square three on the next round, and so on, but do not slide the rock into the turning zone. When the rock is on square six, pick it up from the turning zone.

The rules are as follows: If a player makes a mistake, he must remove his rock, await his turn, and start over. A player must start over if he slides his rock into the wrong square, onto a line, into the turning zone, or out of the course; if he puts down both feet or a hand, or if he falls; if he hops onto the same square with his rock; if he hops onto a line, into a wrong square, or out of the course; or if he fails to pick up his rock. The winner is the player who first hops the entire course six times in succession without making a mistake.

◆ Pitching games that require that an object be tossed at a target require much skill and practice.

Victor Smith described the basic form. One played the game called Washers with either plain or colored metal washers or with silver dollars. It is a double-cousin to horseshoes, pitching marbles or pennies, and various other games involving small objects pitched toward lines or holes. The players dig three holes lined up, each at a farther distance from the first hole. The players stand at least fifteen feet from the first hole and throw their washers at each hole in turn. A washer that lands one washer's width from the hole earns one point; a washer that leans against the side of the hole earns two points; a washer that lands flat in the hole earns three points. The winner is the one who first earns twenty-one points, or whatever number is agreed on to "make a game."

Hopscotch
by
Elton Miles

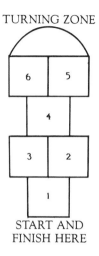

Playground Hopscotch (Richard S. Orton).

Washers
by
Kenneth Davis

Dan Moore of Ennis described a simpler form of the game. The players dig only one hole. Each player has the same number of washers. The one who gets the most washers in the hole wins the game. Each player pitches all his washers before the next player has his turn. In some parts of Texas, silver dollars are still used as washers, but few present-day informants have seen these expensive washers used in recent years.

Tim Short of Shallowater reported the popularity of pitching washers not only on school grounds but also on large ranches in West Texas. The version of the game he cited requires two four-inch holes dug about ten yards apart. Two players pitch their washers alternately at the holes. A washer that lands in the hole scores three points; a washer that hangs over a hole without quite falling in scores two points. The player who earns the most points with his five washers wins. Other versions of the game require the use of milk cans and colored washers, but the objectives are about the same as for those versions played on schoolyards with simple washers and dirt holes. Some school children will gamble on this or on any other game of skill. (Description also sent in by Gayla McLain Sanders)

◆ The first game of Horseshoes I ever saw was played with real horseshoes. I was amazed and surprised by the large size of store-bought game horseshoes, when I finally ran across a set.

Horseshoes
by
Kenneth Davis

Schoolchildren in elementary grades through high school take delight in games involving the manipulation of objects. Horseshoes, a still popular game in parks and backyards, was popular in a number of Texas schools until after World War II. In some remote areas, particularly in the ranching country, the game is still played at recess times and during the noon hour. Mrs. Nan O'Connor recalled playing the game when she was a child in Gilmer. Few variants of the game exist. The rules for pitching horseshoes are simple. Two players must have two horseshoes each and a pair of wooden sticks, generally referred to as stobs. The stobs are driven into the ground about twenty-five feet apart [Editor's note: forty feet is regulation]. Each player has a turn at tossing his horseshoes, one at a time, at the stob opposite him. His opponent then throws his horseshoes. When both players have had a turn, they pick up their horseshoes and in turn throw them toward the other stob. A shoe that lands one shoe's length from a stob earned one point; a shoe leaning against the stob earned two points; and a shoe circling the stob earned three points. Total points required to win a game could be twenty-one, fifty, or whatever number the players agreed on. Because school grounds are now better kept than they were from 1900 through World War II, few unsupervised Horseshoe games can be found, but some grandparents still teach grandchildren how to pitch horseshoes. Kelly Rhodes of Magnolia recalled playing the game when she was in junior high school in 1981, so there is hope for this game's survival.

◆ We knocked a caddy around in Palestine, but we did it primarily to see who could hit it the farthest. We never knew the rules, but some of the big boys who played it must have. Caddy went through a short-lived popularity with our group after we saw Stan Laurel and Oliver Hardy play it in a movie. Then I never thought of it again until I received the following description from Compton Sylvest, who had a description of the game written out by his uncle Rucker B. Ellisor, who had played the game in Sabine and Port Arthur.

Caddy
by
Rucker B.
Ellisor and
Compton
Sylvest

The game Caddy was usually played by two with the use of a caddy made of a round piece of wood about four inches long and one-and-a-half inches in diameter, with each end tapered to a point. The caddy stick was of the same diameter, about eighteen inches long. [Editor's note: We made the caddy and the caddy stick out of a broom or mop handle.]

The first one up would hit the caddy on the end, making it fly almost straight up about two feet into the air, and then he batted it out into the field. From the point of landing the other player would pick up the caddy, take three long steps or jumps, and then throw it at the caddy stick that had been laid on the ground at the place of the original batting. If the caddy hit the stick the batter was out, but if it came close the batter would measure with the stick the number of stick lengths the caddy was from the stick. Then the batter would get to take that many

Caddy, or Spud Jack
(Richard S. Orton).

bats (as originally described). Then the other boy would be up. And after repeating the above, the one who had hit farthest away from the original batting area would be the winner.

◆ W. E. Souchek played a caddy game that he called Spud Jack or Shinny-On-Your-Own-Side: A four-inch piece of broom handle was sharpened at both ends like a pencil. Any number could play, at least three to each side, and each player had a cudgel that he used to knock the caddy, or jack, between goal-posts. The game started with two centers squared off over the jack. At the referee's count of three the centers tried to hit the jack into the air. When it was finally whacked into being air-borne and spinning, the other players would try to hit the spin-ning jack toward their goals. Whichever team made the most goals won. The flying jack [or caddy or puck] and the swinging sticks made this an interesting game, always on the verge of bloodshed.

Shinny on skates was a favorite game when I was a kid during one short period of time, probably for two seasons. We played at the bottom of John Street hill, and we skated with a reckless abandon that I shall not experience again. We used sticks of all sorts; mine was made from a chinaberry limb. Pucks were the small Carnation milk cans and were good standing targets for about five minutes of play. Then they became solid masses of metal that were deadly to shins, which I guess is why the game is called Shinny? Surely not. James Winfrey describes the field-hockey type of Shinny that he played two generations ago.

Shinny
by
James
Winfrey

Shinny was an unregimented battle, patterned after field hockey. We played wherever we could find a vacant lot. Dimensions of the field of play depended on space available. We played Shinny in the fall while the high school boys played football.

Shinny sticks were all homemade from whatever material we could find. A good stick could be made from six or eight inches of a two-inch-diameter tree limb, if it had a one-inch branch at forty-five to sixty degrees. Since such limbs were hard to find, we made sticks from one-by-two-inch moulding, with the six- or eight-inch club end nailed on at an angle to suit the user. A stick could also be sawed out of a wider board. The shinny object, the *puck* in ice hockey jargon, was a small tin can or a wooden block sawed from a 2×4.

As in most children's games, we chose sides. Any number could play, but there were usually only three or four on each side. The tin puck was placed in the middle of the playing field with the two leaders facing each other. The other players lined up with their leaders. Play started with the leaders placing their shinny sticks on the ground near the can or block. Then, after counting "one, two, three" in unison, while touching their sticks

Tin-can Shinny
(Richard S. Orton).

together above the object on each count, each leader tried to knock the object toward his opponent's goal.

Play never stopped until the object crossed a goal or was knocked out of bounds. There was some team play, but it was mostly a one-on-one melee. If an opponent got in your way or was on your side of the object, you shouted, "Shinny on your own side," and hit him on the shin.

I do not remember any serious injuries or fights while play-ing Shinny, but there were occasional cuts from a flying tin can, and bruised shins. It was the most exciting game we played when I was about twelve years old.

◆ Kenneth Davis reports that in the Texas Panhandle this game was called Dust Bowl Hockey or Cow Pasture Stick Ball.

Natalie Ornish tells about playing a type of shinny, or what she calls Palm Frond Polo, in Galveston, where palm fronds are available. The boys played Palm Frond Polo on skate scooters, hitting the puck or cupping and throwing it with their palm frond sticks, as in lacrosse.

Annie Over

Contributors sent in more versions of Annie Over—Auntie Over, Andy Over, Annie and Over, etc.—than any other single game. Frances and I played it in the Panhandle when we were first learning to throw. We had a black-sock ball that we at a very early age could throw over the two-room shack she and the other four members of her family lived in. Whoever had the ball would holler, "Annie," and the one on the other side of the house would reply, "Over." Then Annie would throw the ball over the house in the direction of Over's voice. If Over dropped the ball then he became Annie. If Over caught the ball, he would dash around the corner of the house and try to hit Annie with the ball before Annie could run the opposite way to Over's side, where Annie would be home free. Annie Over is best played with two teams, one on each side of the house. Then the one who is hit after a successful catch is either out of the game or must join the winner's side. (Benjamin Capps, Ralph E. Miller, Janet Jeffrey, Ida Hall, Tammy Thompson of Texas Tech, Gayla Sanders, and numerous others I talked to on the streets and in the hall)

◆ In Texas, basketball, football, and baseball are the main games that children play. Adults have stepped in and have organized these games to such an extent that playing simply for the fun of it—instead of for the score and a city championship and putting on a performance—is out of the question. One of the early revelations in my life came when I shifted from the sheer, spinning fun of sandlot (really the Carnegie Library lawn) football and baseball to the grim games and practice fields of high school sports. I loved sports and played sandlot so much and to such detriment of grades and everything else that my parents threatened (idly, I might add) to send me to a military school; I lasted through one year of campus sports.

We have had a basketball post and hoop at the end of the driveway for over twenty years. The net is shredded and awful, and I will have to cut it off the hoop just to improve the looks of our backyard, if that is possible. I should take the whole thing down, but every time the boys are hanging around in the back, they start shooting goals. I wouldn't deprive them—and my grandson will get the hang of it someday. They played all sorts of games, usually a one-on-one variety of one-hoop basketball. W. David Whitescarver describes two nonstandard basketball games, Horse and 'Round the World:

Horse and 'Round the World
by
W. David Whitescarver

The object of the game Horse is to make a shot that your opponent cannot. Every time a player misses a shot he takes a letter from the word H-O-R-S-E. With five misses, the player is a "Horse" and loses the game. Any number can play the game, although most often two or three play. To start the game each player shoots a free throw. The player who makes the free throw begins the game. If both players make the free throw, both continue shooting until one misses. If, for example, Player A begins the game, he may shoot any type of basketball shot he wishes (jump shot, hook, behind the back, etc.) from any place on the court. The more exotic and difficult the shot, the better, though some players take an easy shot to keep the lead and put pressure on their opponent. Player A might wish to shoot his best shot, or one he thinks his opponent will miss (his opponent's weakest shot). Thus, knowing your opponent's shooting ability determines your strategy. If Player A intends to make a backboard shot, he must call it before shooting. If Player A misses his shot, then Player B takes the lead and may shoot any shot he wishes. The strategy is then reversed and the tension mounts. Each player is allowed to "psych" his opponent before the shot with whatever comments seem appropriate. For example, reminding one's opponent that his hands are sweating or shaking or that his girl friend's honor is at stake is a necessary though verbal part of the game. There are, of course, infinite variations on the psychological game. If Player B makes his shot, then Player A must also make that same shot. When either player gets to H-O-R-S-E, he may then exercise his "free throw option." Each player has three free throws to get back into the game. He may shoot them all at one time or use one each time he becomes a H-O-R-S-E. For example, if Player A has missed five shots and has become H-O-R-S-E, he may shoot the first of his three free throws. If he makes one, he stays in the game as H-O-R-S. Should he elect to shoot all three free throws and makes them, he becomes H-O. Eventually one player uses up all his options and is out of the game. The game continues until only one player is left.

Any number can play 'Round the World, but usually only two or three play. The object is to make a series of shots from various positions on the court. As a player makes his shot, he moves to the next position, thus working his way around the court. The game begins at the free throw line. If the player makes that shot, he moves to the next position, which is under the basket. From there he moves to the far right side of the basket, then to the right side of the key, then to the top of the key, then to the left side of the key, then to the left side of the basket, then underneath again, and finally back to the free throw line. If he misses any attempt, his opponent is then allowed to shoot. A player must stay at each position until he has made that shot. The first player to move "round the world" (make all the required shots) is the winner. Of course, on most home courts the free throw line is a line dug with one's heel at the approximate distance, and instead of other regulation court positions, one may find himself shooting from "that tree stump to the right of the basket" or from "next to the garbage cans" or from "behind the doghouse." Players may add as many shooting positions to the game as they desire. These obstacles and added shooting positions only make the game more challenging.

◆ Five Hundred is a football game played at the convenience of those assembled with a football. Parents are not expected to come and watch, a marked-off playing field is not necessary, nor is a grownup required to referee the game. Chris Carter describes the game as it is played on the Blackland Prairie:

Five Hundred
by
Chris Carter
of Paris High
School

Perhaps the greatest asset of the game Five Hundred is its simplicity. The only necessities are a football and a large grassy playing area. At least three people are needed to play Five Hundred, but as many as ten can play without creating total chaos.

The rules of Five Hundred are fairly simple. First, a kicker is chosen to kick the ball to the other players, who form a line facing him. The kicker then punts the ball high into the air, and the players race to catch it. In the event that more than one player has equal opportunity to field the ball, a simple cry of "Mine!" reserves the fielding rights to one player. This cuts down on confusion and collisions. When a player realizes that he is not going to be able to field the ball himself, he becomes the defense. The defense may heckle the offensive player, the catcher, in any manner as long as he does not touch him or the ball.

The point system of Five Hundred is based on how the ball is caught. A player receives one hundred points if he catches the ball before it hits the ground, fifty points if he catches it after one bounce, or twenty-five if it is rolling. However, if the ball is fumbled, the number of points the player would have received for a catch is instead subtracted from his total score. The first player to attain five hundred points is pronounced the winner and is awarded the coveted position of kicker.

◆ Variations on Abner Doubleday's baseball game were many. Ben Capps sent in the rules for Scrub, which is similar to Work Up and One-Eyed Cat—or Two-Eyed Cat, if there are enough players to warrant two running bases instead of one. Elton Miles described his kinds of sandlot baseball, which he called Townball, Longball, and One-Eyed Cat:

Townball, Longball, and One-Eyed Cat
by
Elton Miles

Stick Ball.

In rural Coryell County before and after 1900, A. L. Miles and others played Townball—their name for baseball—when enough boys came together. In Townball two teams can be formed by as few as seven or eight players using home plate and three bases. With four on a team, you have a pitcher and three basemen, with one of the "in town" players helping the opposing team as catcher. With fewer than four to a team, extra work may fall on two boys manning three bases. With more boys, there can be at least one outfielder. A little thought produces many workable combinations.

As played by the Llano County boys, regular baseball rules were followed, with one exception. If a fielder could return a long grounder to the pitcher before the batter reached his base, that runner was out.

A. L. Miles recalled, "We rarely had numbers enough to have two teams, so we resorted to Longball, with only two bases: home plate and one base several yards from home plate." In the 1950s in Alpine three of us would play this version; we called it One-Eyed Cat. A specialist in sports history, Dr. Wayne Sheehan of Sul Ross State University, observed that Longball bears some resemblance to cricket in that the batter runs to only one base, or in cricket, a "wicket."

The object of Longball, or One-Eyed Cat, is for a player to score the most runs to win over his two or more opponents. There is only one base. In our three-man version, each player takes turn as batter, catcher, and pitcher, in that order. When more than three play, others are fielders, and rotation for batting and field position is agreed on. Sometimes the game is called Rotation. The rules for Longball are as follows:

1. If the batter strikes out or his hit is caught, he is out, and the players switch places: as we played it, batter to catcher, catcher to pitcher, pitcher to batter.
2. If the batter hits a fair ball, he must run and touch the base and run back and touch home without being thrown out. If he chooses, he can run on a wild pitch or if the catcher fails to catch a pitch.
3. The runner is out if another player throws the ball between him and the base he is headed for. He is *not* out if the ball crosses his path on a bounce or is rolling, or if the ball touches the ground during a double throw put-out attempt.
4. If the runner scores, he stays "in town" until he is put out.

"To get started," as explained by A. L. Miles, "two of the boys chose players, first choice, second choice, etc. First choice went to the winner of 'hand over hand' when the bat was pitched to one of the leaders." As "hand over hand" is described by Ernest Speck, one fellow tosses the perpendicular bat, handle up, to the other, who grabs it with one hand, usually about the middle. If, however, he catches the bat at the handle tip, covering it, he instantly wins. If he does not, the tosser then grips the bat, his hand above and adjacent to that of the holder. The holder places his other hand immediately above his opponent's, and so on, both alternately placing both hands on the bat until the outcome.

There is variation in deciding the winner of "hand over hand." Sometimes the last gripper loses if there is not enough bat left to accommodate his entire hand. Or, if the last gripper can cover the handle tip with three fingers, he gets first choice. Or, if he can hold the bat at all, even with his fingertips, and not drop it, he wins, but sometimes on one of two conditions. One is that he must hold the bat suspended tightly enough that the other boy cannot kick it loose on one attempt. Or he must throw the bat back over his shoulder for at least ten feet.

In Townball (with two teams) this ritual also determines which team bats first. In Longball the "hand over hand" winner bats first. The loser then performs the rite with another player, that player with another, and so on to determine playing position and batting order.

More recently Longball, or One-Eyed Cat, is usually played with an unlively softball because every player has to run about a great deal in pursuit of a good hit, a wild pitch, or a bad catch. Early in the century the A. L. Miles bunch played with string balls and willow-wood bats they wound and carved themselves. Any old thing makes a base or home plate—a rock, a board, a bucket lid, even a sturdy stick.

XII

Marbles

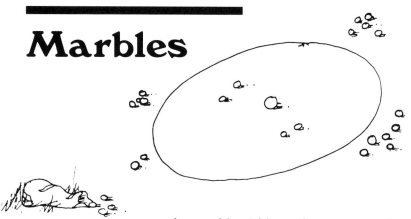

I never was very good at marbles. I blame this on my mother, but in reality it was probably my lack of manual dexterity coupled with poor hand-eye coordination. Whatever the cause, my aim was always troubled by problems of morality. I lay my ineptness at the feet of my mother's Presbyterian-Baptist conditioning, which would not allow gambling of any sort. I learned this early on—in the fourth grade, I think it was—when I came home triumphantly sporting a sack of marbles that I had won in an after-school game of Cat Eye. Most lectures on behavior rolled easily off my back like glassies on a slope. For some reason, I remembered this one. Mother explained the evils of gambling, lectured me on the multitudes of sins involved in playing keepsies, and told me in no uncertain terms to return the marbles to their original owner(s). I am sure that I promised I would; I don't remember that I did. But I do know that I never flashed my winnings, rare that they were, around the house thereafter, and I blamed my lack of expertise on a vague uneasiness that hovered over me when I played. And worn knees and grubby knuckles and nails always cried out, "This kid's been playing keepsies!"

In spite of which, we played a lot of marbles at Rusk Elementary in Palestine in the Thirties. The games I best remember are Cat Eye, Four Square, and Bullring—"Knucks down!" and "Slips don't count!" Teachers, who had gotten the gambling lecture either from my mother or from their own, forbade the playing of keepsies on the school ground and looked with distrustful eyes on marble playing of any sort. Any boy caught looking over his treasures during class had them snatched precipitously from his grasp and plunged into a teacher's drawer that emptied into a hole that reached to the center of the earth. It was a bourn from which no marble ever returned. So the wise ones among us kept their marbles in their jacket pockets in the cloakroom and either played funsies or tallied up on the way home after school.

I once had an aggie taw that I swapped a treasured pocket-knife for, an apt illustration of an aggie's value. It had a good feel and afforded me a fair amount of status. I had a cigar box full of glassies and several steelies of various sizes for use when I got a close shot in the bullring. I had a big, blue lagging crock that would land and stick like a bullfrog. I had others, but these are the ones that I remember. I am sitting here now, wondering where those marbles are. Solid glass and steel and agate are al-most indestructible, so they should be somewhere, probably buried a foot deep in red East Texas dirt, waiting for some twenty-first-century archaeologist to dig them up, or maybe at some flea market. I think I would recognize my brown aggie if I saw it.

Perhaps the gambling-gained marbles have been spirited back to their original owners by some prevailing anti-gambling justice. Properly so, in those cases when I fudged or didn't shoot knucks down. And I blush to remember putting the ratsy-puke on one schoolmate and causing him to miss shots. Using this ploy, I would spit on my finger and draw an X between his taw and the target, and he would usually miss and have a hissy fit. I hope the prevailing powers have with poetic justice delivered to him all those lost marbles of my sporting youth—but just the glassies and steelies, not my aggie taw.

Collecting marbles for illustrations in this book has been a pleasure, as well as a rekindling of an old love affair. I used to spill my marbles out on my bed and pore over them with all the avaricious satisfaction of a conditioned miser. Jack Clevenger did the same thing when I went over to his house to get a sixty-year-old sack of well-used marbles. He poured them out in a dish on the kitchen table and fingered them with fond memories. He had at least a dozen aggies, several beautiful spirals, both solid and glassy, blue Benningtons, some crocks and clays, and some

Beginner's Bullring
(Richard Orton).

steelies and peewees. Jack knew every marble by name and reputation, and they were still dear to his heart. Mike Worsham, one of those hard-eyed shooters that fired his taw with the speed and accuracy of a .30-.30, claimed to have won at least ten thousand marbles in his career. Lin Cross had a classic brown aggie that he once carried in a snuff can filled with lard to clear the moons it incurred during a hard game's shooting. Jessie Wyatt had eighteen beautifully clean agates—one perfect tiger eye—that her husband, John S., had lovingly looked after in his youth. Iva Johnson had a cake box full of marbles, and Mrs. McAllister Smith had thirty of her husband's agates that had been bought and used before the turn of the century. I wanted—no, I lusted after—each and every one of them.

At one time the Veterans of Foreign Wars sponsored a national championship contest for marble shooters. Towns all over the United States had shootouts to determine local champions who were sponsored and sent to this great event. And do you know that now among all the students in my classes I did not find a single one that knew how to play marbles!

On the other hand, two generations back, numerous marble games were popular. Ralph E. Miller played a game called "marble drop" that began with a hole in the dirt the shape and size of half a grapefruit. Two boys took turns dropping marbles from about two feet above the hole. Both boys put five marbles in the hand of the boy doing the dropping. If after dropping the ten marbles the number in the hole was odd, the dropper got all the marbles. If even, the nondropper got the ten. Jack C. Phipps sent in a variant of Bullring and a game called "Killings": "In Bullring, the participants placed one or more marbles in the center of a ring about six feet in diameter and then shot at them with their taws as fast and as accurately as possible from the edge of the circle until all of them had been knocked out. In Killings, the participants put one or more marbles in a two-foot ring and shot in sequence. The purpose was not only to knock the marbles out of the ring but also to kill the opponents' taws. The last shooter alive was the winner."

Cat Eye

CAT EYE:
Six-by-fifteen-inch
cat eye, four-foot
shooting line.

Cat Eye could be played with as few as three marbles, one on each end and one in the middle. It was a two- or three-boy game, and the number of marbles across the middle depended on common agreement and the size of the cat eye, usually about fifteen by six inches. Cat Eye started like most marble games, with the players lagging to determine the order of shooting, the closest to the lag line being first, the farthest last. The players shot from an agreed-upon distance, around four feet. Marble players use a lot of "ground rules," deciding on shooting distances, the numbers of marbles in the pot, and other game matters on the basis of their own abilities and the nature of the playing ground. Cat Eye is a simple game. The first player shoots from the line and if he knocks a marble out of the cat eye, he shoots again. It his taw sticks in the eye, the shooter is "dead" and out of the game.

In Four Square the player shoots the four corners off and then shoots the center. If he accidentally hits the center marble before cleaning the corners, he owes the square a marble. If he sticks in the square, he is dead. Four Square shooters, like Cat Eye shooters, shoot from an agreed-upon distance. Keen shooters started off eight or ten feet away.

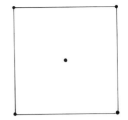

Four Square

FOUR SQUARE:
Twelve-inch square,
four-foot shooting
line.

The Story of Marbles

by Ellisene Davis

We all know the excitement of touching an antiquity, an object existing beyond our life's experience. Finding misshapen crock marbles in an old trunk is to touch the childhood of a loving grandfather, to discover a special toy savored and cherished beyond the remembrance of three generations. Ultimately, the adventure is in the research of a tale, and another, and still another.

Used long ago in play by adults and children, marbles represent one of the earliest games ever enjoyed. In Nayad, Egypt, archaeologists found marbles together with a set of ninepins and three rectangular bricks, dating to the fourth millennium B.C., in a child's grave. Some believed the bricks provided an arch through which the child rolled the marbles. In 2500 B.C., a center at Chanhudaro made marbles and beads of jasper and agate for use in games. Later, in 1453 B.C., Minoan boys played with knucklebones and pebbles. Favorite treasures of soldiers, the glazed marbles belong to a period about 200 A.D. During the seventeenth century a prisoner in the Bastille invented a game of solitaire played with marbles on pegs on a round board. In earthen monuments of North American Mound Builders archaeologists have found decorated marbles made of flint and clay (White, 31–33).

Roman children played marbles as early as 27 B.C. Literature reveals that marbles reached a peak of popularity in the Roman Empire about the time of Emperor Augustus, a century before the beginning of the Christian Era. In the first century A.D., when the Romans made the final conquest of England, they took with them marbles made of stone. Later the English created new balls made from real marble and from dried or baked clay (Baumann, 7).

The oldest sporting event in England is the annual marble championship held at Tinsley Green. Since 1588 the games have been conducted in the courtyard of the Greyhound Inn on Good Friday. Eight teams, six men to a team, participate. The second-prize winners receive a barrel of beer. The first prize for the event is a suckling pig (Baumann, 9).

Marbles belong to any age from prehistoric times to the present day, but how and where they are made determines their place in time, their individuality. Round pellets of clay found in England dating from 312 B.C. had designs similar to those of the stone balls from the Stone Age. In England in 1788 a man by the name of Hoffman took out an English patent for a machine he invented to make marbles for children. Now displayed in Pollock's Toy Museum are glass marbles from Bristol, a town noted for glass manufacture. The Englishman J. Pitts sold beautiful marbles from every era at his Toy and Marble Warehouse on 8 Great Street, Saint Andrews Street, London (White, 33).

No one knows the exact place or time that glass marbles were first produced. The old Venetian glassblowers of Lauscha and Sonneberg created glass marbles in small factories called glass cottages. The English called these marbles monstrosities because their fragile quality made them useless in many games. A Venetian cottage worker invented a new tool called a Marbel-schere, or marble scissors. This invention marked the beginning of the sale of marbles to the public (Baumann, 35).

Before World War I craftsmen of Germany produced most of the china and glass marbles found in collections in this country. A few desirable antique marbles were made in the United States and even India (DiNoto, 151). In the province of Thuringen, East German zone, the first glass marbles known as German swirls were created. Collectors believe some of the earliest glass spirals could have been made in Amsterdam, Holland. By 1800 the Germans were also producing hand-painted china marbles. Craftsmen used squares, diamonds, bull's eyes, leaves, stars, flowers, and concentric rings for designs (Baumann, 32–33).

Within the category of glass marbles are a kaleidoscopic array of patterns, designs, swirls, and colors. Some even contain images of birds, animals, and people made from china, clay, gypsum, or kaolin. Goldstones, sometimes thought to be made of stone, are glass marbles containing particles of copper (Baumann, 35).

In America, J. H. Leighton opened the Iowa City Flint Glass Manufacturing Company and made glass marbles until the company failed twenty months later. Another American company, Navarre Glass Marble Company of Navarre, Ohio, produced small spiral and sulphide types containing images of birds, people, and animals. Excavation at the old factory site of Boston and Sandwich Glass Company in Massachusetts revealed many broken and imperfect marbles (Baumann, 37).

Many stone marbles were also made in Germany. Expert agate grinders came from Oberstein, Idar-Oberstein, Bundenbach, and Niederworresbach. Although the Tiger Eye marbles were made in Germany, the stone comes from mines in Griqualand West, South Africa. Rose quartz, bloodstone (green chalcedony), a petoskey stone (fossilized coral found near Lake Michigan), and jasper are all used to make stone marbles (Baumann, 17).

Crock marbles are known as Benningtons. Although Bennington has become a generic term for a mottled brown ware, the name actually is a town in Vermont where two important potteries were located (Huxford and Huxford, 53–54, 316–17).

In 1793, two years before Vermont became a state, Captain John Norton established a pottery works to produce the simple wares required by the community—jugs, crocks, milk pans, plates, etc. Bennington did not manufacture marbles as production items (Barret, 3). Some believe workers molded spheres from extra clay to make marbles for their children. The marbles were coated with a thin clay slip or were dusted with powdered lead and were fired to form a hard, transparent glaze. Like the pottery, the marbles were either blue or brown; some were speckled. Occasionally solid pink crockery marbles were made. A few crock marbles were white with colored swirled lines. A few of the swirled marbles contained marks like the eyes found on other crock marbles (Baumann, 30–32).

In the mid-1800s when crock marbles were favorite toys, potters worked for fifty cents a day. How surprised the potters would be to see that the simplest marbles they made now sell for six dollars or more each. The large fancy Bennington marbles can sell for as much as twenty dollars. Crock marbles aren't considered rare like Clambroth, Lutz, Indian Swirls, Peppermint Swirls, and Sulphide glass marbles or even the machine-made comic strip marbles, but the Benningtons are sought by collectors and will increase in value (Rinker, 314–15).

Although it is exciting to touch and collect a variety of marbles, it is the memory of the games, the socialization and competition, the warmth of sharing that is revered by each generation. Long ago, Caesar Augustus stepped from his litter to join in a game of nuts and marbles with young boys, to relive for a brief moment his childhood (White, 33). Then, as now, the boys must have played "for keeps"—learning the pleasure and pain of competition—or "for funsies"—simply enjoying practicing their game skills.

A treasure of antique crocks (Ellisene Davis).

Ring Taw: A Bullring Game

Ring Taw territory is a one-foot ring in the bull's-eye of a six-foot ring. Each player puts marbles in the inner ring and takes his first shot anywhere around the outer ring. Any marble he knocks out of the six-foot ring is his, and he may shoot again if his taw remains in the big ring. If he rolls out of the big ring or is later knocked out by another player, he shoots from the big ring when his turn comes up again. If he misses and his taw remains within either ring, he must leave it there to be shot at. If he is shot out, he must hand over a marble to the shooter. No taw can be taken, and it can be shot at only once. The game continues until all the marbles have been shot out of the ring.

RING TAW (A BULLRING GAME): Six-foot bullring, one-foot bull's eye, bullring is shooting line.

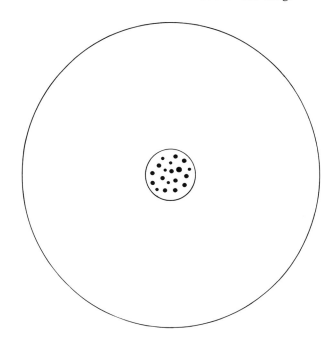

Picking Plums

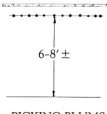

6–8′ ±

PICKING PLUMS: Six- to eight-foot shooting line, preferably with a backstop.

In Picking Plums the players place their marbles on a line with at least the width of two marbles between each marble. A shooting line is drawn parallel to the marble line and six to eight feet away. Each player takes his turn to shoot once at the "plums." Those he knocks off the line are keepers. If he misses, he gives one of his marbles to the line. Picking Plums is best played against a wall backstop.

Marbles for Keeps

by Tom Davison

One of the pressing moral dilemmas confronting the fifth-grade class at Nacogdoches' Central Grammar School in 1930 was the "Marbles for Keeps" question.

"Do you play marbles for keeps?" Katherine, a pretty little girl from the Anti-Keeps bloc, asked me pointedly. I felt as though an improper answer would bring down the wrath of God on my shoulders.

"No," I answered piously. What Katherine didn't know was that I was a rather poor left-handed scattershooter who refrained from playing for keeps only because I would have been a heavy loser. But that didn't keep me from watching, and greatly admiring, the boys who rushed out at recess for as many games as the fifteen minutes would allow. I never bothered to question that if playing for keeps was wrong, was watching people play for keeps also wrong?

Our classroom seemed about equally divided between the anti's and the pro's. Most of the opposition was from the girls, and they didn't play marbles anyway. Most boys were for it, particularly if they were good at it.

Our game consisted of a taw line where players lagged their shooting taws to determine who got first crack at the small elliptical circle of marbles entered by each contestant. The player who lagged closest to the dirt-drawn taw line got first shot at the circled marbles, usually about eight feet away. Since this was all performed on dirt, fifth-grader fingernails never seemed to be clean.

"Hard-down knucks!" was the cry the lead shooter most often heard as he squatted to take his shot. This meant he must keep all his knuckles down in the dirt and shoot without raising his hand.

Shooting taws were greatly prized, and some players could even afford "agates," a superior marble of near-perfect circumference that gave more accurate results, at least in some hands. I remember trading one agate my grandmother had given me for the then-princely sum of fifty cents to a small tow-headed boy named Maurice, who used it to knock marbles out of the center ring with regularity.

The idea, of course, was to knock as many marbles as possible out of the ring with your shooting taw. Those you could keep. Naturally, nobody put any very fine specimens in the circle, and some of the old glass marbles were pretty badly chipped. Some were so bad that their entry was rejected by a vote of the other players.

There was a lot of shouting and heckling when a player got ready to take his shot at the prize marbles in the ring. One classic disclaimer could always be used by the shooter if yelled in time, voiding any limitations on the way he had to make his shot. *Anything* was the magic word. If you could yell "Anything!" before anybody else yelled some other restrictive command, then you could shoot any way you wanted. It was often shortened to "Anys!" for practical purposes.

"You heard my 'anys,'" I can still remember one particularly alert player saying disdainfully as he beat some "hard-down knucks" shouter to the draw. Frank was a master at saying the magic word first as it came his time to shoot. I don't remember his ever having to make a hard-down knucks shot.

Occasionally the heated games would overrun the recess bell, and boys who returned late to the classroom would get a

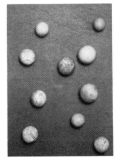

(Mark Weatherly)

(Mark Weatherly)

trip to see the principal, H. H. Hall. Mr. Hall would sit his culprit down on a bench beside him, place his hand in friendly fashion on the boy's leg, and speak reassuringly for a few moments. Just when you might have thought he was going to let you go back to your homeroom, down would come his hand with a resounding slap on your knickered leg. It didn't hurt much, but the anticipation of when the next lick would come could be nerve-wracking. Most boys got off with three or four leg slaps and a short lecture about punctuality.

After recess there was a lot of conversation about winnings and losings. "I'm four loser," one would say, "and I ain't got but five marbles left."

"I'm six winner," another would brag, "and I'm gonna win that much more next recess with this here new taw I got."

A player would take his marbles home after school, put them in an old cigar box with his other treasures, finger them awhile, and dream about how many he would win tomorrow.

"Knucks Down!"

by James W. Winfrey

My memory of schoolboy playground and backyard games is from the early 1920s, most of which was when I was eleven to fourteen years old in Durant, Oklahoma. There was no organized play or exercise at school, so we played games of our own choice during the fifteen-minute recess periods, morning and afternoon, and before the morning school bell. We were not allowed to stay on the grounds after school let out at four P.M., so we would play in our own backyards or on vacant lots.

The games we played changed with the seasons, from marbles and tops, which were warm-weather games, to mumble peg, one and over, and shinny.

Marbles required a great deal of skill and a considerable investment for a boy of limited means who was making about two dollars a week delivering a paper route. The serious player needed a large number of a variety of marbles.

First and most important was his "taw," the shooting marble. Depending on the size of the boy's fingers and his shooting technique, it needed to be from one-half to three-fourths an inch in diameter. My favorite taw was a beautiful brown five-eighths-inch agate that cost me seventy-five cents. Agates had to be bought at the drugstore where they were displayed in a glass jar for us to admire. The larger ones could cost a dollar or more. Everybody preferred agates, but if you did not have one for a taw, you could use a steel ball bearing (a "steelie") or a cheaper marble that could be bought at a racket store for a nickel or a dime.

An agate was a treasure to be carefully guarded. After considerable use, an agate would develop surface fractures, called "moons," that marred its looks, particularly if you wanted to trade it. If you soaked it in lard for a few days, the moons would disappear.

The next-lower level in value was the imitation agate, which we called "immies." They were of opaque glass, generally about one-half an inch in diameter, and came in a variety of variegated colors. Most boys who did not have an agate would use an immie for a taw. To compete in a marbles game, you needed a handful of immies.

Just as pretty but less valued were the "glassies" and "crocks." The glassies were of transparent glass with internal color streaks, like antique paperweights. They came in various sizes, some being as large as three-fourths an inch. They were rarely used for a taw, but you would need a few for playing and trading. Crocks were glazed ceramic, brown or blue mottled, similar to the common water pitchers of the 1920s. Their diameter was from three-eighths to five-eighths, but they were rarely used for a taw because they were not perfect spheres.

Some players would have a few "chalks," which were very lightweight and were usually larger, up to three-quarters of an inch.

The most numerous in the marbles player's arsenal were the "peewees," a small, unglazed ceramic marble, about three-eighths-inch diameter, and costing a penny. A player would have a pocketful of peewees.

To take care of such an array of marbles, you needed a box or sack. My mother made me a bag of cotton domestic, six or eight inches long, with a drawstring top like a Bull Durham sack.

The best technique for shooting marbles was to hook the thumbnail under the curled middle finger second joint and hold the taw between the end of the index finger and the thumb joint. Shooting was done from a kneeling position with the back of the hand flat on the ground, "Knucks down." When the thumb was released, the thumbnail struck the marble, propelling it airborne. An expert with an agate taw using this technique, called "plunking," could hit a target marble two feet or more away without the taw touching the ground.

Some players used a steelie taw (a steel ball bearing), which was too heavy for plunking. It was held between the thumbnail and the index finger first joint and was shot with the side of the fist on the ground. The steelie rolled on the ground and was usually used for shots of only a few inches.

The object of most marbles games was simply to knock marbles out of a ring drawn on hard ground, called a bullring, and the game was called Bullring. The ring was usually three or four feet in diameter, but could be larger, the size being drawn by agreement and depending on the number of players. Each player would put in the middle of the ring an equal number of each type of marbles: immies, glassies, crocks, and peewees. The more valuable marbles would be placed in the center of the ring, surrounded by the less valuable, with the peewees on the outside. A straight line was drawn on the ground and each player tossed his taw (lagged) at the line from about ten feet away to

(Mark Weatherly)

ROLEY HOLEY:
Two-inch holes three
feet apart, four-foot
shooting line.

determine the order of shooting. The one nearest the line won the first shot.

The first shot was from anywhere outside the ring. Successive shots were from wherever your taw stopped. Your turn to shoot continued as long as you could knock marbles out of the ring without your taw leaving the ring. If you were "playing for keeps," which our mothers frowned on, marbles knocked out of the ring were yours. However, your taw was not in jeopardy. If your taw was knocked out by another player, he could select one of your other marbles in lieu of your taw. Taking turns, players continued the game until all marbles were out of the ring.

Movement of the hand on the ground while shooting was not allowed. "Knucks down" at all times. Violation meant loss of a turn.

In games not "played for keeps," the winner had the privilege of shooting his taw at the knuckles of the poorest player at a distance of about one foot.

There were no doubt many variations of Bullring, depending on the imagination of the players. One version was to tee up only a few valuable marbles in the center of the ring, with all the shooting done from outside the ring.

Another very popular marbles game was Roley Holey. Four holes were dug three or four feet apart, two or two-and-a-half inches in diameter and an inch or two deep. Three holes were in a straight line with the fourth at a right angle from the third hole. Starting at a shooting line three or four feet from the first hole, the player tried to roll his taw into each hole in succession and return. As in playing croquet, you could continue to shoot as long as you made holes without missing. Steelies were popular for Roley Holey because they would roll further than the lighter marbles. It was not easy to plunk into a hole.

◆ The following is a contribution from the 1978 staff of *Loblolly*, the Gary (Texas) High School publication directed by historian Lincoln King. Johnny Smith of Gary tells about his father, John Wesley Smith, who was one of the local marbles champions several generations ago.

Tennessee and Seven-Up

by Johnny Smith

They played marbles ever since I remember—way back. I've known my daddy to walk down there (to Woods Post Office). That's about three miles. After dinner on Saturday he'd bathe, put on fresh clothes, and be off for some serious marble shooting. After he got to be about seventy, the playin' kinda drowned out over at Woods Post Office, and he started going to Gary. He played with Uncle Jim Applegate and Uncle Jesse McGee. Aus Downing played with them some. Cousin Johnny Hooker was often my daddy's partner. He had a brother named Jed Hooker. He played, as did old Uncle Henry DeBerry.

My daddy used to carry marbles in his pocket, and when he had some free time, he'd take 'em out and practice. He was one of the best around. He loved to play marbles anyplace, anytime, and against anyone. It was a pretty big deal in those days. They even went up to Beckville for a tournament one time. But they lost that one. They were serious in their playing. Old Dr. Parker and Cousin Johnny Hooker got into a fight one time. It was some argument about the rules. They made up, though. No one got hurt; it was a friendly fight.

The taw was the "thumping marble," or the one you shot with. The other marbles were just called ring marbles, and they were larger than the taws. You placed the ring marbles in the playing area to set up your game. The marbles were mostly made of stone and weren't all different colors like the glass ones you see now.

TENNESSEE: A four- to six-foot square, six-foot shooting line.

To see who would shoot first, the players would toss their taws, to see whose got closest to the center of the square. Then they'd take turns. When they played, it was usually one of two different games. The first one was called Tennessee. When they first started playing they had a big square. Oh, I 'spect it was maybe four or six feet square. They put nine marbles in there, one on each corner, then one in the center of each side, and one in the middle. They played where the one who got the most marbles won the game, you know. You had to knock at least five of the nine out of the square. Your first shot would be from about six feet away and then you'd shoot from where your taw had landed. On that game they could play partners. If the other team killed your partner (hit his taw with theirs), you could give him a marble (a ring marble you had previously knocked out of the square), that is, pay him out. The way they killed your partner, or you for sure, was they'd shoot one of you and your partner didn't have a marble to pay you out. Then you were dead and your team lost.

SEVEN-UP: A two-foot square, ten- to fifteen-foot shooting line.

Well, they'd quit that one and start playing the other game that was called Seven-Up. They had a little square about two feet square. They put a marble in each corner and one in the middle. You'd have to win seven games to call it Seven-Up. You had to stand back about ten to fifteen feet away, and if you hit that middle marble and knocked it out of the square, well, you got a game. I've seen my daddy knock that middle marble out seven shots in a row, and win. They played partners on that one too. If you didn't hit the center marble out on your first shot, you had to try to hit all five out of the square. And, if your taw stayed in the square after a shot, you were "dead," or "fat," and were out of the game.

XIII

Tops and Knives

Tops and knives are toys that are used in games of competition. A top can, of course, be a toy used as a pastime also, and kids have spun tops with a twist of their fingers or a flick of a string or a lash of a whip for thousands of years. They have spun them just for the joy of seeing them spin or for the satisfaction of mastering a skill. Spinning a top is a real skill, you know, like shooting a marble or jumping a rope or walking on stilts, and if you have not spun a top in a while, you

Mexican-style tops
(Joe Graham).

will probably bounce it all over the place before you recover the art and stand it spinning on its toe like a ballerina. Young boys quickly master the art in a playground world where certain skills are equated with dominance. And to prove their mastery, they are soon competing.

Knives fit a bit strangely into a chapter on toys, because when a boy gets his first knife he doesn't think of it as a toy. A knife is a grown man's accoutrement and is his most useful tool. If you are ever cast adrift in a wilderness and can carry only one tool, let it be a knife—a Texas Bowie, a Malaysian parang, a Nepalese Ghurkha-kris, a Mexican machete—any blade that has authority. And whatever you do, don't go dulling its edge by sticking it in the dirt, which is exactly what young boys do as soon as they get their first Barlow. And keen for competition, they are soon involved in knife games.

Pico and the Splits in Port Isabel
by Tom McClellan

When I turned ten, my folks and I were living in a trailer on the west bank of the channel that made Port Isabel, Texas, "technically an island rather than a peninsula," so my dad told me. Dad also told me the reason you couldn't catch mangrove, snapper, or flounder in the channel anymore, just hardhead and sailtop catfish. It had to do with waste from the boats and the fisheries around the bend to the south of us in what they called the shrimp basin; the industry was improving, and there were more people and more pollution.

Our school building was a barracks, hastily put up to house the unexpected influx of children begotten near the beginning of World War II, and our playground was packed dirt, kept hard by endless games of free-form football, tag, and tackle-the-big-kids. To the big kids, eighth and ninth graders, we must have seemed like tenacious kittens, easy to toss about, and when two or three of us managed to dump a big kid on his rear, we whooped our victory. But mostly we chased one another across a football field whose endzones were sidewalks and whose boundaries were school buildings.

"You're gonna catch it now."

"Huh? Whyzat?"

"You tackled Rucho. *Nobody* tackles Rucho."

It turned out Rucho didn't mind—maybe he figured a skinny kid with glasses wasn't worth the trouble—and by the eighth grade, Rucho was gone, and Jose with him, to work on the boats; and by the ninth, Emilio and Fernando, and Dominga, rumored to be pregnant; and by the tenth, Maria Elena, her virginity spattered, it was said, all over the interior of Eduardo's brother's car.

But before all that we played *pico*, at least that is the word for our way of playing tops that my memory digs up. The object of the game was to bust open one of the fifteen-cent tops (blue, red, or forest-green) spinning or—God forbid!—dead on its side in the ring. The ring never exceeded three feet in diameter and could go as small as two-and-a-half feet. It was scratched into the dirt with a top *pico* (the beak, or point). Then the two-to-five players would slam their tops into the ring, pretty much simultaneously, with a vigorous overhand cast that ended with a sharp snapback of the cord intended to bounce the top out of the ring, still spinning and safe. If you could manage that, and could scoop the spinning top onto your palm, you got "dropsies." That is, you could play bombardier onto someone else's top—or start over if you didn't want to risk becoming a target yourself. It was understood that everyone would have filed the harmless half-inch of the store-bought top's tip to needle sharpness, if not replaced it with a nail ground to a murderous beak up to one inch in length. In this last case, I am thinking of an innovator by the name of Bill Morgan. It was this same Bill (probable descendant of the pirate) Morgan who forever ended our class's mild interest in marbles with an inch-and-a-half steel ball bearing. But I digress.

The *pico* player was expected to have two tops, if not three. The more battered, gouged, and chipped one would be thrown first, as a decoy to lure the newer weapons into play. I even recall seeing a three-fourths remainder from some previous battle cast whirring into the ring mainly by force to sputter still and face its final demolition, while its owner brought forth the gleaming means to his revenge, already spiralled to the hilt with new cord. This was serious business. The top that gyrated from the ring showing raw wood was a wounded ego, and a battered one with no paint on its *pico* was a loser's life in the making. Eight years down the road, the eyes that surveyed, the brain that estimated, the wrist that measured its own flexion, might be engaged in a state tennis championship—I believe that was so in one case—and five years past the top-playing stage, I shocked myself by ending a lizard's life with an arrow, drawn and loosed almost absentmindedly, that exactly clipped off its head.

We graduated from *pico* to a knife-throwing game called "splits." Incidentally, the ability to slap a knife into a nearby target was not the sole property of adolescents. I saw this demonstrated by a young shrimp house employee whose skill with a palmed pocketknife was such that the blurred whip of his arm could bury it half-blade deep into a wall ten yards behind him. Mumbletypeg required a three-bladed knife, which few of us had; besides, it was too tame. Splits demanded trust, trust in one's own invulnerability or in the other player's knack for planting the knife—any stickable knife would do—into the earth near one's foot or between one's legs. [Editor's note: This is a "chicken" or nerve game called Split the Kipper or Black Foot in Great Britain. Ken Davis sent the game in from the High Plains, and he called it Stretch or Chicken.]

The two players would face one another about four feet apart. If the first throw of the knife was not ceded by either player, one side of the blade would be dampened with spit and the knife flipped like a coin. The player not in control of the knife was to "call it in the air." Whoever won the toss had the first throw that left the knife sticking into the ground near his opponent's foot—twelve inches or a span or a knife's length or whatever distance was decided. This required the target to "do the splits" until his foot touched the knife. Then he would pluck it from the ground and try his best to put his antagonist in a similar position. Thenceforward, any failure to stick the knife would free the intended victim to return to his starting stance.

If the knife could not be reached by further stretching, the player was to pivot on the foot nearest the knife to bring the other foot into contact with it, so that his back was turned, and he would have to throw the knife behind him. To force one's opponent into such a position was not always good strategy. The farther away one's opponent, the farther away he might plant the knife, and a "stick" unreachable by any stretch was an automatic win. Better to chunk it into the ground between his legs and enough behind him so that he could not reach it. This would require him to turn his back and place his feet together, the most awkward position to throw from.

We played other games, more common ones: foot-to-foot handshake battles called "Indian wrestling" and the inevitable game of tackle anywhere we could run a football—and more serious combats that were not games at all. I recall a friend's face twisted into denial of any intended offense against the calm-voiced boy who pointed four inches of stainless-steel blade into his belly, and another face smashed bleeding and purple by a large lad who finally cried out, "For God's sake, stop him, he's crazy! Stop him before I kill him!" This before any of us showed even peach fuzz. And a knockdown hair-pulling match between two eighth-grade girls ended any illusions I might have had about femininity.

I do not mean to overdramatize. Doubtless every play-ground reverberates with contained savagery. Still, my memories of the Gulf Coast town where I grew up are filled with images of easy violence.

Three of us high schoolers got into a clod fight once. We'd gone out to plink or shoot birds with .22 rifles, but there was nothing to shoot. We fanned out around a stock tank and rested a bit, and one of us chunked a clod. Soon we were back to fifth grade, laughing and throwing and ducking. I got Ronny a good one on the hip, and he was still laughing as he picked up his semiautomatic and, making spitting "gun noises," sprayed a half-dozen rounds across the bank I stood on.

We stopped playing then.

Top Games

The simplest kind of top is one sent in by Elton Miles. It consists of a round piece of cardboard with a stick stuck through the

center, and it is twirled by a twist of the fingers. A popular form of the homemade top was the wooden spool, whittled to a cone shape, with a stick through the center hole. Ruben Villareal sent in the spool top, as well as a true game top that was whittled out of a piece of mesquite that had a nail driven through the center for the spinner. The mesquite top was wrapped and spun with a string.

Anytime two or more kids (or goats or mockingbirds or Sunday School teachers) get together, they will peck for dominance, one way or another. If they happen to have tops, they will spin them to see whose top will spin the longest, or who can do more tricks off the string with it, or who can throw it at such an angle to make it walk or travel the farthest.

Shinny
by
Jack C. Phipps

A form of shinny was also played with tops. This was a team game with an equal number of participants on each side. The puck was usually a small block of wood or an old top that had lost its spinner. Two goal lines were established about fifteen yards apart, with the puck placed halfway between them. The attacking top propelled the puck by striking it a glancing blow in an attempt to score by knocking it across the goal line. The team garnering eleven scores first was the winner.

A top with a rounded spinner would not penetrate the ground as deeply as one with a pointed tip and was my preference in one top game. The targets in this game were bottle caps, which were placed cork-side up in a ring that might vary from two to three feet in diameter. The object of the game was to knock the caps from the ring without the top's sticking in the ring. If a player's top stuck in the ring, that player could not continue plugging at the caps until another player knocked that top out of the ring, for which the knocker could exact one cap from the knockee.

[Editor's note: Ben Capps sent in the same game, but he and his friends used a different kind of prize and target: "We chose for our 'dakes' (somebody check the etymology of that word) the small metal tags stuck on plugs of chewing tobacco. A Brown's Mule tag was a little red mule; an Apple tag was a red apple; Tinsley had a dignified black and gray tag; and Star had a star. At the end of a game, the big winner would have a pocketful of little metal tags to shake in his pocket and for bragging purposes." Ben also recommended using a top with a rounded point that wouldn't stick and die in the ring, losing the player a throw.]

Tops
by
**James W.
Winfrey**

Twelve-year-old boys playing tops was far different from the child's pastime of merely spinning a beautifully colored top to see how long it would spin. The way we played, it was total war.

Our tops were about one-and-one-half inches in diameter and one-and-three-quarters inches high. The cone angle was forty-five degrees, which was steeper than the usual decorative top. The cylindrical spindle on top was about one-half inch in diameter and one-eighth of an inch high to accommodate a large spinning cord. The cone point was tipped with an iron sphere, about one-eighth of an inch in diameter.

The spinning cord, about an eighth of an inch in diameter, was much larger than the common top cord. We called it a "calf rope." It took eight or ten turns to cover a top. You tied a knot in the end, wrapped it around the spindle crossing over behind the knot, then pulled it down tightly to the tip and wrapped in the reverse direction, coming up the cone from the tip to near the largest diameter. The cord was cut to length to fit your hand, and a knot was tied near the end.

After the cord was wrapped on the top, you cradled it between the thumb and forefinger knuckle with the point toward you, holding it firmly in place with the forefinger, while the cord was held tightly between the middle and fourth fingers by the knot. This gave you complete control in casting the top. With an overhand movement, you would cast the top downward, like throwing a ball, then with a flick of the wrist, you would add to the spin just before the cord was completely released. An expert could make his top land accurately, spinning on its point after hitting another top.

As in marbles, the players made up some of their rules. Usually a three- or four-foot circle would be drawn on the hard ground, and each player would put one or more tops in the ring. You took turns trying to knock tops out of the ring. It did not count if your top did not continue to spin after hitting an object top. The next player could try to hit your spinning top before it stopped. If he did, you did not get to keep the top you knocked out of the ring.

Some of the boys with a vicious streak would sharpen their top's point and try to split the other boy's top.

Top Plugging
by Dorothy Howard

When neighbor families came to visit and big boys and men took to top spinning, top plugging was a favorite pastime. For top plugging, a circle was scratched on the ground—some two feet in diameter. The first spinner (determined by drawing straws or matches) threw his top into the circle; the second spinner, in throwing down his top, tried to strike the first top at an angle to knock it out of the circle. Successful, he claimed the top. Unsuccessful, he left his top in the circle along with the first top. The third spinner attempted to plug one of the two at an angle to make it leave the ring in such a way as to knock out the other top also, or he simply tried to plug and strike one top out of the circle and, if successful, claimed the top and the right to try to plug the second one in the ring.

Knife Games

Some knife games, like Tom McClellan's Splits or Charles Martin's Slicing the Pie, are dueling games, battles fought for dominance and territory, and the contest is with an individual. The

Knives for sticking.

most widespread knife game in Western culture—European, British back to the sixteenth century, and American—is called by some Mumblepeg, or Mumbletypeg, and is a contest of skill. As in all folk games the rules from one part of Texas to another vary with the players, as do the name of the game and the names of the positions. Ken Davis sent in West Texas forms of "Mumbley Peg" games. Davie Gibson Tunnell's description includes such throws as "Break the Chicken's Neck," "Climb the Ladder," "Shaving Old Pete," "Mark the Pigs," and "Find the Turkey's Nest." The loser definitely loses and must "mumble the peg" or "root the peg" (American parlance); that is, he must pull a peg out of the ground with his teeth. (For a discussion of Mumblepeg and other children's knife games see Opie and Opie, 219–23.)

Mumblepeg
by
James W. Winfrey

The most popular knife game was the traditional "Mumblepeg." We did not call it "Mumbletypeg" in Hunt County, Texas. It was played on soft ground, usually grassy, with an ordinary jackknife, which had a one-half-inch-wide blade about two-and-one-half inches long in one end and a smaller blade in the other end. Only the long blade was used to play Mumblepeg.

Two or more could play the game, with the objective being to complete the most maneuvers without failing to stick the blade in the ground. Who would go first was determined by a preliminary contest of knife throwing at a target a few feet away on the ground. After this, contestants formed a circle on their knees, and the leader would start with a manuever of his choice. Each player in the circle would attempt the same. If the contestant was successful, he stayed in the game to attempt the next maneuver. If he missed, he was out. If the leader missed, he was out and the next player in the circle became the leader. Play continued with the leader attempting a great variety of maneuvers of his choice until all but the surviving leader were eliminated.

The usual maneuvers were in the following order, with each maneuver being done first with the right hand and then repeated with the left hand:

Hold the knife by the blade tip, handle down, and flip it one-half turn, underhanded.

Hold the knife firmly by the blade and throw for one-half turn overhanded.

Lay the knife on the fist, blade up. Hurl to the ground while turning the hand over.

Hold the blade by the tip, handle down, with the point against the nose. Flip for one-half turn.

Do the same with the blade tip touching the right ear, the left ear, the right eye, the left eye.

Rest the blade tip on top of the head, holding it in place with a finger on the end of the handle. (A cap is recommended.) Flip the knife forward.

Repeat the head maneuver with the blade tip on the right and left shoulders, right and left knees.

If more than one player remains, these maneuvers can be repeated with variations in the number of knife turns.

Mumblepeg
by Dorothy Howard

Mumblepeg, played with a two-bladed pocketknife (both blades opening from the same end of the knife), was a game for spring or fall weather in Hunt County. Winter was too cold for sitting on the ground, and in the summer the ground was too dry. Moist soil, neither too wet nor too dry, was a necessity, as was a grassy turf where the grass was not too high. Bermuda grass was best with its intricate web of roots to hold the knife blade upright once it stuck. Two or three well-matched players—not more than three—made for a good game.

Each player owned his own mumblepeg knife, a Christmas or birthday gift likely, and chosen for that purpose; the weight, size, shape, and length of the handle were important in proportion to the length of the two blades, and the ratio of the lengths of the two blades was equally important. Each player played with his own knife, with which he had practiced long hours at every opportunity, for the game was long and depended on skill (more than luck) learned by watching and copying skilled players.

The game started with the easiest of all tricks of skill and ended many plays later with the losers "rooting the peg." First play: the player held the knife (with the long blade open) by the tip of the blade between the thumb and forefinger and flipped it outward from him to make the blade stick into the ground upright. (Rule: when the knife slanted, the slant must allow the thrower's finger to pass between the knife handle and the earth; otherwise the thrower lost his turn to another player.) The player flipped the knife thus three times.

Second play: a fist was made, first of the right hand; the open knife, placed across the fist (palm up) with the blade thumbward, rested in the trough made where the fingers clenched the palm. The fist then described a half-circle in the air counterclockwise, carrying the knife with it, giving the knife momentum in the downward movement to plunge blade-first into the ground. This move was repeated with the left hand.

Third play: the open knife was held on the palm of the outstretched right hand, blade pointing away from the body. The hand and arm were then moved swiftly upward, describing an arc declining toward the body to make the knife describe a half-circle toward the body with enough momentum to plunge into the ground. The player usually kneeled, prepared, if necessary, to move backward from the descending knife. This move was repeated with the left hand.

Fourth play: the open knife was held on the hand as in the third move except that the back of the hand instead of the palm held the knife. The movements of the third move were duplicated.

Fifth play (called "breaking the chicken's neck"): the knife was held horizontally with its blade secured and balanced by the forefinger and middle finger of the left hand (on top of the forefinger and under the middle finger). The right forefinger struck the knife handle quickly, dislodging it, making it flip to describe a half-circle clockwise and plunge into the ground.

Sixth play: the knife was held in the right hand with the blade pointing down. The forefinger of the right hand pressed on the end of the handle, which was secured between the thumb and the other three fingers. The point of the blade was poised on the tip of the thumb and the forefinger (pinched together) of the left hand. The knife was then flipped by the right forefinger outward to describe a circle and plunge into the ground. Next the thumb and middle finger (left hand) formed a tip on which to poise the blade for another flip and plunge. Next, the thumb and ring finger and last the thumb and little finger.

Seventh play: the blade tip was poised on the back of the left hand, was flipped, and plunged into the ground; then, in turn, it was poised on the wrist, on the elbow, on the shoulder, on the chest, on the top of the head.

Eighth play: the arms were crossed (right arm inside) so that each hand could grasp the tip of an ear. The right hand held the knife blade by the point and from the ear flipped the knife outward to stick into the ground. Then arms and hands were changed, and the move was repeated.

Ninth play: the knife was held by the thumb and forefinger, handle down, by the blade tip, with the blade tip touching the chin; then it was flung out by a head and body movement carrying the knife into a counterclockwise half-circle; next it was released, point downward, to plunge into the earth. The play was repeated with the knife tip held, in turn, to the mouth, the nose, each eye, and the forehead.

Tenth play: the knife tip was held by the right hand (thumb and forefinger), and the knife was thrown over the left shoulder to stick into the earth behind the thrower. This move was repeated with the left hand over the right shoulder.

Eleventh play (called "bucket in the well"): a circle was formed with the thumb and the forefinger of the left hand, and the knife handle was held (blade down) by the right thumb and forefinger and dropped through the circle (or hole). Then the thumb and middle finger formed a second "well" to drop the "bucket" into, then the thumb and ring finger, and last, the thumb and little finger.

Twelfth play: the shorter blade was half-opened to form a right angle with the long blade. The knife was then placed on the ground, blades down, and was pushed gently until the blade tips sank into the earth and anchored the knife to stand alone. The player, kneeling, gave the knife handle a whack upward and forward, sending the knife rotating through the air to land—and with good luck and skill—to stick into the ground, handle up, some ten to fifteen feet distant.

The first player to accomplish all twelve plays was the winner. He would then rule that all losers must "root the peg," or he could allow the other players to play the game out until only one peg rooter remained. A small sturdy stick or twig was driven into the ground (with a knife handle as a hammer) so far that the rooter (required to remove it with his teeth—his hands behind him) got a mouthful of dirt in the process.

Two people played. They drew a circle on the ground with a knife and cut it in two. This was the pie, or territory, depending on the name of the game. Each person took turns throwing his knife at the other person's half. If the knife stuck point-first in the other person's half, the pie was sliced in line with the knife blade, and the knife thrower took the smaller portion and threw the knife again. He kept throwing as long as the knife would stick blade-first into the ground. If he cut the other person's property down

Slicing the Pie, or Territory
by
Charles B. Martin

Slicing the Pie, or Territory.

to an "island," he could win it by the next three throws, if they all stuck in the ground. The person to gain all of the circle won. If he missed (i.e., his knife landed in the wrong territory or failed to stick), he lost his turn and the other person got to try.

Another Territory Game
by
Jack C. Phipps

Territory consisted of a ring about eight feet in diameter divided into as many pie slices as there were participants. The sequence of play was determined by how near each contestant stuck the knife to a line, much like lagging in marbles. The first player would stick his knife from a standing position into an adjacent territory, dividing that territory at the angle at which the blade stuck into the ground. The stickee would usually choose the larger segment of the division, and the sticker would add the unselected portion to his territory. The knife was passed on when a participant failed to stick it into the ground or missed a target territory. A player was eliminated when he could no longer place his foot into his remaining territory. The winner was the participant who acquired all the territory, the entire eight-foot ring.

Root the Peg
by
Copeland Pass

You take a knife with two blades in it, a little blade and a big blade, both opening from the same end, and you open the big blade straight down and the little blade straight out perpendicular to the handle.

You put your big blade into the ground at an angle and you flip your knife with a finger under the handle. The way the knife lands and sticks determines the score. If it falls with the big blade sticking in the ground, it counts one hundred points. If it falls with only the small blade sticking and the handle and big blade clear of the ground, it counts seventy-five points. If it falls with both blades sticking and the handle clear, it counts fifty points. And if the small blade sticks and the butt of the knife touches the ground, it counts twenty-five points. If you don't stick the knife, you lose your time. Five hundred points is a game.

If you lose, you take your knife and sharpen a match stem about an inch long. You stick it into the ground, and the winner takes his knife handle and shuts his eyes and hits the match stem three licks. The loser has to use his teeth and root the peg.

Root the Peg.

XIV

Rhythm Games

Children come into the world naturally—genetically—prepared to respond to rhythmical beats and chants. In addition to having ancestors of primeval antiquity who were naturally selected to survive on the basis of an active metronomic gene, a child also is newly arrived from nine months in a mother's womb where it listened to and was comforted by the steady tha-thump, tha-thump of the mother's heartbeat in continual and regular iambic feet. It is no wonder, then, that most children respond unrestrainedly to marches and chants and start bobbing to the beat as soon as they can stand. Children are rhythmically bounced, counted, and clapped before they can be talked to with any hope of getting a response. To a steady beat they ride cockhorses, count piggies, and pat cakes. When they

are old enough to play their own games, they count out, bounce balls, play hand games, and jump rope to beats that are as natural as their genetic history and maternal conditioning.

The rhythmical activities in this chapter—clapping games and rope jumping—are not really games, in the sense that games involve competition with others, but these activities do qualify if one stretches the definition of games to competing with one's self. The child competes with the beat, trying to keep his concentration and not miss a coordinated slap of the hands or swing of the rope. (For another discussion of both pastimes, see Knapp and Knapp, 112–37.)

Clapping Games
by Maggie Abernethy Duffin

How far back rhythm games actually go, I don't know. Without the need for any materials but a song and two pairs of hands, a game like Pease Porridge Hot or Pat-a-Cake could be played anywhere anytime. In *The Color Purple*, a movie about southern blacks in the early 1900s, two of the characters played a rhythm game as children. When meeting thirty or forty years later, they rebonded themselves by playing the game. Rikki Lee Jones, a contemporary singer, uses part of a rhythm game chant in her song "Danny's All Star Joint."

Rhythm games are exercises that develop a great deal of hand-eye coordination. The children that play the games, however, are more interested in the fun of the game than a purpose. Some of my day-care class at Discovery Playhouse in Nacogdoches, Texas, can play these simple games quite well at the early age of five. Sixth and seventh graders play with amazing speed and complexity. I suppose that by the time one reaches high school these games are considered a bit childish. I haven't found any that age that admit to playing rhythm games.

Basically, a rhythm game is played with a series of pat-a-cake slaps. Two children get together and clap and slap hands together to the beat of a song or chant.

The easiest pattern begins with two participants slapping both hands palms down on their own knees. Then both clap their own hands together. With palms facing outwards, they slap the other one's palms in sort of a double "high five" gesture. Each participant then slaps his or her hands together again. They repeat all of the steps over again until the end of the chant.

As players become better the speed increases as well as the complexity of the slaps, all variations of the basic pattern. Every other movement is a clap of the hands. Alternate hands are slapped together singularly as well as both hands of the players simultaneously. In some chants that use descriptions, gestures are used.

Have you ever, ever, ever in your long-legged life
Seen a long-legged sailor
And his long-legged wife?

When the phrase "long-legged" is sung the players throw out their arms to indicate just how long these legs are. In the following verse, when it is a short-legged sailor, the hands are held close together, showing how short the legs are. When the sailor becomes bowlegged the arms curve outward to indicate the bowedness. Some play it by bowing the legs out instead, depending on who taught them or how their imaginations run.

When I was going around to different schools asking children to show me some of their rhythm games, I ran into several children I had worked with at day-care centers. These children at first were totally embarrassed that their after-school teacher was there and might single them out. After getting over the first case of red face and giggles they, along with the rest of the class, wanted to teach me. I remembered some of the steps and songs from school and Girl Scouts but was feeling uncoordinated by the time the lessons were through.

I did have the good fortune to be teaching some of these children at the time, and they deigned to tutor me after school in my class. Melissa, aged ten, and Vonda, aged eight, showed me a clap I had not seen before. It was done by placing both hands palms together and hitting against the backs of the others' hands similarly placed. That started the chant "1418 Alligator Street." It was also used as a counting-out game.

My mama, your mama
Lives across the street,
1418 Alligator Street.
Every night they have a fight
And this is what they say:
"Boys are rotten, made out of cotton.
Girls are sexy, made out of Pepsi."
Icka backa soda cracker
Icka backa boo
Icka backa soda cracker
Out goes you.

This next chant and game is one that my father remembers as a song from his childhood, that I remember from my childhood, and that was brought to mind again by seven-year-old Brooks Starr Martin, one of the little boys in my after-school class.

Say say oh playmate,
Come out and play with me,
And bring your dollies three,
Climb up my apple tree.
Look down my rain barrel,
Slide down my cellar door,
And we'll be jolly friends
Forever more.

Three sisters work in the same day-care center I do. In the summer of 1987 one of their nieces spent a few weeks with my class and filled in many gaps in my repertoire of chants. These next three verses are from Keisha, nine years old, who has a vast store of knowledge concerning rhythm games. These three are done with the basic clapping pattern described earlier.

Uno dos y eska
Said uh east uh west uh
I met my boyfriend at the candy store.
He bought me candy, he bought me cake,
He brought me home with a bellyache.
Mama, Mama, I'm so sick;
Call the doctor quick, quick, quick.
Doctor, doctor, will I die?
Count to five; I will be alive.
1-2-3-4-5
I'M ALIVE! YAY!

Finding out who likes whom is pretty big stuff in the early grades. The following is not exactly a surefire method but gives material for teasing.

Ice cream. Soda water. Lemonade.
Tell me the initials of your boyfriend's name.

The alphabet is then run through until a mistake is made in the clapping, that letter supposedly being the initial of the boyfriend.

Want to ride a bull, bull too black.
Want my money back.
So I went downtown, saw Mr. Brown.
He gave me a nickel so I bought me a pickle.
Pickle was sour so I bought me a flower.
Flower was dead so took it instead.

One can pick up songs and games from anywhere if the ears are kept open. This rhyme was being chanted by a young black girl about eight years old on the Lake Nacogdoches beach one hot August weekend.

Psycho-dilly.
Your mama eats chili.
Bet you five dollars
She'll knock you silly.

Discovery Playhouse was one of my major sources for songs and games. The children had picked up numerous chants from school, Girl Scouts, Cub Scouts, and neighborhood friends and brought them in to us.

Miss Susie had a steamboat.
The steamboat had a bell.
Miss Susie went to heaven;
The steamboat went to—

Hello, operator, get me number nine.
If you disconnect me
I'll kick you in the—

Behind the 'frigerator
There was a piece of glass.
Mary sat upon it and cut her little—

Ask me no more questions
I'll tell you no more lies.
The cows are in the pasture
Making chocolate pies.

The more off-color the chants are the more widely known they are, so it seems. My friends and I sang the above rhyme when we were kids and thought how daring we were. The next two versions of a similar chant brought peals of laughter from

Brandon and Shean, five years old, of Discovery Playhouse, and Lacy, a second-grader from Nettie Marshall.

> Miss Polly had a dolly;
> She named him Tiny Tim.
> She threw him in the bathtub
> To see if he could swim.
> He drank up all the water;
> He ate up all the soap.
> He tried to swallow the bathtub
> But it wouldn't go down his throat.
> Quick call the doctor.
> Quick call the nurse.
> Quick call the lady with the alligator purse.
> I don't want the doctor.
> I don't want the nurse.
> I don't want the lady with the alligator purse.
>
> Miss Lucy had a baby;
> She named it Tiny Tim.
> She put it in the toilet bowl
> To see if it could swim.
> He swam to the bottom;
> He swam to the top.
> Miss Lucy got so excited
> She flushed him down the pot.

Tracy and Bailey, second and fourth graders respectively, were part of a threesome that could slap out the rhythms at amazing speeds. They donated this next one, but the handwork that goes along with it defies transcribing into words.

> Apples on a stick
> Just make me sick.
> Makes my tummy go 2-4-6.
> Not because I'm hungry.
> Not because I'm clean.
> Just because I kissed a boy
> Behind the magazine.
> Hey, girls, wanna have fun?
> Here comes [name] with his pants undone.
> He can wibble,
> He can wobble,
> He can do the splits.
> But I bet you five dollars that
> He can't do this.
> Close your eyes and count to ten.
> 1-2-3-4-5-6-7-8-9-10.
> If I say it again he'll be a fat hen.
> 1-2-3-4-5-6-7-8-9-10.
> He's a big fat hen.

Vonda, nine years old, was the third member of the above-mentioned group. She taught the other two this rhyme and a

hand pattern to go along with it. The rhyme was all that I could ever do with any accuracy.

> Ronald McDonald
> Biscuit biscuit
> Ronald McDonald
> Biscuit biscuit
> Oo shoo shi wawa a biscuit
> I've got a boyfriend a biscuit
> He's such a sweety a biscuit
> Just like a cherry treaty a biscuit
> Ice cream soda water cherry on top
> Ice cream soda water cherry on bottom
> Down down baby down by the ocean
> Sweet sweet baby I'll never let you go
> Just because I kissed a boy doesn't mean I love him
> So shimmy shimmy coca water
> Shimmy shimmy bang
> Shimmy shimmy coca water
> Shimmy shimmy bang
> Ice cream soda water lemonade
> Tell me my boyfriend's fairest in the lane
> Not 'cause he's dirty, not 'cause he's clean
> Just 'cause I kissed him behind the magazine.
> Hey girls wanna have fun? [etc.]

Ms. Cheryl Tucker, from Christ Episcopal School, and her fourth-grade class gave me the next two rhymes. The school was extremely helpful. They stopped the regular lessons and just let me have their class for as long as I needed. Several of the songs were repeats of earlier ones I had gathered, but the following were songs I had not heard before.

Eeeny meanie popsa deanie
Ooh pop popsa deanie
Education liberation
I love you
Tutti Fruiti
Down Down Baby
Down by the roller coaster
Sweet Sweet Baby
No place to go
Shamrock Shamrock
Shimmy Shimmy coco pop
Caught you with your boyfriend
Naughty Naughty
Want a piece of candy
Greedy greedy
Don't do the dishes
Lazy lazy
Jumped out the window
Crazy crazy
Eeenie meanie popsa deanie
Ooh pop popsa deanie
Fascination generation
I love you
Tutti Fruiti

This next is an example of the slightly risque subjects broached in these chanting games. It took the girls singing it three times to get through the second verse.

When Pebbles was a baby, a baby, a baby,
When Pebbles was a baby
She went like this;
Wah wah, give me a sucker, two plus two is four.
When Pebbles was a teenager, a teenager, a teenager,
When Pebbles was a teenager

She went like this;
Wah wah, give me a sucker, two plus two is four.
Ooh ah I lost my bra, I lost it in my boyfriend's car.
[When Pebbles was a mother/Look at all these children]
[When Pebbles was a grandmother/Oh my aching back]
[When Pebbles was a ghost/1-2-3-4-5-6-7-8-9-10-Boo!]

This next game involves the whole body in the rhythmic pattern of the song. A second-grade student from Nettie Marshall by the name of Reanetteress taught all of us this one.

Sweet, sweet baby,
I'll never let you go.
Baby down the roller coaster,
Baby down the roller coaster,
Grandma, Grandma sick in bed,
Called for the doctor,
The doctor said:
Get in the rhythm of the head. Ding dong. [Head bends once
    left, once right.]
Get in the rhythm of the head. Ding dong. [Head bends once
    left, once right.]
Get in the rhythm of the feet. Ding dong. [Stamp left foot once,
    right foot once.]
Get in the rhythm of the feet. Ding dong. [Stamp left foot once,
    right foot once.]
Get in the rhythm of the hands. Ding Dong. [Clap twice.]
Get in the rhythm of the hands. Ding Dong. [Clap twice.]
Get together what you find.
Ding dong [Head bends left then right six times.]
Ding dong [Stamp feet six times.]
Ding dong [Clap hands six times.]

Tracey is one of my day-care center friends who was also enrolled at Nettie Marshall Elementary school in the second grade during the fall of 1987. She and her friend Lacy, also in the second grade there, played these next two songs for me until I got it all down on paper.

Miss Susie, Miss Susie,
Miss Susie from Alabama,
Sitting in a rocker,
Eating Betty Crocker,
Watching that clock go
Tick tock tick tock anamanama
Tick tock tick tock anamanama
A-B-C-D-E-F-G
Wash that stuff right off your knees
Mushicalla mushicalla mushicalla
FREEZE!

Miss Rita, Miss Rita,
Miss Rita from Pasadena,
Sitting in a rocker,
Eating Betty Crocker,
Watching that clock go tick tock

Tick tock namanamanama
Tick tock namanamanama
Tick tock namanamanama
Oh my goodness, three o'clock,
Time for the kids to get out of school.

Jameshia was another friend in Tracey and Lacy's class. She was so shy that I nearly didn't hear the words over the handclapping.

Mama's having a baby;
Daddy's going crazy.
If it's a boy I'll give it a toy.
If it's a girl I'll give it a curl.
Roll it up in toilet paper
Singing lalala
What's it gonna be?
A boy, a girl?
A boy, a girl?
I cannot tell.

When I visited the fifth-grade class at Christ Episcopal, it was something like Talent Night. All the girls got up and sang and clapped together. They were really good.

Three sailors went to I I I
To see what they could I I I
But all that they could I I I
Was the bottom of the deep-blue I I I.
Three sailors went to C C C
To see what they could C C C
But all that they could C C C
Was the bottom of the deep-blue C C C.
Three sailors went to U U U
To see what they could U U U
But all that they could U U U
Was the bottom of the deep-blue U U U.
Three sailors went to I C U
To see what they could I C U
But all that they could I C U
Was the bottom of the deep-blue I C U.

I called a friend of mine to help me remember the words to this next one. I believe it may go back as far as the 1920s, to an old Tin Pan Alley song. The rhythm game is a later addition that has kept the song alive with the younger generation. When we were growing up it was very popular among the Girl Scouts I knew. The further along in the song one gets the faster the hand movements are. One slaps the thighs twice then claps twice. The third movement involves first shuffling the right hand over the left twice then the left hand over the right. The next step is rather hard to explain. The hands are held at the shoulders and the fingers are brought together at the tips, kind of like making shadow birds in front of a screen projector. This is done twice right above the shoulders then the arms are lifted a little higher and it is repeated once. Try and follow that!

> Please play for me that sweet melody
> Called the doodley do, doodley do.
> I like the rest but the part I like best
> Is the doodley do, doodley do.
> Simplest thing there isn't much to it.
> You don't have to sing, just doodley do it.
> I like it so, wherever I go
> I just doodley doodley do.
> Come on and waddley acha waddley acha,
> Waddley oh, waddley oh.
> Waddley acha, waddley acha.
> Waddley oh, waddley oh.
> Simplest thing there isn't much to it,
> You don't have to sing, just doodley do it.
> I like it so, wherever I go
> I doodley doodley do. Woo woo.

Rhythm games, or clapping/slapping patterns done to the beat of a song or chant, can be done by one's self, but they lose a lot of the fun if not done with others. Usually the simpler games are done by children around kindergarten age, with the games growing more complicated as the children get older. The speed increases with coordination. It is fascinating to watch a group of children going ninety miles an hour and never missing a beat.

Roundup clapping game (Richard S. Orton).

◆ Violet Sone's following article on jump-rope rhymes is two generations old, but I haven't found any significant additions to her repertoire. Children are still jumping rope to rhythmical chants, and some physical education departments have turned rope jumping into an art seldom found outside a boxers' gym. It is a skill that has been rejuvenated during our present fitness craze. Rope jumping usually stops during the junior high years as glands activate and new interests appear, but there was a time when schoolyard rope jumping in the fifth and sixth grades was a vigorous—and dangerous—activity, an exacting sport that challenged the most vigorous boys and girls. No sweet chants were sung. The rope was swung in a vicious cutting circle, and only the most agile and energetic could get in and get out without getting whapped. Only the practiced athletes survived with a hot-pepper, high-water, double-rope swing.

Rope-Jumping Rhymes

by Violet West Sone

When mesquite trees put out their leaves, and boys bring out their marbles and girls their skipping ropes—why, it's spring in Texas. In Rockport School, way down South on the Gulf, the skipping ropes are always much in evidence. Lithe young figures with nimble feet dance hot pepper, high water, rock the cradle, and double rope all over the sidewalks. But the most interesting part of the procedure is the chanting of rhymes in time to the regular swing of the rope. Some of these rhymes are adaptations of familiar verses, but most of them show evidence of recent composition and of the fertility of childish imagination. One of the familiar ones used is:

> "Mother, Mother, I am sick,
> Call the doctor quick, quick, quick!"
> "Doctor, Doctor, will I die?"
> "Yes, my darling, bye and bye."
> "How many hours will I live?"
> One, two, three, four, five, . . .

And so on the counting goes until the nimble feet miss. This rhyme is also said with: "How many hearses will I have?" instead of "How many hours will I live?" Another familiar one is:

> One, two, three, four, five, six, seven,
> All good children go to heaven.
> All the rest go down below
> To eat supper with Old Black Joe.
> How many bad ones go below?
> One, two, three, four, five, . . .

The old button-counting rhymes have been taken over by the rope jumpers:

Learning to jump rope (Marvin Gorley).

> What shall I be when I grow up?
> Rich man, poor man, beggar man, thief,
> Doctor, lawyer, merchant, chief,
> Tinker, tailor, cowboy, sailor,
> Butcher, baker, music maker, . . .

A machine-age supplement goes:

> What shall I drive when I grow up?
> Lincoln, Chrysler, Chevrolet, Ford, . . .

Of course, the name the jumper misses on answers the question. Usually the girl says, "Who shall I marry when I grow up?" instead of, "What shall I be?" Then when that important question is settled, the jumper says:

> What shall I wear on my wedding day?
> Silk, satin, calico, rags, silk, satin, . . .

A rhyme peculiarly suited to the Rockport region is:

> Down by the ocean,
> Down by the sea
> Johnny broke a bottle
> And he blamed it on me.

I told Ma, Ma told Pa,
Johnny got a lickin'
And a Haw! Haw! Haw!
How many lickin's did he get?
One, two, three, four, five, . . .

A number of these counting rhymes are based on the love theme, such as:

Cinderella, dressed in yellow,
Went upstairs to kiss her fellow.
How many kisses did she get?
One, two, three, four, five, . . .

Another version of the Cinderella rhyme is:

Cinderella, dressed in yellow,
Went downtown to buy an umbrella.
On the way she met her beau,
Who took her to a ten-cent show.
How many kisses did she get?
One, two, three, four, five, . . .

The same theme with a different setting is used:

Down in the meadow where the green grass grows
There sat Rosemary sweet as a rose.
Up jumped Johnny, and he kissed her on the cheek.
How many kisses did she get right quick?
One, two, three, four, five, . . .

Instead of using "Johnny" and "Rosemary" every time, the children supply the names of the jumper and her boyfriend.

Jumping the long rope (Richard S. Orton).

Another amusing rhyme is:

> My mother is a butcher,
> My father cuts the meat,
> I'm a little hotdog
> Running down the street.
> Hot many hot dogs do I sell?
> One, two, three, four, . . .

Not all the rope-jumping rhymes are counting rhymes. Some use letters of the alphabet:

> Ice cream soda, Delaware Punch,
> Spell the initials of my honey-bunch:
> A, B, C, D, E, . . .

And so on down the alphabet. The letter the jumper misses on is the initial of the best beloved. If she fails to miss on the first round, she starts off with A again, and the speed of the rope is increased. Sometimes the letters of the alphabet are said without the preliminary "Ice cream soda," etc. Then when the initial is determined by a miss, the jumper continues with "Yes, no, maybe so, certainly, yes, no, maybe so," etc., to determine whether he loves her.

All the rhymes mentioned so far can be jumped with either a skipping rope or a long rope. The "rock the cradle" variety requires a long rope. The throwers swing the rope back and forth instead of over for this one:

> Grace, Grace, dressed in lace,
> Went upstairs to powder her face,
> How many boxes did she use?
> One, two, three, four, five, . . .

A combination of "rock the cradle" and "over" is used for this one:

> Blue bells, cockle shells,
> E-ve, I-ve, over.
> I like coffee, I like tea,
> I like the boys, and the boys like me.
> Yes, no, maybe so, yes, no, maybe so, . . .

The word *over* is the signal for the throwers to stop rocking the cradle and to throw the rope over.

Hot pepper is always a favorite with jumpers. A good way to get started off is to say:

> Mable, Mable, set the table,
> Don't forget the RED HOT PEPPER!

The chant comes in on regular cadence rope swinging, but as soon as the swinger shouts, "RED HOT PEPPER!" the swingers accelerate the speed.

It is no mean accomplishment to jump "double rope." The throwers keep two long ropes going at once, throwing one with the left hand and the other with the right. The proficient jumper learns not only to keep her feet clear of both ropes but also to enter and run out at will, either "front door" or "back door," and to jump "high water," in which the rope is not allowed to touch the ground.

Most attractive of all are the action or gesture rhymes jumped with the long rope. The words suggest to the jumper what to do:

Jumping hot peppers (Richard S. Orton).

Amos and Andy, sugar and candy,
    I pop in.
Amos and Andy, sugar and candy,
    I pop down.
Amos and Andy, sugar and candy,
    I pop up.
Amos and Andy, sugar and candy,
    I pop out.
Amos and Andy, sugar and candy,
    I pop through.

This is the most interesting action rhyme of them all:

Shirley Temple went to France
To teach the ladies how to dance.
This is the dance she taught them first:
Heel, toe, around we go,
Heel, toe, around we go,
Salute to the Captain, bow to the King,
Make a dirty face at the ugly old Queen.

A similar action rhyme is:

Last night and the night before
Twenty-four robbers knocked at my door.
I asked them what they wanted,
And this is what they said:
"Spanish dancer, do the split,
Spanish dancer, show your shoe,
Spanish dancer, that will do."

The first rhyme that I ever saw jumped was "Teddy-Bear."
There are several versions of this rhyme, one of which is:

Teddy-Bear, Teddy-Bear,
Turn around.
Teddy-Bear, Teddy-Bear,
Touch the ground.
Teddy-Bear, Teddy-Bear,
Show your shoe.
Teddy-Bear, Teddy-Bear,
Skit, skat, skiddoo!

And the jumper runs out. She may return with this version:

Teddy-Bear, Teddy-Bear,
Go upstairs.
Teddy-Bear, Teddy-Bear,
Say your prayers.
Teddy-Bear, Teddy-Bear,
Turn out the light.
Teddy-Bear, Teddy-Bear,
Say Goodnight.

XV

Play-Party Games and Songs

Bleakwood was a sawmill town near Thicketty Creek in Newton County. It was born in a yellow pine forest, grew up around a post office and a schoolhouse, and died in 1943 when the pine forest was a field of stumps. But for a few years it was home to the men who hauled and sawed the logs and the women who put the biscuits and sawmill gravy on the table and the children who were born and raised to the sound of mill whistles. Then the timber was gone, the mill was closed down in 1942, and the families departed, the young men to the Big War and the old ones to the shipyards.

Twenty years later the kids came back with their own kids to see each other and the woods grown up again. They met in the old school gym, they ate and laughed and hugged each other—and they had a play-party, or a Josie party, as it is frequently called in East Texas.

The play-party was a tradition of their growing up. It was a song-accompanied dance and was practiced either because musicians were scarce or because the religious beliefs of the area did not permit fiddles and dancing. But even those fundamentalists who believed the fiddle was the devil's instrument and dancing was the heathen's pastime had the urge to respond in measured steps to the rhythms and sounds of music, so they rationalized with the Josie party. The Josie party was technically not a dance; it was a game or a march. The music was provided by some leather-lunged singer who could beller out the verses above the

noise of the crowd, and the players joined in on choruses. They marched in rings and reels but seldom in squares, and under the strictest rules they swung their partners by the hand, never by the waist. The latter sort of contact was too much like touching bodies.

These East Texans from Bleakwood started the Josie after a picnic supper. A father-type character in a flannel shirt with a tie stood on a chair and slowly sang their favorite starter, "Coffee Grows on White Oak Trees":

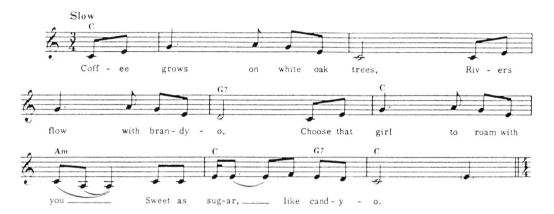

And a big ring made up of three generations began slowly turning to the right. The two lead couples peeled off and joined hands in the middle of the ring and were swinging when the leader reached the chorus. Everybody sang the chorus, speeding the tempo, moving from a walk to a skip to almost a run:

Somebody hollered, "Domino!" at the end of the chorus, and the next two couples took the swingers' place, and the circle marched again as the leader started a second verse, slow like the first. He sang:

Coffee grows in a white oak stump,

and someone was thinking about the rich East sandy loam where the white oaks grew and where their ancestor-settlers had cleared the ground to plant their first crops.

Rivers flow with sugar lumps;

Their old grandads had come to Texas with a long hope in sweet rivers flowing through a wealthy land. And they brought women with them who were bred strong for the course.

> Choose that girl that you love so,
> Sweet as sugar like candy-o.

They had come and they had survived—and their children had survived, and their children's children—and they sang their songs of celebration.

> Hold my mule while I dance Josie,
> Scat the cat and let's dance Josie,
> Clear the floor and we'll all dance Josie,
> Hello, Susie Brown.

They met and mixed and held each other's hands. They marched together to the same beat to songs they had known all their play-party lives. They were bonded again into the comfort and warmth of a familiar society.

They "Shot the Buffalo," sang "Joe Clark" and "Dan Tucker," and reeled up and down the line to "Weevily Wheat." They danced—really, they marched—late into the night, went to church the next morning, and were back in Houston or Beaumont or wherever Sunday evening, still wondering how all those years had passed so quickly.

That reunion at Bleakwood was years ago, and I did not hear of a play-party again until I discovered that Kenneth Munson had revived the tradition in San Marcos. He taught the songs and steps to a church group of young people, and they got so good that they were invited to demonstrate this old song-and-dance tradition at the Texas Folklife Festival in San Antonio.

Play-Party Songs of Hope, Texas
by Kenneth Munson

Hope, Texas, and hundreds of other small rural communities all over America were blessed in frontier days with a form of entertainment called "play-parties." These play-parties were a type of dancing but could not be called that. Dancing was forbidden. Circuit-riding preachers condemned it as a sin, and the young people of these settlements were not allowed to go to the dance halls that were being operated in predominantly Catholic villages. Occasionally, Saturday night dances ended in drunken brawls, and this was condemned by the circuit-riding preachers also.

With no social life or entertainment on Saturday night the young people soon learned to meet at a neighbor's house and provide their own. Singing the songs they could remember was fine. This could include folk songs, or popular ballads, or even some songs that included square-dance calls. Some of these songs were not recalled accurately, but changing them or adding verses of their own was part of the fun.

After a few such sessions, groups began to think of "games" that could be used with some of the songs. These games were sometimes half-remembered dances. By singing certain songs and playing some of these games they could improvise movements or steps to go with them and have lots of fun singing and swinging. No one condemned them for this until instrumental music was added. The old folks drew the line there. When a fiddle and guitar were used, it was no longer a game; it was dancing, and that was a sin.

To meet at a neighbor's house to sing and swing without instrumental music soon became acceptable. They were not dancing. They were singing and playing games, and finally this activity was given a name, a "play-party." Play-parties spread from place to place and from generation to generation but were changed in the

Students at Hope School, 1925. The second boy from the left on the second row is Kenneth Munson.

process. Songs, verses, and games were added. Some were forgotten. Soon no two community parties were identical, but the surprising part is that so many were similar.

Play-parties were a vital part of rural life during the first four decades of the twentieth century. In fact, most of the entertainment for rural young people during the Roaring Twenties came from them. This lasted during the Depression years but died out and went into oblivion during or soon after World War II. Seemingly, they were resurrected in one place only—Hope, Texas. Hope, like other rural settlements, was eventually invaded by "civilization," but let us examine its development before telling of its demise and of the ending of play-parties in Texas.

Before 1836, while Texas still belonged to Mexico, a man whose last name was Hope started an Indian trading post on the banks of Little Brushy Creek. This was on the Coastal Plains and between the (at that time) nonexistent towns of Victoria and Hallettsville. Hope remained a trading post during the years of the Republic of Texas and later became the first stop for the stagecoach going north from Victoria and the last stop going south.

Before the Civil War, a general merchandise store was built about three miles north of the trading post with a post office in it. Since the mail was brought from Victoria on the stagecoach, this stop was designated as the Hope Post Office. The surrounding area became known as the Hope Community.

In 1876, a two-story frame building was constructed for the Masonic Lodge upstairs and the Methodist Church downstairs. Later, in 1899, the building in use today as the Methodist Church was constructed about one hundred yards south of the older building. The downstairs part of the Masonic Lodge became the Hope School. About 1894, the Baptist Church was built north of the lodge and the cotton gin across the road from the Hope Store.

These buildings—the Hope Store, the cotton gin, a blacksmith shop, two churches, and a school with the Masonic Lodge upstairs—remained the buildings involved in life at Hope until the 1920s. During the Roaring Twenties another store, another blacksmith shop, and an ice cream parlor were added.

It was during the Roaring Twenties that Hope was most active as a community. Most families replaced their buggies with cars, which could be driven the twelve miles over mud roads to Yoakum, but wagons continued in use for gathering corn, hauling cotton, and transporting larger groups.

By 1927, many women had "bobbed" hair. Flapper days were in full swing. Skirts were worn above the knees. Being able to dance the Charleston was the mark of an up-to-date flapper. Towns such as Yoakum and Hallettsville had "moving picture shows" that became "talkies" in the next few years, and one radio came into use at Hope.

As a rule during the flapper days, the teenagers at Hope were able to talk someone into "giving a party" on Saturday night. Word spread quickly and no invitation was necessary to attend. Boys could bring girlfriends, but girls or boys could attend without a partner—they just came "dolled up" in their Sunday best.

If the crowd was too large for the house, kerosene lanterns could be hung from tree limbs and the party continued outside. Refreshments might be served but were not required. After an hour of games, the parties usually stopped for a "breather." Quiet games such as Spin the Bottle, or Heavy, Heavy Hangs Over Your Head, or Knock-Knock, or Fruit Basket, Turn Over were played. Occasionally an older man would dance a jig, and at one party, the Charleston was demonstrated before the old folks had a chance to prevent it.

During the flapper days, this author was a teenager and very much involved in the Hope play-parties. The songs reproduced here were the ones used at that time. Each song had a certain game to be used with it. There were twelve games to go with the twenty-six songs noted in this publication. However, the simplest game was used (with minor variations) with thirteen different songs. This section will explain each game, how it was played, and how it was used with certain songs.

The simplest game, the one used with thirteen songs, consisted of (1) a promenade, (2) a right and left, and (3) a full swing right and left. What does that mean, for the uninitiated? For most songs, the promenade meant that each boy began with his partner on his left. They held hands between them with right hand to right hand over left hand to left. They marched that way counterclockwise about one step behind the couple ahead. This created a circle with boys on the outside and girls on the inside.

At the proper time in the song (the beginning of the second verse in most of them) left hands were dropped and the boy swung his partner in front of him to the outside with his right hand. This left her facing in the opposite direction and ready to catch left hands with the boy behind her partner. Boys continued forward and the girls went clockwise swinging right and left until the partners met on the opposite side of the ring.

As partners met, they hooked arms at the elbow and swung a full circle. When this circle was complete they were in position to hook the opposite arm with the next person and swing a full circle in the opposite direction. This continued until all partners were together again or until all verses of the song had been sung.

Instead of hooking arms for the full-circle swing some boys preferred to grab both of the girl's arms slightly below the shoulders and swing. Also, fancy footwork could be used for the promenade, for the right and left, and for the full swing right and left with only one requirement—keep in step with the singing.

The game described above of (1) promenade, (2) right and left, and (3) full-circle swing right and left was used with the following thirteen songs: "Old Joe Clark," "I Sent My Brown Jug Down to Town," "Railroad, Steamboat," "Shoo, Shoo Fly," "Walking on the Green Grass," "Rowser," "She'll be Comin' Around the Mountain," "Cindy," "Buffalo Gals," "Jingle Joe," "All Dig Taters," "Dance Josie," and "Skip to My Lou."

(Kenneth Munson)

OLD JOE CLARK

Old Joe Clark is dead an' gone! I hope he's do-in' well. He

made me wear the ball and chain. It made my an-kle swell.

Refrain

A- round an' a- round Old Joe Clark! A- round an a-round I say. A

round an a- round Old Joe Clark! I ain't got long to stay.

2. If you see that gal of mine,
   Just tell her if you please,
   Before she goes to roll that dough
   To roll them dirty sleeves.

3. Went upon a mountain top,
   Gave my horn a blow,
   Thought I heard a pretty girl say,
   "Yonder comes my beau."

4. Went up to Old Joe's house,
   Found him sick in bed,
   Ran my finger down his throat
   And pulled out a loaf of bread.

5. Met a possum in th' road,
   Told him, "Take a tree."
   He turned around and whipped my dog
   And bristled up at me.

6. Wish I was in heaven,
   Sittin' on a rail,
   Sweet potato in my hand
   And a possum by the tail.

I SENT MY BROWN JUG DOWN TO TOWN

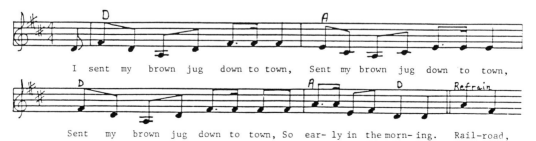

I sent my brown jug down to town, Sent my brown jug down to town,

Sent my brown jug down to town, So ear- ly in the morn- ing. Rail-road,

See "Railroad, Steamboat" for a refrain.

RAILROAD, STEAMBOAT

1. Rail-road steam-boat en-gine on the track. I lost my true lov-er and I

don't want her back. Oh she's gone, gone, gone. Let her go, go, go, Oh she's

gone, gone, gone to her last fare ye well. 2. Rail - road, steam - boat,

riv-er and ca-nal. Yon- der comes a suck-er and he's got my gal.

SHOO, SHOO FLY

Shoo, shoo fly don't you both-er me. Shoo, shoo fly don't you both-er me.

Shoo, shoo fly don't you both-er me for I be-long to some-bod-y. I

feel, feel, feel, I feel like a morn-in' star. I feel, feel, feel, I

feel like a morn-in star. I feel, feel, feel, I feel like a morn-in star. And its

WALKIN' ON THE GREEN GRASS

Walk- in' on the green grass, dust, dust, dust. Come on you pret-ty.

fair maids and walk a-long with us. Pret-ty and as fair as I take you for to

be, Gim- me hold your lit-tle white hand, I'll lead you cross the sea.

O'er the world, Chase the squirrel. My true love's a pret- ty lit-tle girl.

O'er the world, Chase the squirrel. My true love's a dan- dy.

Bin-go he loves but- ter and cheese. Bin- go he loves brand - y.

Cause I love to kiss the girls Be- cause they come so han- dy.

ROWSER

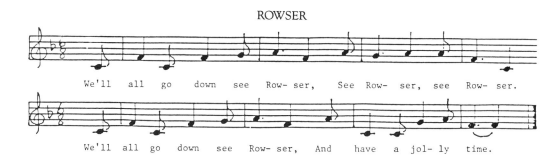

We'll all go down see Row- ser, See Row- ser, see Row- ser.

We'll all go down see Row- ser, And have a jol- ly time.

2. Rowser is a jolly boy, Rowser is a jolly boy, Rowser . . . . and has a jolly time.

SHE'LL BE COMIN' AROUND THE MOUNTAIN

2. She'll be drivin' six white horses when she comes.
3. We will kill the old red rooster when she comes.
4. We will have chicken and dumplin's when she comes.

This following refrain was used to extend the song above and also
"New River Train":

CINDY

I wish I was an ap-ple A- hang-in' on a tree, And ev'- ry time my sweet-heart passed, She'd take a bite of me, Git a-long home, Cin- dy, Cin- dy. Git a- long home, Cin -dy, Cin -dy. Git a- long home, Cin -dy, Cin -dy. I'll mar -ry you some - time.

BUFFALO GALS

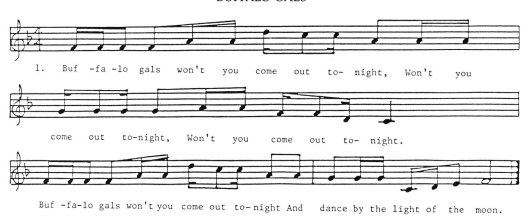

1. Buf -fa -lo gals won't you come out to- night, Won't you come out to-night, Won't you come out to- night. Buf -fa-lo gals won't you come out to- night And dance by the light of the moon.

2. Danced with a gal with a hole in her stockin'.
   Her knees kept a'knockin' and her toes kept a'rockin'.
   I danced with a gal with a hole in her stockin'.
   As we danced by the light of the moon.

JINGLE JOE

Round and round and a-round we go. Skip one win-dow, ty-de-o.

Skip two win-dows, ty-de-o, We all go jin-gle, jin-gle Joe.

Jin-gle, jin-gle, jin-gle Joe, We all go jin-gle, jin-gle Joe.

ALL DIG TATERS

All dig ta-ters in San-dy-land. All dig ta-ters in San-dy-land.

All dig ta-ters in San-dy-land A-way down be-low.

Swing to the right and then to the left. Swing to the right and then to the left.

Swing to the right and then to the left, A-way down be-low.

DANCE JOSIE

We're float-ing down the riv-er. We're float-ing down be-low. We're

float-ing down the riv-er To ol' Shi-loh.

1. Choose you one and come dance Jo-sie. Choose you one and come dance Jo.

Choose you one and come dance Jo-sie. Hel-lo Su-sie Brown.

2. Wheel about, whirl about, can't dance Josie.
3. Two in the middle and I can't dance Josie.
4. Black cat, yellow cat, can't dance Josie.
5. Ride my mule while I dance Josie.
6. Chew my tobacco while I dance Josie.

SKIP TO MY LOU

Green leaves, green leaves, growing on a vine. Go choose you a part-ner, the

pret-ti-est you can find. Chick-en on a hay-stack, shoo, shoo, shoo.

Chick-en on a hay-stack, shoo, shoo, shoo. Chick-en on a hay-stack, shoo, shoo, shoo.

(continue tune as verse)

Skip to the Lou my darl-in'. Skip, skip, skip to my Lou.

2. Lost my partner, what shall I do?
3. Get me another one, prettier, too.
4. Can't get a pretty girl, an ugly one'll do.
5. Little red wagon painted blue.
6. Back band broke and traces, too.
7. Ma churned butter in Pa's old shoe.
8. Pa said, "Ma, that butter won't do."

Five couples ready for the promenade (Kenneth Munson).

The only variations in singing one verse for the promenade and starting the right and left with the beginning of the second verse occurred in the songs "Dance Josie" and "Skip to My Lou." Each of these has a preliminary part. "Dance Josie" begins:

We're floating down the river;
We're floating down below,
We're floating down the river
To old Shiloh.

Boys could get partners and join the promenade while this part and the first verse, "Choose you one and come dance Josie," were being sung, but beginning with the next verse, "Wheel about, whirl about," the tempo became faster for the right and left full swings.

The preliminary of "Skip to My Lou" was as follows:

Green leaves, green leaves
Growing on a vine.
Go choose you a partner,
The prettiest you can find.

That part was followed by "Chicken on a haystack, shoo! shoo! shoo!" and the right and left began with the chorus. Since the chorus says "skip," all participants skipped while doing the right and left and the full-circle swings.

Another game that was used with more than one song began with couples paired off into sets of four all around the room. For "Rare Back Chicken" and "Jack Shot a Rabbit" the four caught hands and circled right for the first verse, did a simple right and left for the second verse, and a full-circle swing right

and left for the remaining verses. At that time they were ready to trade for a new foursome.

"Shoe Dye" began as described above. At the words "Right hands cross" the two boys clasped right hands, the two girls did also, and they all circled left. At the words "Left hands back," they changed hands across and circled right. At "Break and swing" they did a right and left until reaching the chorus. The chorus says "Double L swing," which means two full-circle swings right and then two full-circle swings left. At the end they were ready for a new foursome. At times, as groups of four were changed, the song and game were changed also. Quite often they began with "Shoe Dye" but used "Jack Shot a Rabbit" and "Rare Back Chicken" before all couples had been together as a foursome.

RARE BACK CHICKEN

Rare back chick-en and crow for day. Flop your wings and fly a - way.

Sat - ur - day night and Sun - day, too, Pur - ty girls on my mind.

Mon - day morn -in' just 'fore day Old folks had me gwine.

2. Wish I had a big white house
Fourteen stories high
And every story in that house
Filled with chicken pie.

3. Once I had an old banjo,
Strings all made of twine.
The only tune that I could play,
I wish that gal was mine.

JACK SHOT A RABBIT

1. Jack shot a rab-bit shoo-la-lay. Jack shot a rab-bit, shoo-la - lay.

Jack shot a rab- bit, shoo-la-lay. Shoo - la - lay.

2. Shot him with a beanstack, shoo-la-lay.
3. Gonna get married, shoo-la-lay.
4. Next Sunday mornin', shoo-la-lay.

SHOO-DYE

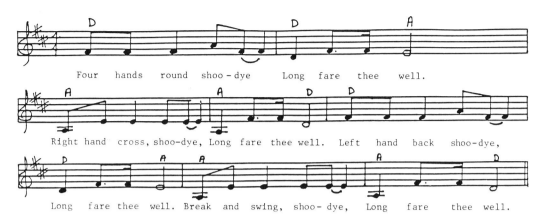

Four hands round shoo-dye Long fare thee well.

Right hand cross, shoo-dye, Long fare thee well. Left hand back shoo-dye,

Long fare thee well. Break and swing, shoo-dye, Long fare thee well.

Refrain:
Double L swing, shoo-dye, Long fare thee well. (repeat)
Don't care if I do die, Long fare thee well. (repeat)

"Oh, Lady Go Center" began with a promenade with girls on the outside while they sang two lines of the music using "La, la, la" in place of words. As they sang "Oh, lady go center" each boy swung his partner in front of himself with the left hand. This turned her so that she was ready to travel in the inner circle of girls in the opposite direction. As partners passed on the opposite side, each boy swung a circle and a half to the left with the girl behind his partner and promenaded with that girl on the outside. The above was repeated again and again until they had "promenaded all" and got back to their original partners.

OH, LADY GO CENTER

Oh, la-dy go cen-ter, go form a ring. Go half way round be-fore you swing.

And when you swing, re-mem-ber the call, And don't forget to prom-e-nade all.

La, la, la, la, la, la, la, la, la, la, la, la, la, la, la, la, la.

"The Irish Trot" began with a large circle with girls to the left of their partners, all facing toward the center and holding hands. A verse was sung and they began singing "All hands up in the Irish trot." With hands up, everyone rushed (trotted) towards the center and back. After "Away down below" each boy

swung his partner a full circle and promenaded with the girl
behind her. All of the above was repeated until partners were
back together.

THE IRISH TROT

All hands up in the I-rish trot. All hands up in the I-rish trot.

All hands up in the I-rish trot. A - way down be-low. If I'd leave her she'd go wild.

2. Oh you tell her I forgot.
3. I'm my mama's darling child.

"Shoot the Buffalo" began with singing the chorus and partners together for the promenade with girls on the outside. As
they sang "Ladies to the center" boys swung with their partners
but left them standing in the inside circle, facing out, while the
boys circled counterclockwise in the outer circle. They went all
the way around, passed their partners, and swung and promenaded the next girl. This was repeated until partners were together again.

SHOOT THE BUFFALO

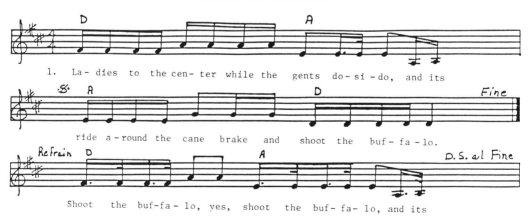

1. La - dies to the cen - ter while the gents do - si - do, and its

ride a - round the cane brake and shoot the buf - fa - lo.

Shoot the buf - fa - lo, yes, shoot the buf - fa - lo, and its

2. I shot him in the head and I shot him in the heel,
   And I shot him in the middle of a forty-acre field.
3. I shot him in the heart and I shot him in the head,
   And I know good and well that the buffalo's dead.
4. Eagle chase a hawk and a hawk chase a crow,
   And we'll ride around the cane brake and shoot the buffalo.

"First Two Gents" has neither a preliminary part nor a promenade. All catch hands to form a circle facing toward the center
with the girls to the left of their partners. Two boys on opposite
sides of the circle danced (cut a caper) across the hall and swung
the other boy's partner with the right hand, danced back, swung
their own partners by the left hand, and "promenaded the girl

behind." This was repeated ("Same ol' two") with the new partners until the two boys were back to their original partners. As
they sang "Next two gents" the next two repeated all of the above.

FIRST TWO GENTS

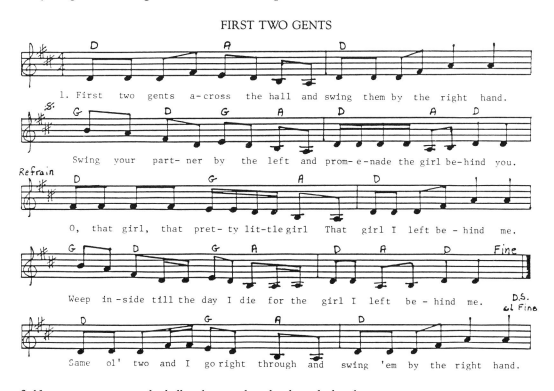

1. First two gents a-cross the hall and swing them by the right hand.

Swing your part-ner by the left and prom-e-nade the girl be-hind you.

Refrain

O, that girl, that pret-ty lit-tle girl That girl I left be-hind me.

Weep in-side till the day I die for the girl I left be-hind me.

Same ol' two and I go right through and swing 'em by the right hand.

2. Next two gents across the hall and swing them by the right hand.

"Blue-Eyed Raleigh" began with a large circle with girls to the left of their partners and all holding hands facing towards the center of the circle. As they sang "Circle right" the entire group circled to the right. At "Right back this way" they circled to the left, and as they sang "All in a motion" the entire group rushed toward the center and back while still holding hands. At verse four, which says "Treat your partner," partners swung a full circle plus one-half so that a new girl was on the boy's left. They repeated all the above with the new partners until original partners were brought back together.

BLUE-EYED RALEIGH

2. Right back this way
   Blue-eyed Raleigh. . .

3. All in a motion
   Blue-eyed Raleigh. . .

4. Treat your partner
   Blue-eyed Raleigh. . .

For "New River Train" four couples formed a square facing each other. The first two couples, holding hands as in regular promenade, went forward, met, and went back to their original positions. The second two couples then went forward and back. Now the boys of the first two couples went across, swung the girls on the opposite side, and went back to swing their own partners. The second two couples repeated the swings done by the first two, and they were ready to trade for new couples.

NEW RIVER TRAIN

2. Oh my darling you can't love but one.
   Oh my darling you can't love but one.
   You can't love but one and have any fun.
   My darling you can't love but one.

"Miller Boy" was a mixing game that could be played with extra boys or girls involved or with an equal number of boys and girls. It began with the usual promenade counterclockwise with the girls on the inside—right hand to right and left to left. As the verse ended with "turn right back," all couples turned to promenade clockwise without having to change hands.

The verse was repeated for this "backward" promenade but ended with "Ladies step forward and the gents turn back." The ring of girls going one direction and boys in the opposite direction continued while the first refrain was sung. As they came to the "better be quick in the motion" part, boys grabbed girls for a quick full circle swing and the promenade started again as from the beginning but with new partners.

On this second time around the movements were the same but ended with the second refrain and the words "Lost my true love and right here I find her." The game repeated all the above several times before "steady" couples felt compelled to get together again and start a new game.

MILLER BOY

Hap-py was a mil-ler boy lived by the mill. The mill turned a-round with its own free will. A hand on the hop-per and the oth-er on the sack, Ev'ry time the mill turns,

turn right back. / gents turn back.   Sail-in', Sail-in', west Sail-in' o-ver the o-cean. / La-dies step for-ward and the

Say, young, man, if you want a part-ner, you'd bet-ter be quick in the mo-tion.

Rain-ing, hail-ing, cold storm-y weath-er. You and the true love lurch a long to-geth-er.

You run the reap-er and I'll run the bind-er. Lost my true love and right here I find her.

"Got a New Pig in the Parlor" was a game for mixing partners and required one boy without a partner. He was the "pig in the parlor" as all others caught hands and formed a ring around him with girls to the left of their partners. All circled right and sang

(Kenneth Munson)

the first part of the song. As they came to "Right hand to your partner," boys did left and right clockwise and girls counter-clockwise. The "pig" grabbed a hand and did a left and right with the others, and as they came to the promenade one boy was left without a partner. He would be a "new pig in the parlor" or "the same old hog."

GOT A NEW PIG IN THE PARLOR

"Topsy" was another game for mixing partners. Several boys without partners could enter this game. The promenade was slightly different in that partners were side by side circling counterclockwise with boys on the outside—boy's left hand on girl's right shoulder and girl's right hand on boy's left shoulder. As they began to sing the second part, "Here comes Topsy through the window," partners caught hands above their heads and left room for Topsy, the extra boys, to come between them. Topsy usually managed to steal a partner by being in front of a favorite girl as the second part ended and they were ready to sing "All promenade with hands on the shoulder." This game usually ended after four or five rounds. Sometimes another game or two could be played before the original couples could get together again.

TOPSY

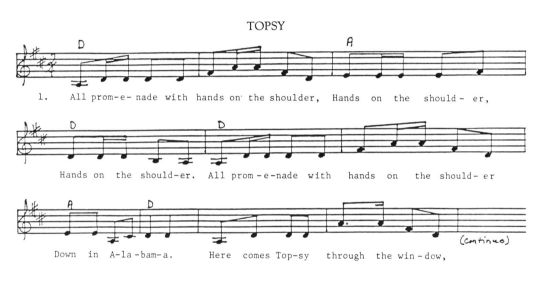

1. All prom-e-nade with hands on the shoulder, Hands on the should-er,

Hands on the should-er. All prom-e-nade with hands on the should-er

Down in A-la-bam-a. Here comes Top-sy through the win-dow,

(continue)

"Come, Come, Girls, Let's Go to Boston" at times began with a promenade until someone in a good position to be the head of the line stopped and suggested this game. The circle then moved on around to form a straight line with girls to the left of their partners. Every couple moved about six feet apart facing each other to form a line of girls on one side and boys on the other. As they sang "Come, come, girls" the girl at the head of the line led a parade of girls in a circle to the left and back to their starting places. As they sang "Saddle up boys" the boy at the head of the line led a parade of boys in a circle to the right and back to their starting places.

The next verse began "Uh-oh [first boy's name], I'll tell your mama." That boy and his partner grasped both arms and skipped sideways between the two lines back and forth but took their places at the foot of the line as the verse ended. Since this put the next couple at the head of the two lines, they led the parades for repeating the process. In this way each couple eventually came to the head of the lines and led the parades.

COME, COME, GIRLS, LET'S GO TO BOSTON

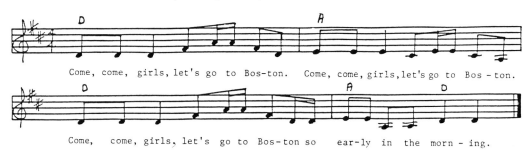

2. Saddle up boys and let's go with 'em. . . . . so early in the morn-ing.
3. Uh-oh Allen I'll tell your mama. . . . how you go a - court-in'.
4. Court Miss Anna and then can't get her. . . . . so early in the morn-ing.

"Come, Come, Girls,
Let's Go To Boston"
(Kenneth Munson).

The twelve games and twenty-six songs named above were the Hope play-party games and songs during the Roaring Twenties and during the Depression; but boll weevils, paved roads, automobiles, radios, television, movies, and school consolidation hit Hope a few years after World War II. It will never be the same again. In fact, by 1980, both stores, both blacksmith shops, the cotton gin, and the ice cream parlor had all fallen and rotted away. All that remained were the two churches on either side of the vacant, deteriorating three-room school built in 1925 from the lumber of the oldest structure in the community.

In 1986, this building was renovated, and play-parties returned. The school is being used for the young people of Hope to learn these songs and games—perhaps the only place in America where this has happened. The Hope, Texas, Sing and Swing Group performed at the Texas Folklife Festival in San Antonio on August 7, 8, and 9, 1987. With that performance they may be instrumental in showing other young people a way to have fun without having to watch television.

After more than fifty years away from the Hope community, I was unable to recall all songs and games for this publication. For the help given by my brother Allen Munson and his wife, Anna Lou, who remained at Hope and taught these games and songs to the next generation, I wish to express my sincere gratitude. My daughter, Karen Munson, is due my profound thanks for transcription of the music and preparation of the manuscript. She has added chord symbols for instruments for the convenience of those who wish to use them. To end this article we quote a favorite verse from "Old Joe Clark," a widely popular play-party song:

> I wish I was in heav'n,
> A settin' on a rail,
> A sweet 'tater in my hand
> And a 'possum by the tail.

Part Three

Essays on Toys and Games

XVI

Folk Toys in Texas

by
Lee Haile

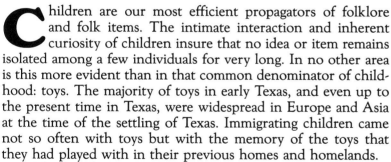

Children are our most efficient propagators of folklore and folk items. The intimate interaction and inherent curiosity of children insure that no idea or item remains isolated among a few individuals for very long. In no other area is this more evident than in that common denominator of childhood: toys. The majority of toys in early Texas, and even up to the present time in Texas, were widespread in Europe and Asia at the time of the settling of Texas. Immigrating children came not so often with toys but with the memory of the toys that they had played with in their previous homes and homelands.

The fact that Texas was a frontier when the Europeans settled here had a big effect on the toys that children played with. Frontier society was thrown back into a more primitive form. Stores were few, distances were great, and money, when available, was needed for more important things than toys. Although the toy industry in Europe had been well established since the 1600s and was in its early beginnings in America, Texas was still a raw frontier in the 1800s. As a consequence, "if you couldn't make something yourself, you didn't have it." Which brings us to a definition of folk toys: toys made with natural or available materials by amateurs in the tradition of the area's culture and ancestors for personal rather than mercantile reasons.

Children have always been great scavengers, partly by nature but mostly by necessity, and as a result, common folk toys were simple, easy to make, and made from whatever was available. Early Texas toys were very similar to the toys found in ancient history and among the more primitive societies of the world. Only the materials used and the way they were played with differed.

Many of the toys found in Texas are universal folk toys. They are found in almost all cultures, recent and ancient. Dolls, balls, bow and arrows, bull-roarers, stick horses, boomerangs, and buzzers were already present among the Native American Indians when the Europeans brought them to the New World. A few toys or variations were adopted directly from the American Indians by the Europeans settling in the eastern United States. These were later brought west to Texas. In this category were corn-shuck dolls and slip-bark whistles.

The rest of the folk toys found in Texas came from Europe to the New World and then to Texas in three ways. First, there was the European (Spanish) movement north from Mexico. Then there was the westward expansion of Europeans from the east coast. Along about this same time, beginning in the 1840s, there was the immigration of Europeans directly through Texas seaports, particularly Indianola and Galveston.

Many of the toys that came from Europe had their origins elsewhere. Those toys in Texas that originated in ancient Asia, mostly China and Japan, were kites, string and whip tops, diabolos, stilts, and yo-yos. Jacob's Ladders, or folding blocks, originated in recent Japan and were imported directly to America in about 1900. Ancient Greeks and Romans played with hoops, and the cup and ball and the spin top had several different ancient origins.

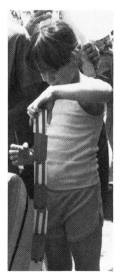

Jacob's Ladder
(Karen Haile).

Cup and ball
(Karen Haile).

Toys that originated in Europe from the Renaissance period through the 1800s were helicopters, parachutes, windmills, English jumping jacks, acrobats, peashooters, and popguns. When the rubber band was invented by an Englishman in 1830, a number of toys came about using this new power source. The most common in Texas were paddle boats, spool tractors, rubber-band guns, and slingshots.

A few other toys found among the children of Texas have relatively recent but obscure origins. There are the Whoopee Stick, the Sky Piercer or Whip Dart, the clothespin or match gun, and the flying Whirlygig.

Toys were not always just for children. Some of the toys that escaped the realm of childhood and became very popular among adults were the cup and ball, the whip top, and the diabola.

At the present time almost all these toys can still be found in Texas, primarily among the rural folk. Now many of the toys are mass-produced and are bought, instead of being made at home. Folk toys are still frequently handmade in eastern areas of the state and along the border of Mexico. They are commonly sold in the border towns.

The children of Texas had a lot in common with their ancestral counterparts, and the toys they played with reflected this. Thrust into a new and primitive environment, children soon learned to make do with the same pioneering spirit of their parents. They had to learn what was available to work with in the environment that they found themselves in. Slip-bark whistles, which were made with hickory in the East, were made with willow in the West, where no hickory grew. In the East, kite sticks were made of river cane, and in the desert West of dead yucca stalks. All it took was a gathering of two children for toys to pass between them and then among their friends. Younger ones learned from older ones, and so for the children, these toys lived on.

Diabolo (Karen Haile).

Spool tractor
(Karen Haile).

Rubbing the notches—Whoopee Stick (Karen Haile).

XVII

Toys on the Frontier

by
Joyce Gibson Roach

Toys are a part of heritage and history, but unlike so many elusive facts, figures, names, places, and dates, some toys are traceable to prehistory. According to Pauline Flick, an English toy historian, toys "have always re-flected the child's attempts to imitate grown-ups" (Flick, 4). She mentions making mud pies, sailing a piece of bark, and using acorn cups for bowls as examples of imitation. The "purpose-made toy—the artifact created specifically as a child's plaything," she goes on to say, may be traced back to toys or miniature objects used as funeral offerings in Egypt in about 2000 B.C. A wooden tiger with movable jaws, a wooden cow without legs, and papyrus balls are all among collections of toys in the British Museum and are all Egyptian in origin, dating from about 1000 B.C. Likenesses of Greek and Roman toys were found on deco-rated vases. Mention of the same toys is found in literature and from archaeological excavations. Both Greek and Roman chil-dren had a wide variety of toys such as clay rattles, jointed clay dolls, rag dolls, handcarts, hobbyhorses, miniature furniture, hoops, and tops.

In the Middle Ages toys continued to be simple and much like the playthings of the Greeks and Romans. Tops, hobby-horses, puppets, and windmills appear in medieval illuminations. Flick makes an interesting observation that purposeful toy mak-ing "flourishes only in the context of a settled way of life, where houses have space for playthings to be kept, and where there is leisure enough for them to be enjoyed. More important still,

society must have an indulgent attitude towards its children"
(Flick, 5).

It was during the late Middle Ages that the German toy
industry began to flourish, and it was the Germans who played
the most important role in the toy trade worldwide, especially in
items carved from wood. By the sixteenth century, regions such
as Oberammergau, the Graden Valley, Berchtesgaden, and Sonneberg specialized in toys. Traders, peddlers, and travelers spread
the toys, along with other trade goods, throughout Europe.

Professional toy makers and distributors encountered a philosophy in the eighteenth century that virtually assured their
success. The English discovered that children had a right to be
individuals for their own sakes instead of merely existing as
miniature grown-ups. Flick explains:

> The idea of play for its own sake was foreign to a society still
> deeply influenced by puritan values. Now, however, far more lib-
> eral views were found reflecting the opinions of enlightened edu-
> cationalists like John Locke and Isaac Watts; parents began to
> realise that their children had a right to enjoy themselves, and
> that sometimes lessons could be learned more quickly if they
> were combined with an element of entertainment. And with this
> realisation came—at least from the upper classes—an unprece-
> dented demand for toys (Flick, 5).

It seems fairly safe to assume from studying other aspects of the
English-linked history of the United States that not only the
toys but also the same ideas about children traveled across the
ocean and then from frontier to frontier.

Perhaps the telling phrase in Flick's account is "upper
classes." Manufactured toys seemed at first destined for only
those who could pay for them, and this might account for the
division between folk toys and manufactured toys. This explanation considers folk toys as those fashioned from readily available,
free, usually natural materials, accessible to many classes or
groups and made by skilled or unskilled hands at no monetary
cost and not necessarily for sale. Manufactured toys are those
made from materials of any source including metals and intended to be bought at a price commensurate with the cost of
materials, labor, and distribution and sold for a profit. One kind
brings no more pleasure than the other and is no more valuable
in the eye of the beholder. Children possessing one of the two
types probably wanted the other kind as well as what they had.
A toy was a toy was a toy, but there obviously were two types by
the sixteenth century.

Mentioning the history of toys in Europe and the movement of toys to the colonies and then on to Texas is not to say
that toys were not manufactured or distributed in other areas of
the world. Oriental, African, Indian, Polynesian—virtually every
culture on the face of the earth produced toys of some kind, and
evidences and influences of toys from everywhere in the world
have been found within the boundaries of the United States at

one time or another. It is in the history of European toys, however, that one can stand in the middle of the folklore bridge and see most clearly in both directions from familiar to familiar.

Lists of early manufactured toys are available because of illustrated catalogues that were prevalent even before 1800 from—who else?—those incomparable German craftsmen who knew better than any other group how to carve and fit together toys or anything else. Although it is merely speculative, I would venture a guess that on a frontier—Texas's or any other—any wagons driven by German immigrants would have had toys, or better yet, would have had settlers with the ability to make them.

Not only catalogues but also museums exist to illustrate a long list of toys. After two weeks spent seeing and visiting the toy museums of the United Kingdom, it occurs to me that surely there must be more museums or at least portions of museums dedicated to toys than to any other kind of collections. Patent office records also identify kinds of toys. Consider the list of which immigrants would have been aware: dolls (wooden, cloth, pottery, china, paper), doll furniture and clothes, dishes (wooden and pottery), ships, trains with working parts, pull-along toys, rocking horses, soldiers (wood, paper, and metal), paper toys (people, imaginary characters such as jumping jacks, rooms of houses, gardens, dolls that were known as "English" dolls even in Germany, doll clothes, peep shows, pictorial alphabet cards, juvenile books, and board games), dissected map puzzles made of wood, miniatures made of wood or metal with working parts (either for collecting for dollhouses or for hanging on Christmas trees), mechanical figures and objects, optical toys (kaleidoscopes, thaumatropes consisting of a cardboard disk with a related drawing on either side, stroboscopes using moving pictures, zoetropes), roller skates, farming equipment (tractors, gardening tools, wagons, buggies), Noah's arks (considered Sunday toys and played with only on that day), drums, magic lanterns, banks and money boxes, blocks, and "gee gaws" and "thingamajigs," such as wiffle sticks, rope-climbing figures, whirligigs—and the list goes on and on.

With such a lavish historical background in toys, frontier people were well equipped to provide their children with toys. It is easy to believe that folk toys were merely simple devices created by simple folk from simple materials found at hand and fresh from the minds of clever frontier fathers and mothers. But such a definition of folk toys is only surface truth. Beneath the surface is the fact that most settlers from rich to poor to yeoman class knew much about toys, were prepared to create them or imitate and adapt materials to make them, and even had some examples along with them. Ann Patton Malone in *Women on the Texas Frontier* notes an important distinction about the pioneering women, who were contributors to toy making or creating, and that is that not all women were of one class or kind. She distinguishes the "elite," who were accustomed to a Victorian social system in which women were "passive, childlike, unreflective, self sacrificing, and dependent." Another group of immigrant women were ideally suited to making do even in strange terrain: "The peasant or agricultural societies from which many European immigrant women came prepared them well for the hard labor and role adjustments they would en-counter in Texas" (Malone, 21). The largest group and the one most comfortable on the frontier, "the yeoman class, or middle rank," were "wives, daughters and other kin of yeoman farmers, small slave holders, craftsmen and tradesmen." At the bottom of the pioneer heap were the poor, "whose existence was at best marginal."

A discussion of various female social classes is not necessary to make the distinction that the kinds of toys little girls played with may have depended on their rung on the frontier ladder. Some classes, of course, did better than others at making toys, just as some built better homes than others. Some cooked better food, some plowed and planted better, some were just better folks morally, socially, and monetarily, but all had access to ideas about the world of toys. And yes, males and females were proba-bly equally good at creating specialties in toys. Nevertheless, frontier folk in the wilderness of Texas knew perhaps as much if not more about toys and their making than they did about any-thing else in that place of new beginnings. In fact, they were probably on much more secure ground making toys, say, than they were building a dugout or a soddie.

And who in truth can deny that kingdoms were lost and won, great ideas forged and literature written, and nations cre-ated over what toy one little boy or girl had—or didn't have—to play with, what toy one coveted from another child, or what toy one was denied because of birth or circumstances. The impor-tance of toys in children's lives should not be underestimated. One of the most pathetic comments on the Ethiopian famine, for instance, was shown in a film of dying children, as they starved and played a game at the same moment of their short lives.

Li Bo's paper-made toys.

XVIII

Folk Games of Texas Children

by
Martha Hartzog

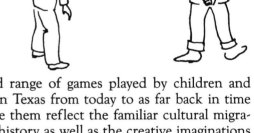

The variety and range of games played by children and young adults in Texas from today to as far back in time as we can trace them reflect the familiar cultural migration patterns of Texas history as well as the creative imaginations of children.

There are the games played by the prehistoric and historic Indians, faint outlines now like the fading images of their rock art. There are the games brought by the children of the first Spanish settlers, reflecting a Western European culture, which would later be blended into the mestizo culture. These games would find counterparts in the games played by the nineteenth-century European immigrants who came to Texas directly by sea and those who came to Texas after first stopping for a few generations on the Atlantic seaboard and in the inland southern United States. Finally, there are the games played by Afro-American children, only now being fully recognized for their unique blend of the European and the African.

The folk games of Texas children, like the games of today, played the same roles as they have from the very beginnings of the human race: they amuse, instruct, and inspire. They reflect the values and beliefs of their parent cultures. Providing children with a chance to act out roles, make choices, and experience the thrill of winning and the disappointment of losing, the games help small minds and imaginations mature.

Games that developed toughness and physical endurance were especially favored by the boys. In the nineteenth century, Plains Indian boys were observed staging mock buffalo hunts, in which some of the little boys went out on stick horses to hunt other little boys who were the "buffaloes." The "buffaloes" defended themselves with prickly pear leaves mounted on sticks. Indians played many forms of ball games. Kickball, a simple form of field hockey, was enjoyed by Plains Indian girls, and a game the French were to name lacrosse was played throughout the Indian world. Indians especially loved guessing games and gambling games and developed a large number of these, which the adults played (Capps, 19–22, 87–88). Their children must have imitated the parents, as children always do, and played at least simpler versions of these games.

By the Middle Ages in Europe and the British Isles, there was an established set of common cultural ties, among them the games that children played. Many of these—like tops and marble games and jacks—can be traced back to Greek and Roman times. Some of these games are played with rhymed formulas, often set to song, which have been handed down from generation to generation. Many are grounded in superstition, religious belief, historical events, and celebrations tied to specific times of

the year. They exhibit such themes as courtship, warfare, stolen children, and the magic of numbers and prophecy. They are often built around the joys of motion and jest. They exist in numerous variations (Newell, passim).

Successive waves of immigrants from throughout Europe brought these games to the North American continent. In Texas, the first European children arrived in significant numbers in the early part of the eighteenth century, when Spain began to attempt to colonize the area on the East Texas frontier, along the Rio Grande, and around San Antonio. Games played by Mexican-American children in the early part of the twentieth century are a good illustration of this pan-European culture. La Puerta Esta Quebrada (The Door is Broken) is a variant of the well-known London Bridge. In both games, two children form an archway with their hands; the other children file through as a song is sung. As the song ends, the last child to file through is caught in the arch and must pay a penalty or choose between joining the side of good or evil, represented by the two arch makers. Often, after each child has been caught by the arch and has joined one side or the other, a tug-of-war ensues to determine the victor. The Germans also brought this game to Texas when they began to establish their colonies around such places as Fredericksburg. There it was called Zieh Durch (Gonzalez; Hall; Estill, "Games"). London Bridge has been traced in recognizable form to the year 1553 and occurs at that time simultaneously in such countries as England, Italy, and Germany. It apparently had its beginnings in a very early belief that a bridge would be opposed by evil spirits and that a human sacrifice would be required to keep it from falling down (Newell, 204–11).

Another consistent theme in the pan-European games was the stealing of children by the devil or an old witch or a buzzard. The children of Anglo pioneers in Texas played Chickimee Craney Crow, German children played Kluck mit Heunkel (Hen with Chickens), and Mexican-American children played Colores, in which the children were assigned colors and the devil had to pay a forfeit to win the color or child desired.

Variations of the familiar Hide-and-Seek (or I Spy) and Blindman's Buff were also played by Anglo, German, and Mexican-American children in Texas. These are also very old games, described by Pollux in the second century and played throughout Europe. In Fredericksburg the variation of Blindman's Buff was Blinde Kuh, Ich Fuehre Dich (Blind Cow, I'll Lead You).

Special games for certain seasons of the year were notably played by both German and Mexican-American children. And the Mexican-American culture inherited a particular love for wordplay, with riddles, sayings, or *dichos,* along with animal fables, being favored by young and old alike.

The theme of courtship is a perennial favorite with children as well as young adults. A ring game with courtship implications was played in South Texas in the early twentieth century. It was introduced into that area directly from Mexico, illustrating the continual cultural interchange between the two areas that has always taken place. In Maria Blanca (called Dona Blanca in Mexico), the children form a ring. A girl is chosen to represent Maria Blanca, and she stands in the center of the circle; a boy called Jicotillo (The Hornet) is outside the circle. The game ends with Jicotillo chasing Maria Blanca until he catches her. In German Fredericksburg, the girls pretend to be little birds and flutter inside a circle drawn on the ground; the boys are "buyers" and must bid for the girl they desire by handclaps. This game is called Voegel zu verkaufen (Birds for Sale).

Jump-rope games became very popular in Texas in the first half of the twentieth century. These often have courtship themes, linked to prophecy through numbers, the numbers being functions of the number of times a girl could jump the rope without missing. Some of the rhymes are adapted from familiar verses, like the button-counting rhyme "Rich man, poor man, beggar man, thief." Newer verses expressing romantic themes include "Cinderella dressed in yellow" and "Ice cream soda, Delaware Punch." A particular favorite on the Gulf Coast of Texas, showing how region can influence popularity, was the one that began "Down by the ocean, down by the sea" (Sone, 195–99).

Very popular in frontier Texas where strict church precepts forbade dancing were the ring and longways games played at play-parties, or Josie parties, a uniquely American development. Many of the songs sung at play-parties had their origins in Europe, but the words were distinctly and peculiarly American.

Many of the songs have words that could have come only out of the southern or western experience: "Shoot the Buffalo," "Wish I Was a Cowboy," and "Raise Big 'Taters in Sandy Land" (Owens, Abernethy, Dudley and Payne, Payne, Gates).

With the southern emigrants to Texas came the Afro-Americans, mostly as slaves, sometimes as free people. They brought with them their own cultural mixture—a blend of the European with the African, developed within the conditions of slavery and rural life. Black children played and sang games out of the Anglo tradition, like Chickimee Craney Crow and Lil' Liza Jane. As to be expected, many of these game songs, like those of Anglo children from the South, exhibited regional flavor, referring to raccoons in persimmon trees, collard greens, and even hangings. Although most of the Negro games seem to be European in origin, it is now increasingly recognized that they have been significantly modified by the strong oral traditions and the love of rhythm originating in Africa. The handclap games of black children, like Mary Mack, Mack, Mack, exhibit more syncopated rhythms than do handclap games of Anglo or Mexican-American children, and there is a much greater willingness to experiment with sounds for their own sake (Hughes and Bontemps, 421, 424).

The ring games and the line games, like "Little Sally Walker," played by black children are really primarily performance games, with the child in the middle of the ring or the line actually putting on a dance or a mime. In this the games also reflect the heritage of African dances (Stoeltje, 33; Eckhardt, 57, 75).

The folk games played by children in Texas have an important role to play in the development of the children. Through game playing, children act out the war between good and evil and learn moral lessons. Games instruct children in the folklore of a culture as well as in the mental and physical skills required of them as adults. They teach children about courtship and marriage and about power and cunning and luck; they help them learn about humor; they show them how to think by solving riddles and how to make choices. And finally they are a child's outlet for often secret hopes and fears and dreams.

XIX

Children's Games and Socialization in the Texas Hill Country

by
Lera Tyler Lich

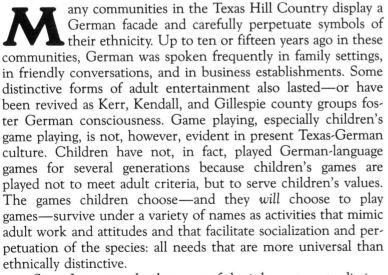

Many communities in the Texas Hill Country display a German facade and carefully perpetuate symbols of their ethnicity. Up to ten or fifteen years ago in these communities, German was spoken frequently in family settings, in friendly conversations, and in business establishments. Some distinctive forms of adult entertainment also lasted—or have been revived as Kerr, Kendall, and Gillespie county groups foster German consciousness. Game playing, especially children's game playing, is not, however, evident in present Texas-German culture. Children have not, in fact, played German-language games for several generations because children's games are played not to meet adult criteria, but to serve children's values. The games children choose—and they *will* choose to play games—survive under a variety of names as activities that mimic adult work and attitudes and that facilitate socialization and perpetuation of the species: all needs that are more universal than ethnically distinctive.

Since I was not clearly aware of the inherent contradiction that I will describe in this paper, I began with a search for folk games German children played. I talked first with older adults who had spoken German as children. They readily mentioned German riddles and were always, always telling of childhood pranks, jokes, gossip, and games of mimesis; but they remembered few games and recalled those by English names only. The names of games learned from other Hill Country settlers—Anglo-Americans of the upper and lower South, Hispanics, Scots, English, and blacks—had apparently replaced most German-sounding games fifty or sixty years ago.

A survey of material previously gathered on folk games of the Texas Hill Country provided little new information. In a Texas Folklore Society article entitled "Children's Games in Fredericksburg" (1954), Julia Estill reminisces about childhood games she and earlier generations of Fredericksburgers played, indicating that German names for games were still popular around 1900. Estill describes chasing games, like "Voegel zu verkaufen," and ring games, like "Blinde Kuh, ich fuehre dich." Their repertoire even included a German version of London Bridge called "Zieh durch" (Estill, 231–36).

Gilbert Jordan, who carefully recorded the folk traditions of Mason County in *Yesterday in the Texas Hill Country* (1979), described rhymes and games of his generation. One German game, "Mummela" or "Sautreiben," is apparently a variant of Estill's "Blinde Kuh." Jordan too remembers riddles. "We even got a double dose of riddles, in English and in German," he wrote. The English version of one popular riddle for a plum or cherry,

> First white as snow,
> Then green as clover,
> Then red as blood,
> Tastes good all over,

is similar to the German,

> Erst weiss wie Schnee
> Dann grun wie Klee,
> Dann rot wie Blut,
> Schmeckt allen Kindern gut.

Bilingual children of Jordan's Willow Creek community had German counting-out games (Abzahlverse), like "Ich und du und Mullers Kuh,/Backers Esel, das bist du," along with the English "Eenie, meenie, miney, mo." While examples of such German rhymes and sayings fill Jordan's volume, his accounts of recess play mostly describe games we associate with America—baseball, Crack the Whip, Red Rover, horseshoes, and mumbletypeg (Jordan, 105–6, 112–14).

Having only this small collection of material from oldsters and researchers, I could have confirmed Mac Barrick's statement in *German-American Folklore* (1987): "The role of games in the life of children has changed considerably in the past generation. Once an essential part of the educational and social process, the game is now an incidental form of entertainment" (Barrick, 124). If I had agreed, I would have been quite misinformed. I had just been asking the wrong people, for children's game lore belongs to children, and children—or near children—remember it best.

Consequently, I asked my sixty-four senior English students at Ingram Tom Moore High School to record and explain games they had played in childhood and adolescence. Their descriptions of over sixty-five different games (and more were mentioned but not recorded) show that a folk game tradition is quite alive in the hills of western Kerr County. Mr. Barrick, and anyone who believes that "the repertory of games that today's child plays pales by comparison with the long lists remembered by his ancestors" (Barrick, 124), should consider this evidence.

As we discussed games in class, I did, however, ask myself why some games are held so long in the collective memory of childhood while others pass from the playground. Why didn't German-speaking children continue to play German games as they continued to speak German together? Why were my students so enthusiastic and responsive to game collecting? What was the relationship between retention and culture? Couldn't these questions be answered in part by the function of children's games?

Voluntary games such as those my students recorded are played anywhere—classrooms, school buses, cars, backyards, chaperoned and unchaperoned parties, and, of course, playgrounds. Even with sophisticated technology at hand, young people occasionally draw on these simple games. Young boys, and girls, abandon their BMX bikes to play King of the Mountain on a tempting pile of dirt or sand. Teenagers, even when they have cars equipped with expensive car stereo systems, may choose to play Cockeye or Slug Bug while driving country roads. These games

continue because they satisfy some needs that toys, vehicles, or adult-made board and computer games cannot satisfy.

Improvisation that comes from such unstructured play may perhaps better allow children to be themselves, since they are not restricted to any level of verisimilitude or accountability. This play becomes a way of socializing and imitating adult worlds. "When my brother and I were around ten years old we used to play Indians," Dawn Bocock of Hunt wrote. "I was the sister who worked in the camp. I smashed the berries, ground rocks to use as soap, made pretend meat out of mud. Jamie was the hunter. He would bring in imaginary saber-tooth tigers and big snakes. I would cook them and skin them. We used moss for the animals' hides and pretended as if we were going through the tanning process." Popular children's pastimes like Indians—and house, spies, and forts—are bound in rules. Children consider them games, but they are basically pastimes and are noncompetitive, built on fantasy and escape.

While creative play occurs privately—in homes, backyards, and open fields—school groups often generate play of an intra-competitive nature. These games usually serve other functions, but they too assist in childhood socialization and act as a child's imitation of the adult world. They reflect the conservative nature of children, their demand for rules. Elementary children may quickly change opinions about friends, teachers, and popular culture figures, but they tolerate little change in rules they have made because altering rules usually serves the interest of an individual or a small group rather than their established community. Peer attitudes govern dress, speech, and competitive play, especially on the public school playground. Ironically—or appropriately—during recess, that period of official freedom within the confines of school authority, children establish especially strict social rules. Children learn how to act in these structures as authoritative older boys and girls pass on rules, games, rhymes, and stories to younger ones without adult interference. Old lore creates new. Names and words may alter, but many games my students described I had known as a child in East Texas thirty years ago.

Among young children, Hide-and-Seek, Red Rover, and Hopscotch are still popular. Freeze Tag has many versions, including Chinese Freeze Tag (a person is freed when someone crawls under his or her spread legs) and TV Tag (a person is saved by shouting out the name of a television show). Boys play Dodge Ball and Kick the Can along with popular sports like football, soccer, and basketball. (Girls occasionally join in these games, but most elementary playgrounds are voluntarily segregated by sex.) Girls appear to perpetuate more traditional games than boys. They still jump rope to rhymes like Cinderella, Cinderella and play clapping rhymes like Miss Suzie. Both sexes remember choosing and counting games such as One Potato, Bubble Gum, and Inka, Binka—played "when we were trying to decide who goes first sitting in the front or who gets to pick the

movie." Both boys and girls also describe more formal games—like Mother, May I; Fruit Basket Turn Over; I Spy; and Duck, Duck, Goose—often encouraged by adults "when we were told to play quiet, nonactive games."

These early childhood games fulfill important needs of that age group: to show strength and agility, to be the center of attention, to make decisions, to prove popularity, and to be a part of a group. As children grow closer to adolescence, the nature of their games shifts as additional needs must be met: to show daring, to alleviate boredom, to trick others and show superiority, and to create tension and thrills. When "waiting for class to be over," preteens and teens play paper games like Football, SOS, Hangman, Tic-Tac-Toe, or Airplanes. When "Mom was inside the grocery store, and we were told to stay outside," siblings play I Spy. Young people know at least three paper contraptions that will tell fortunes. In cars they play versions of Cockeye as well as alphabet games and a more risky amusement called Chinese Fire Drill. Strength or endurance is tested with Slap King, Suicide, Bloody Knuckles, Arm Wrestling, Pea Knuckle, and Mercy.

At mixed parties, especially when unchaperoned, drinking and courting games are popular with older adolescents. Quarters and Red/Black were the most frequently mentioned drinking games. Truth or Dare becomes more risky too as children grow into adolescence. Several old courting games like Post Office and Spin the Bottle are still popular (although the forfeitures are allegedly more serious than a generation ago). New games have emerged. In Credit Card, often played in the back of school buses, young people try to pass a piece of plastic from person to person using only their lips (the game is also known as Suck and Blow).

Whatever game is played, it is chosen because it serves to assist in socialization with peers. Although adults may generate some games, especially ones played by primary-age children, most are peer taught and suggested. And those learned from peers generally become more popular than those that are introduced by adults. Games associated with older generations are usually not as interesting, perhaps because they are tamer or perhaps because their purposes—to keep children quiet, busy, or under control—are more desirable to adults than to children.

And possibly a similar situation fifty or sixty years ago discouraged use of German folk games. American games may have quickly replaced German ones because adults were seldom present to preserve Old World traditions. Traditional American games introduced by Anglo peers met the same needs and were adopted to Texas-German pastures and playgrounds. German games would have excluded those peers, therefore discouraging socialization when it was desirable. German jokes and sayings, on the other hand, remained popular, for they functioned to exclude or ridicule—and that is what they were intended to do.

Spontaneity and freedom keep the folk game alive. As Tracy Hesson notes of the ever-popular Slug Bug, "This game is always being played; in other words it's continuously running. It can start up whenever and wherever—but only when the person sees a VW bug." In a child's own game, "You can quit when you want." Games played for adults, however, on occasions as varied as birthday parties and basketball games, are seldom spontaneous. In the presence of a spectator, participants become performers. The situation becomes rhetorical as players and audience send messages to each other—generally related to who will win—that alter the intent of the games. Players then try to win not only for themselves but also for their audience. They play not to socialize but to win a prize—either the high esteem of adults or an actual material object. A backyard game of Smear the Queer evolves into a more systematic version of football. Children play knowing an audience expects a product, a measurable end.

Games, or rather sports, associated with popular success naturally attract young people as their need to be a part of the adult world grows. Childhood games are played less and less frequently. Games associated with an exclusive group—whether that group be German-speaking adults or playground children—will not be played if the players wish to be a part of another group, if they wish to socialize with others.

For the Peter Pans of younger childhood, however, the child's immediate world is what matters. Then children's games are played by and for children. Perhaps because these games are so unconscious, so free of trying to appeal to anyone but the players, they are especially expressive and intimate. They function simply to meet the needs of children to be children, to have friends and freedom and a separate world, to be alone together.

Say, say, O' playmate, come out and play with me
    and bring your dollies three.
Climb up my apple tree.
Slide down my rainbow into my cellar door,
And we'll be jolly friends for evermore,
    more, more, more, more.

So sorry, playmate, can't come out and play with you.
My dolly has the flu. I think I have it, too,
Can't slide down your rainbow into your cellar door,
But we'll still be jolly friends for evermore,
    more, more, more, more.
(Clapping game remembered by Lisa Alford.)

XX

Games and Recreation

by
F. E. Abernethy

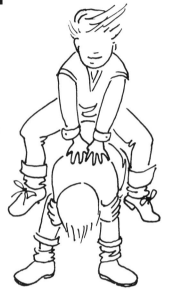

The genetic makeup of man—the sum total of his inherited characteristics—demands that he has recreation; and as people differ because of their inherited characteristics, so do the kinds of recreation they require and the kinds of games they play.

The Stimulus Struggle

Man is the supreme opportunist among animals. Very early in his evolution his survival depended on nonspecializing, on availing himself of everything at hand in the way of food and shelter. The result was that nature selected to survive as man a hyperactive, extremely curious animal that must always be exploring and prying and poking at something. Desmond Morris in *The Human Zoo* (Chapter 6) explains that one result of this genetic aspect of man is what he calls "the stimulus struggle," the continual pursuit by this hyperactive animal of the optimum amount of stimulation to keep him interested in life. Optimum does not mean maximum; one can be overstimulated as well as understimulated. Morris compares it to adjusting the volume of music: "too low and it makes no impact, too high and it causes pain." Somewhere between the two extremes of stimulation man seeks the mean between boredom and panic, and this seeking is his recreation, his games and pastimes.

The stimulus struggle is one explanation for the phenomenon of games and pastimes among people. The more stable our social system, the more we are free from want—the closer we are to a four-day work week—the more necessary play is for variety's and excitement's sake. In a protected welfare society, one no longer competes directly and obviously for dominance and territory, but the drives are still there and are sublimated into competitive games. Man the hunting animal no longer has to hunt for survival so he hunts and fishes as pastimes and enjoys the chase vicariously in stories and directly in games.

Theoretically the animal that is balancing on the fine, knife edge of survival has no time for games or pastimes. When he is not searching for food, he is resting his body for the time when the search and struggle will resume. Recreation comes to the animal that is fed and safe and still has energy left. The young pups that suck enjoy playing. The old bitch holes up in the den to rest. Human children are more concerned with playing than are adults. Their energy causes them to forego a nap for a game of chase. The old man comes home from work and barely has the energy left to eat and flop down before the television.

The stimulus struggle is the basis for the particular kinds of recreation one chooses. If one is intellectually bored at his work, he will probably seek intellectual stimulation in his play, in bridge or chess or the creation of the arts. If he is intellectually overstimulated, he might turn to handball or volleyball. If he works amid the press of people, his recreation will most likely be private, like hunting or fishing. If his work is isolating, he will go to football and baseball games or make a night on the town with dancing where there are a lot of people. One turns to recreation for the refreshment of mind and body through activities that are diverting and different from the activities that are necessary for survival.

The Ethological Implications of Recreation

The basic drive for recreation is man's struggle to find just the right amount of stimulation and diversion to satisfy his exploratory nature. The games and pastimes with which he satisfies this nature are also determined by his behavior patterns, both those that are genetically a part of his animal makeup—the ethological—and those that are conditioned by the culture of which he is a part. The main drives in games and pastimes are the need for order, the hunting instinct, sociality, the dominance drive, the territorial imperative, and sexuality.

The Need for Order

Man, like the lower animals, is a creature of order, following the known and familiar paths and patterns of his daily life. Disorder and the unfamiliar frighten and agitate him, and much of his recreation is an attempt to reestablish rules and a sense of order in a world that cannot always be plumbed and squared. The games he plays, no matter how physically violent or intellectually complex, are played under the strictest of rules looked over by Hoyle, the Marquis of Queensbury, and other official arbiters. Spectators enjoy their chosen sports because they observe players involved in a symbolic struggle of life in a framework of known rules and in an identifiable area of operation. Games are played in agreed-upon settings with agreed-upon rules. The arts man creates (cultural play) are the ordering and balancing of fragments of chaotic life into controlled works of literature or music or painting. His recreation, when he feels the world is tumbling crazily about his ears, is something that is logical and ordered and that he can control, perhaps something creative like painting or building model airplanes or throwing pots or perhaps something reassuring like reading the novels of Agatha Christie, who in a perfectly organized plot with easily identifiable good guys and bad guys solves a very understandable problem in a direct and logical way.

The Hunting Instinct

Man is genetically and biologically a hunter, an omnivorous predator, continually on the prowl and longing for a chase, whether he is part of the posse or the mob. Much of his recreation is a literal or figurative satisfaction of this drive, and he is involved in the chase from childhood on. The young, like coyote pups, play continual games of hunt, chase, and capture; and many children's games—like Hide-and-Seek, Tag, Wolf over the River—have evolved in response to this desire. More directly, Americans are a gun culture, and young and old are still involved in the real hunt and chase but now hunt according to strict state and federal game rules and according to season. For some, the deer hunters and bird and squirrel hunters, the kill is important and is like winning a game. For others, the fox hunters, the chase is all, and they wouldn't kill a fox if it were pushing them out of their pickups. Fishing falls under this category also, and between hunting and fishing, Americans spend millions of recreational dollars annually. We no longer have to fish and hunt for survival, but we still can satisfy the age-old instinct directly, but under state and federal rules for the game, or indirectly in games, or vicariously as we watch the dozens of chases that are acted out daily in books, television, and theatres.

Sociality and the Herding Instinct

Man as a herding animal derives satisfaction from gathering in groups with his fellows, whether it is at a rock concert, motorcycle speedway, or Pentecostal revival. In a crowded world where we are continually forced to be hip-and-thigh alongside dozens whose ideas, manners, and way of life we deplore, it is recreational and relaxing to come together with those of the same mind and aims as our own. Playing games, dancing in groups, playing clapping games, and singing harmoniously together satisfy a strong herding urge. And a basic part of man's recreational patterns is the regular reestablishing of the strength and unity of the group. People do this playing dominoes under a chinaberry tree or playing cards on poker night or at bridge club or gathering in a cow pasture to play some form of baseball or on a back street to play Shinny on skates. There is joy and excitement in coming together with friends to play a great game!

Some people have dominance drives that require more satisfaction than their social circles will allow. For those aggressive individuals society has sublimated the drives into socially acceptable games in which they can vent their aggressions without disturbing their society. Although Saturday night barroom brawling is accepted play on some levels, and although boxing, wrestling, and fencing are popular sports, the usual sublimation occurs in cutthroat bridge or in a table-slamming game of dominoes or, for those who are more physically oriented, in tennis, handball, ping-pong, or pool, all games in which a player can figuratively slam a ball down his opponent's throat. Our American culture is sports and dominance oriented. We are a nation that loves winners and a people that are personally and vicariously and continuously competitive in our play. Everybody from the president down to the Podunk Junior High football team chants "We're Number 1" in response to the dominance gene and in response to the fact that we're rich enough and leisured enough to afford continual competition.

In recreation one does not have to compete against another person or team; he can compete against himself, testing his nerve by driving fast airplanes, cars, boats, or motorcycles or testing himself against mountains and caves and snow-covered hillsides or testing himself by invading the domain of sky-diving birds or deep-sea-diving fish. Sometimes playing games—seeking increasingly exciting stimuli, tempting survival itself for the thrill—involves the chancy competition of casting dice or betting the horses or playing poker. The stimulus struggle involves people playing games with their neighbors' wives, with robbery, and even with murder. Man will go to many lengths in search of diverting activities.

The Dominance Drive and the Pecking Order

The territorial imperative is that genetic command that causes individuals and tribes to compete to gain and hold an area that is large enough to support them and their dependents. Both men and the lower animals require an area that will give them space enough to feed and breed in, and they are genetically programmed for this possessiveness. The territorial imperative is strong, and games from childhood to old age have been invented to satisfy the drive in socially acceptable ways. Football, basketball, and soccer are physical battles of territoriality. Each team doggedly defends its own territory while trying to invade the opponent's. King of the Mountain and Musical Chairs are simpler physical struggles for territory. And Chess and Checkers and Monopoly operate more intellectually but on the same principle. These forms of recreation satisfy the natural inclinations to struggle for territory without disordering the social system. The struggles become the playing of games when survival does not depend on winning.

The Territorial Imperative

The sexual drive, so insistent and continual in its summons, is the motivation for many forms of recreation. Dating games,

Sexuality

which involve continual but subtle forms of competition, occupy a large part of the lives of the young, and nonproductive sex is considered a pastime in itself. In our culture male-female dancing is a popular form of recreation for all ages and levels of society. And many social games, which are really no more than mixers or courtship stimuli, require male and female participation, games like Post Office, Spin the Bottle, and Wink.

The Recreation of Cultures

Like man the individual, social groups—cultures—also have their recreation, things that they do that are voluntary, nonproductive, and with no goals beyond themselves. Like individuals also, societies pursue recreation only when they are stable, fed, and rested. The group that is struggling for survival pursues very little recreation. Only after it has a strong hold on survival and is able to afford a leisure "playing" class can it turn to recreation. For a society this comes in the form of creating the fine arts, of financing Sistine Chapels and Michelangelos and Da Vincis to decorate them, and of developing pure exploratory sciences and philosophies, both pastimes where leisured individuals play cerebral games with facts and ideas. All these pursuits are voluntary, nonproductive (in the short run), and of intrinsic value.

And the greatest social recreation of all is war, the most diverting and stimulating of all group activities, and the game that satisfies most of our basic drives. War is initiated when a country is well fed and energetic and when it is bored with too much stability for too long. It is the result of society's continual need for a stimulating political life. War socially bonds the nation and the warriors into a brotherhood and unites the nation against a common foe, satisfying the sociality gene. It is the ultimate battle for dominance and the perfect example of the satisfaction of the territorial imperative. Man the hunter bands together to chase the most dangerous and exciting quarry in the field. And a part of his stated motivations is to establish order in what he sees as a disordered world. War is the periodic recreation to let off steam. The nation then will lay itself down to bleed awhile and rise and fight again.

Bibliography

Abernethy, Francis E. *Singin' Texas*. Dallas: E-Heart Press, 1983.

Abrahams, Roger D., ed. *Jump-Rope Rhymes: A Dictionary*. Austin: University of Texas Press, 1969.

Abrahams, Roger D. and Lois Rankin, eds. *Counting Out Rhymes: A Dictionary*. Austin, University of Texas Press, 1980.

Alexander, Frances. *Mother Goose on the Rio Grande*. Skokie, Ill.: National Textbook Company, 1973.

Anderson, Clay, et al. *The Craftsman in America*, edited by Robert L. Breeden, et al. Washington, D.C.: National Geographic Society, 1975.

Arnow, Jan. *By Southern Hands*. Birmingham, Ala.: Oxmoor House, 1987.

Barret, Richard C. *Bennington Pottery and Porcelain*. New York: Crown Publishers, 1958.

Barrick, Mac E., ed. *German-American Folklore*. American Folklore Series, edited by W. K. McNeill. Little Rock: August House, 1987.

Baumann, Paul. *Collecting Antique Marbles*. Lombard, Ill.: Wallace-Homestead, 1981.

Brewster, Paul G. *American Nonsinging Games*. Norman: University of Oklahoma Press, 1953.

Bronner, Simon J. *American Children's Folklore*. Little Rock: August House, 1988.

Brunvand, Jan Howard. *The Study of American Folklore*. 2d ed. New York: W.W. Norton & Company, 1978.

Caillois, Roger. *Man, Play and Games*. Translated by Meyer Barash. Glencoe, Ill.: Free Press of Glencoe, 1961.

Capps, Benjamin. *The Indians*. New York: Time-Life Books, 1973.

Culin, Stewart. *Games of the North American Indians*. 24th Annual Report, Bureau of American Ethnology. Washington, D.C.: Government Printing Office, 1907.

Curtis, Edward S. *The North American Indian*. 1930. Reprint. New York: Bonanza Books, 1962.

Daiken, Leslie H. *Children's Toys Throughout the Ages*. London: Batesford, 1953.

DiNoto, Andrea, ed. *The Encyclopedia of Collectibles.* Alexandria, Va.: Time-Life Books, 1979.

Dickson, Paul. "Marbles: A Rite Turned Rarity." *Smithsonian* 19, no. 1 (April 1988): 94-103.

Dudley, R. E., and L. W. Payne, Jr. "Texas Play-Party Songs and Games." In *Round the Levee,* PTFS I, edited by Stith Thompson. 1916. Reprint. Dallas: Southern Methodist University Press, 1975.

Dulles, Foster Rhea. *A History of Recreation.* 2d ed. New York: Appleton-Century-Crofts, 1940.

Eckhardt, Rosalind. "From Handclap to Line Play." In *Black Girls at Play: Perspectives on Child Development.* Austin: Southwest Educational Development Laboratory, 1975.

Estill, Julia. "Childrens' Games." In *The Sky Is My Tipi,* PTFS XXII, edited by Mody Boatright. 1949. Reprint. Dallas: Southern Methodist University Press, 1966.

———. "Children's Games in Fredericksburg." In *Texas Folk and Folklore,* PTFS XXVI, edited by Mody Boatright, et al. Dallas: Southern Methodist University Press, 1954.

———. "Customs Among German Descendants of Gillespie County." In *Coffee in the Gourd,* PTFS II, edited by J. Frank Dobie. 1923. Reprint. Dallas: Southern Methodist University Press, 1969.

Ferretti, Fred. *The Great American Marble Book.* New York: Workman Publishing Company, 1973.

Flick, Pauline. *Old Toys.* London: Shire Publications, Ltd., Cromwell House, 1985.

Foley, Daniel J. *Toys Through the Ages.* Philadelphia: Chilton Books, 1962.

Fowler, H. Waller, Jr. *Kites: A Practical Guide to Kite Making and Flying.* New York: Ronald Press Company, 1953.

Fowler, Virginia. *Folktoys Around the World and How to Make Them.* Englewood Cliffs, N. J.: Prentice-Hall, 1984.

Fraser, Antonia. *A History of Toys.* Frankfurt-am-Main, Germany: George Weidenfeld and Nicolson, 1966.

"Fun and Games, Parties and Other Recreations." *Loblolly* 6, no. 1 (Summer 1978). Edited by Marvin Jordan. Published by Lincoln King and the students of Gary (Texas) High School.

Gates, Helen. "Toodala." In *Texian Stomping Grounds,* PTFS XVII, edited by J. Frank Dobie, et al. 1941. Reprint. Dallas: Southern Methodist University Press, 1967.

Georges, Robert A. "Recreations and Games." In *Folklore and Folklife: An Introduction,* edited by Richard Dorson. Chicago: The University of Chicago Press, 1972.

Gomme, Lady Alice B. *The Traditional Games of England, Scotland, and Ireland.* 2 vols. London, 1894, 1898. Reprint. New York: Dover, 1964.

Gonzalez, Rosalinda. "Work and Play on a Border Ranch." In *The Golden Log,* PTFS XXXI, edited by Mody Boatright, et al. Dallas: Southern Methodist University Press, 1962.

Grober, Karl (English version by Phillip Hereford). *Children's Toys of Bygone Days.* New York: Frederick A. Stokes Company, 1928.

Hale, Leon. "A Lesson on Playing Muhle." In *Some Still Do: Essays on Texas Customs,* PTFS XXXIX, edited by F. E. Abernethy. Austin: Encino Press, 1975.

Hall, Ida B. "Pioneer Children's Games." In *Texian Stomping Grounds,* PTFS XVII, edited by J. Frank Dobie, et al. 1941. Reprint. Dallas: Southern Methodist University Press, 1967.

Hart, Clive. *Kites—An Historical Survey*. New York: Frederick A. Praeger, 1967.

Haslam, Fred. *Simple Wooden Toys*. London: Studio Limited, 1945.

Hayles, Larry, and Dwain Lake. "Toymaking." *Loblolly* 6, no. 4 (Spring 1979): 31-41. Edited by Johnny Woodfin. Published by Lincoln King and the students of Gary (Texas) High School.

Henderson, Majorie, and Elizabeth Wilkerson. *Naturally Powered Old Time Toys*. Philadelphia and New York: J. B. Lippincott Co., 1978.

Hertz, Louis H. *The Handbook of Old American Toys*. Wethersfield, Conn.: Mark Haber and Co., 1947.

Hillier, Mary. *Pageant of Toys*. London: Elek, 1965.

Hodges, Lewis H. *46 Step by Step Wooden Toy Projects*. Blue Ridge Summit, Pa.: Tab Books, 1984.

Holme, Geoffrey. *Children's Toys of Yesterday*. New York: Studio Publications, 1932.

Howard, Dorothy Mills. *Dorothy's World: Childhood in Sabine Bottom, 1902-1910*. Englewood Cliffs, N. J.: Prentice-Hall, 1977.

————. "The Rhythms of Ball-Bouncing and Ball-Bouncing Rhymes." *Journal of American Folklore*, 62 (April-June 1949): 166-72.

————. "Rope-Skipping Games: Language, Beliefs and Customs." *Maryland English Journal*, n.d.

Hughes, Langston, and Arna Bontemps, eds. *The Book of Negro Folklore*. New York: Dodd, Mead & Co., 1953.

Huizinga, Johan. *Homo Ludens: A Study of the Play-Element in Culture*. London: Routledge and Kegan Paul, 1949.

Huxford, Sharon, and Bob Huxford. *Schroeder's Antiques Price Guide*. Paducah, Ky.: Schroeder Publishing Co., 1987.

Jackson, Mrs. F. Nevill. *Toys of Other Days*. New York and London: B. Blom, 1968.

Jordan, Gilbert. *Yesterday in the Texas Hill Country*. College Station: Texas A&M University Press, 1979.

King, Constance Eileen. *Antique Toys and Dolls*. New York: Rizzoli International Publications, 1979.

Knapp, Mary, and Herbert Knapp. *One Potato, Two Potato*. New York: W. W. Norton, 1976.

Leonard, Jonathan N. *Ancient America*. Alexandria, Va.: Time-Life Books, 1979.

Lipman, Jean. *American Folk Art*. New York: Dover Publications, Inc., 1948.

Macfarlin, Allan A. *Book of American Indian Games*. New York: Association Press, 1958.

Malone, Ann Patton. *Women on the Texas Frontier: A Cross-Cultural Perspective*. El Paso: Texas Western Press, 1983.

Mason, Benard. *Boomerangs: How to Make and Throw Them*. New York: Dover, 1974.

Metcalf, Harlan G. *Whitlin', Whistles, and Thingamajigs*. Harrisburg, Pa.: Stackpole Books, 1974.

Millen, Nina. *Children's Games from Many Lands*. New York: Friendship Press, 1951.

Morris, Desmond. *The Human Zoo*. New York: Dell Publishing Co., 1969.

Newcomb, W. W., Jr. *The Indians of Texas*. Austin: University of Texas Press, 1961.

Newell, William Wells. *Games and Songs of American Children*. New York: Dover Publications, 1963.

Opie, Peter, and Iona Opie. *Children's Games in Street and Playground.* New York: Oxford University Press, 1984.

Owens, William A. Swing and Turn: *Texas Play Party Games.* Dallas: Tardy Publishing Company, 1936.

Page, Linda Garland, and Hilton Smith, eds. *The Foxfire Book of Toys and Games.* New York: E. P. Dutton, 1985.

Payne, L. W., Jr. "Finding List for Texas Play-Party Songs." In *Round the Levee,* PTFS I, edited by Stith Thompson. 1916. Reprint. Dallas: Southern Methodist University Press, 1975.

Pelham, David. *The Penguin Book of Kites.* New York: Penguin Books Ltd., 1976.

Polkinghorn, R. K., and M.I.R. Polkinghorn. *Toy Making in School and Home.* London: George C. Harrap and Co., 1916.

Provenzo, Eugene F., and Asterie Baker. *The Historian's Toybox.* Englewood Cliffs, N. J.: Prentice Hall, 1979.

Rath, Sura P., guest editor. "Game, Play, Literature: An Introduction." *South Central Review* 3, no. 4 (1986).

Rees, Elizabeth Lodge, M.D. *A Doctor Looks at Toys.* Springfield, Ill.: Charles C. Thomas, Bannerstone House, 1961.

Rinker, Harry L. *Warman's Americana and Collectibles.* Elkins Park, Pa.: Warman Publishing Co., 1984.

Rohrbough, Lynn. *Handy Play Party Book — Authentic Folk Recreation.* Delaware, Ohio: Cooperative Recreation Service, 1940.

Ruhe, Benjamin, and Eric Darnell. *Boomerang: How to Throw, Catch, and Make It.* New York: Workman Publishing, 1985.

Schnacke, Bill. *American Folk Toys: 85 American Folk Toys and How to Make Them.* New York: G. P. Putnam and Sons, 1973.

Sebeok, Thomas A., and Paul G. Brewster. *Studies in Cheremis: Vol. VI, Games.* Bloomington: Indiana University Press, 1958.

Smith, Robert Paul. *How to do Nothing With Nobody All Alone by Yourself.* New York: W. W. Norton and Co., 1958.

Sone, Violet West. "Rope-Jumping Rhymes." In *Backwoods to Border,* PTFS XVIII, edited by Mody C. Boatright and Donald Day. 1943. Reprint. Dallas: Southern Methodist University Press, 1967.

Spizman, Robyn Freedman. *Lollipop Grapes and Clothespin Critters.* Reading, Maine: Addison-Wesley Publishing Company, 1985.

Squires, John L. *Fun Crafts for Children.* Englewood Cliffs, N. J.: Prentice-Hall, 1964.

Stoeltje, Beverly. *Children's Handclaps: Informal Learning in Play.* Austin: Southwest Educational Development Laboratory, 1978.

Streeter, Tal. *The Art of the Japanese Kite.* New York: John Weatherhill, 1974.

Symons, Harry. *Playthings of Yesterday.* Toronto: Ryerson Press, 1963.

Tippitt, James S. *Toys and Toy Makers.* New York and London: Harper and Brothers Publishers, 1931.

Vinton, Iris. *The Folkways Omnibus of Children's Games.* Harrisburg, Pa.: Stackpole Company, 1970.

White, Gwen. *Antique Toys and Their Background.* New York: Arco Publishing Company, 1971.

Wigginton, Eliot, ed. *Foxfire 6.* Garden City, N. Y.: Anchor Books, Anchor Press/Doubleday, 1980.

Wynn, Afton. "Pioneer Folk Ways in Parker County." In *Straight Texas,* edited by J. Frank Dobie. 1937. Reprint. Southern Methodist University Press, 1977.

Zeiger, Helane. *World On a String.* Chicago: Contemporary Books, 1979.

Index of
Contributors

Index of Toys and Games

The Texas Folklore Society Series

Other TFS annual publications available are:

#35 Hunters & Healers: Folklore Types & Topics (1971). Hudson, ed.

#36 Diamond Bessie & The Shepherds (1972). Hudson, ed.

#40 What's Going On? (In Modern Texas Folklore) (1976). Abernethy, ed.

#41 Paisanos: A Folklore Miscellany (1978). Abernethy, ed.

#43 Legendary Ladies of Texas (1981). Abernethy, ed.

#45 Folk Art in Texas (1985). Abernethy, ed.

#46 Sonovagun Stew (1986). Abernethy, ed.

#47 Hoein' the Short Rows (1987). Abernethy, ed.

#49 The Bounty of Texas (1990). Abernethy, ed.

#50 Hecho en Tejas: Texas-Mexican Folk Arts and Crafts (1991). Graham, ed.

#51 Texas Folklore Society 1909–1943 (1992). Abernethy.

#52 Corners of Texas (1993). Abernethy, ed.

#53 Texas Folklore Society 1943–1971 (1994). Abernethy.

#54 Juneteenth Texas (1996). Abernethy, Mullen, Govenar, eds.

#55 Between the Cracks of History: Essays on Teaching and Illustrating Folklore (1997). Abernethy, ed.

Other books of interest:

Singin' Texas. Abernethy, with Beaty, music.